Vocational Education in the 1990s: Major Issues

Edited by Albert J. Pautler, Jr.

With chapters by:
Melvin L. Barlow,
Gerald D. Cheek, Charles R. Doty,
Curtis R. Finch and John H. Hillison,
Angelo C. Gilli, Sr., Lynne Gilli,
John W. Glenn, Jr., and Richard A. Walter,
James P. Greenan, Melvin D. Miller,
Albert J. Pautler, Jr.,
David J. Pucel, Jane Ruff,
Michelle D. Sarkees and Lynda L. West,
and Merle E. Strong

VOCATIONAL EDUCATION IN THE 1990s: MAJOR ISSUES
Albert J. Pautler, Jr., Editor

Copyright 1990 by Prakken Publications, Inc.
Post Office Box 8623, Ann Arbor, Michigan 48107

Second Printing 1993

Library of Congress Catalog Card Number 89-62018
ISBN: 0-911168-78-8

Contents

Introduction 1

Chapter 1
Historical Background of Vocational Education
Melvin L. Barlow 5

Chapter 2
Policy Issues Perspectives
Melvin D. Miller 25

Chapter 3
The Secondary Vocational Program
Gerald D. Cheek 45

Chapter 4
Postsecondary Occupational Education
Charles R. Doty 71

Chapter 5
Vocational Teacher Preparation
John W. Glenn, Jr., and Richard A. Walter 99

Chapter 6
Organizational Structure of Vocational Education
James P. Greenan 113

Chapter 7
Administrative Leadership Issues in Vocational Education
Merle E. Strong 139

Chapter 8
The Curriculum
David J. Pucel 157

Chapter 9
Special Programs for Special Needs Students
Michelle D. Sarkees and Lynda L. West 173

Chapter 10
**The Relationship of History
to the Future of Vocational Education**
Angelo C. Gilli, Sr. 203

Chapter 11
Issues in Vocational Education
Curtis R. Finch and John H. Hillison 223

Chapter 12
**The Image of the Profession
of Vocational Education**
Lynne Gilli 239

Chapter 13
A Vision of the Next Ten Years
Jane Ruff 255

Chapter 14
**The Role of Vocational Education
in Preparing Students for the Future**
Albert J. Pautler, Jr. 265

Special Section
**Bibliography of Review and Synthesis
Literature Concerning
Vocational and Technical Education**
Charles R. Doty 277

The Authors 297

Introduction

IN 1972 Gerald Leighbody's *Vocational Education in America's Schools: Major Issues of the 1970s* was published. The volume is still frequently quoted today by authors in the vocational education field. It was my good fortune to have Gerry Leighbody as my major professor while studying at the University at Buffalo, and he served as a major role model in my own professional development. His book was, clearly, the inspiration for my design of *Vocational Education in the 1990s: Major Issues*. It is my hope that this volume will provide leadership for the field in this next decade much as the Leighbody volume did twenty years ago.

I have invited established and recognized scholars to contribute chapters to the volume. Each was asked to address specific and critical themes in the field. During 1976 I had the opportunity to spend a semester assisting the National Advisory Council on Vocational Education (NACVE) with planning for the Bicentennial Conference on Vocational Education. Two publications emerged from the event—conference papers were published in *The Future of Vocational Education* (1977) by the Center for Vocational Education at Ohio State University, and NACVE published a conference report containing abstracts of presentations from the conference, also entitled *The Future of Vocational Education* (1977). I contributed a chapter, again entitled "The Future of Vocational Education," to both volumes, offering a careful review of the other papers.

I believe that the issues identified in that bicentennial conference remain vital today, and thus they have formed the basis for development of this volume geared to assist and influence decision makers and planners in vocational education in the 1990s. I used a matrix to analyze the papers from the 1976 conference, looking for key word descriptors and common elements, and from that review emerged six major categories of concern in vocational education at that time: a need for a national policy for vocational education; a need for an employment outlook for the future; a need for a match between schooling and work; a need for an improved vocational education; and a need to address the special needs of minorities, women, native Americans, and the handicapped. Each of these areas was discussed in detail in the publications from the 1976 conference.

As I now review this work, completed some twelve years ago, it appears to me that these six categories continue to be suitable for discussing the major issues which face vocational education. On the other hand, it may also be that these categories are too broad to serve as a useful organizing vehicle for ongoing discussion. Such a review of one's own research and writing from twelve years ago is a sobering experience, and allows for much second-guessing. However, I welcome this opportunity to use that earlier work as a starting point for examining vocational education in the coming decade.

This book has been designed to present issues which face vocational education today and in the immediate future, in the hope that it will serve as a potential agenda for confronting those issues and assisting in responsible and responsive policy development, financing, research, and operation of vocational education programs in the 1990s. My assumption is that vocational education programs will continue to exist in the future, but that changes will necessarily occur, dependent primarily on the students (clients) to be served and the needs of employers for a skilled workforce. Such change is inevitable, and all of us in the field must accept and join that process, and work for the most positive change possible.

Three primary objectives have guided all of us who have contributed to this volume. We have sought to discuss major issues which face vocational education at the present time; we have attempted to make suggestions for how best to deal with those issues; and we have raised topics for ongoing research that will best address and resolve the issues at hand. It is my belief that the reader will find the whole to be greater than its individual parts. While many of the foremost scholars in vocational education have contributed to the book, and each chapter is a careful and expert presentation in its own right, the total package has been designed to give the student and the professional in vocational education a broad and deep view of the field as it is today and as it may be in the coming years.

Melvin Barlow, historian emeritus of the American Vocational Association, offers a historical background of the field in the first chapter. Melvin Miller considers both philosophy and policy perspectives in the second chapter. In the third chapter, Gerald Cheek examines the secondary vocational program, followed by Charles Doty's description of postsecondary occupational education in the fourth chapter. The fifth chapter offers a review of vocational teacher preparation by John Glenn and Richard Walter. James P. Greenan considers the organizational structure of vocational education in chapter six. Issues of administrative leadership in the field are the basis for Merle E. Strong's seventh chapter, while David J. Pucel examines the vocational curriculum in chapter eight. Michelle D. Sarkees and Lynda L. West discuss special programs for special needs students in chapter nine. Chapter ten by Angelo C. Gilli, Sr., examines the relationship between the history and the future of vocational education. Curtis R. Finch and John H. Hillison review issues for research in vocational education in chapter eleven. The image of the profession of vocational education is the focus of Lynne Gilli's twelfth chapter. Jane Ruff offers a vision for vocational education for the next ten years in chapter thirteen, and I close the discussion in chapter fourteen with an examination of the role of vocational education in preparing students for the future. The volume also contains a special bibliography of the field prepared by Charles R. Doty.

It is the hope and desire of all of the contributors that this volume will be of interest and value to the vocational education community as well as to the broader educational and policy-making communities as we mutually grapple with the issues which must be overcome in order to offer the best possible vocational education programs to our students in the 1990s.

—**Albert J. Pautler, Jr.**

CHAPTER 1

Historical Background of Vocational Education

By Melvin L. Barlow

THE roots of vocational education reach deep into the historical past. The mores of every culture leaving a written record have included unmistakable evidence of this fact. However, most trade education in the ancient nations was conducted in a father-son relationship. It was not until the advent of apprenticeship, which in itself is very old, that we find distinctive patterns of teaching industrial processes. It was only "this morning," in a historical sense, that attention was given to vocational education as part of the educational program generally provided for youth. It was later yet before any significant gains were made.

The Greeks and the Romans

The structure of "the glory that was Greece" rested upon a self-sufficient system of slave industry and agriculture. Production of Greek sustenance was largely the job of the slave or near-slave population, and therefore was for the most part considered menial. The citizens of militaristic Sparta were forbidden by Lycurgus "to exercise any mechanical trade." The burden of production in Sparta fell upon the Perioecci, a group of the "dwellers about," who were in a sense slaves once removed. Whatever craftsmanship that was needed to support the Spartan citizens came from the Perioecci.

The rise of Athens was accompanied by an increase in the practice of trades required by the growing city. A definite occupational classification developed, regulating various workers into a caste system. The industrial workers, although free people, were generally of the second class. Yet the work of the artisan is our best evidence of Greek achievement. Greece was raised up by manual labor; then new leaders felt superior to manual expression after they had taken over. Although Athens produced a large number of craftsmen, the nature of their training does not seem to have been a matter of public notice or concern.

"The grandeur that was Rome," like "the glory that was Greece," produced little evidence to indicate that either industry or artisanship was ever held in very high official esteem. And yet the great public works—aqueducts, buildings, and roads—required a high level of craftsmanship for their construction.

Throughout a long history, the craftsmen and artisans of Rome were composed of a mixture of slaves and freemen. They acquired their skill in the only way possible, that is, through family apprenticeship. Evidence exists that under the rule of the Roman emperor Commodus (about 183 A.D.) apprenticeships existed.

The references to vocational training found in the records of ancient Roman life are of interest chiefly for the examples they afford us of transition from the apprenticeship to the school system. This transition seems to have occurred first in what are known as the professional vocations, those involving intellectual rather than manual labor. By the fourth century A.D. architects and mechanicians seem to have been trained at least in part by school methods.

The Middle Ages

The so-called Middle Ages account for approximately a thousand years of history between ancient and modern times, beginning in the early 300s and extending into the early 1300s. One of the most important events of the early period was the establishment of a scriptorium by Cassiodorous. Scriptoria became a major religious contribution of the monasteries; large numbers of manuscripts were copied and distributed throughout the Christian world.

It is interesting to note that strong elements of apprenticeship were to be found in the formal training plans of the monks who copied the manuscripts. The famous Benedictine rule, in setting a pattern for the numerous functions of the monasteries, established manual labor in an honorable and preferred position. At least seven hours of manual labor were required of the monks each day.

Agriculture and some phases of the trades composed a large part of the manual labor requirement, and, by the very nature of the work, involved an apprenticeship type of learning. Thus apprenticeship and manual labor were built into the foundations of Christianity and the preservation of learning. Unfortunately, education existed primarily for the church; the masses remained illiterate.

The Renaissance and the Reformation

The Renaissance, a period of about 250 years, began in the fourteenth century with a great revival of learning—for the few. Rediscovery of the literature of Greece and Rome and the escape from medievalism were for the most part of little importance to the great masses of the people. Humanism and the concept of the importance of man were slow to filter down to the ranks of humanity, but a trend was started that would place increased value upon the "here and now" rather than upon the "hereafter." Latin had long been the language of religion and learning, but the man in the street could neither read nor understand that language. The spirit of the Renaissance would not influence the mores of society until the language barrier had been penetrated. The use of the vernacular in writing was popularized by the appearance of Dante Alighieri's *The Divine Comedy* and Giovanni Bocaccio's *Decameron* in the fourteenth century.

During the whole of this wonderful and terrifying period of contrasts and conflicts, we may find the stabilizing influence of industry, trade, and craftsmanship. Society became dependent upon the new burgher class and the arts-and-crafts guilds. The role of industrial education during the Renaissance was the same as it had been from time immemorial—the father-son or master-apprentice system. During the formal period of instruction on the job the apprentice could learn all of the aspects of the trade or craft from his father or master. The length of time—seven years, more or less—was sufficient to provide a large variety of learning experiences; by imitation and emulation the apprentice would acquire the skills and understandings required. In some cases the master was required to teach reading and writing to his apprentices. It would be late in the 1880s before the idea of combining trade and academic education in the school was tried seriously.

Beginnings of Educational Reform

Traditional ideas of educational theory and practice were supplemented generously by the views of educational reformers from the sixth to the nineteenth centuries. As literate use of the vernacular spread, the common man became more important in the eyes of leaders, and his education became at least a matter of casual notice. Now and again, a faint tribute to some phase of industrial education would drop from the pen of some writer or wedge into the common educational experience of some school. Drawing was taught at Mulcaster's Merchant Taylor School after 1561; John Locke thought that trade education might be useful; and Jean Jacques Rousseau desired that Emile learn the carpentry trade, spending one or two whole days each week with a master carpenter. Be it noted that, although Rousseau felt that man needed to work in order to live, he would be sure that Emile would raise himself to the "state" of being a carpenter, not merely to the occupation of a carpenter.

Johann Heinrich Pestalozzi, a Swiss educator, and the "father of modern elementary education," evolved a system of educational theory and practice from which industrial education borrowed heavily during its formative years. The concept that impression resulted from expression was a fundamental principle of Pestalozzi's, and it became the basis of learning in his school, in which the child was allowed to "learn by doing."

Francis Joesph Nicolas Neef taught under Pestalozzi's direction for approximately three years. Later he opened a school in Paris which attracted the attention of Napoleon and Talleyrand, and more importantly from our point of view, the attention of a delegation of men from the United States which included the philanthropist William Maclure. Maclure offered Neef aid in opening a school in

America. His first school failed, but in 1825 he was called to New Harmony, Indiana, to become a teacher in a school organized along the lines suggested by Pestalozzi—physical labor was combined with moral and intellectual culture.

Philip Emanuel von Fellenberg, one-time associate of Pestalozzi, organized and conducted a variety of educational activities at Hofwyl, Switzerland. He paid special attention to the education of the various social classes, including both extremes, in an effort to promote harmony among the classes and improve the general conditions of human life. Agricultural and industrial instruction were combined with some elements of literacy instruction in an educational experiment with strong social implications. Manual activities were stressed for all students, but the emphasis was placed upon literary activities for well-to-do students and upon practical aspects for the poor children. All teaching was inspired by Pestalozzian principles.

Manual labor activities in agriculture were related to school studies, providing a source of real interest in school work for the students. Trade instruction was provided by skilled craftsmen, representing a dozen or more trade areas, who were employed by the school as a part of their regular work.

Many other nineteenth century educational reformers contributed to the growth of the concepts of industrial education, their contributions and views of activity, handwork, and industry all added emphasis to the necessity of industrial education. Industrial education provided a natural avenue for educational reform. It was practical, close to the common daily experience of man, and therefore easily understood.

Apprenticeship in Colonial America

Apprenticeship was practiced throughout colonial America. Laws and conditions of apprenticeship were provided among other instruments of town government; appropriate authorities were delegated responsibility to determine that apprenticeship agreements were honored. There were two kinds of apprenticeships: (1) The voluntary form bound the apprentice by his own free will in order to learn a trade; (2) involuntary apprenticeship provided a means of taking care of poor children and orphans.

In general, apprenticeship agreements provided for food, clothing, and shelter; religious training; general education as needed in the trade; knowledge, understanding, and experience in the trade skills; and, finally, for the "mysteries" of the trade, or the techniques which had some elementary scientific basis. Paying for an education was always a problem in colonial America; the boy who came from a less fortunate family could find opportunities in apprenticeship. A large segment of public elementary education was accounted for in this manner.

The American Manual Labor Movement

An education-conscious labor force developed rapidly in the early years of our nation. A labor movement which strongly favored public education promoted the concept of equal educational opportunity at public expense.

Private charity schools and societies of mechanics came into existence during the early part of the nineteenth century in an attempt to supply the educational advantages of apprenticeship for factory workers.

The General Society of Mechanics and Tradesmen, which was founded on November 17, 1785, had by 1821 embarked upon a full-scale educational program. When public education became generally available, this group relaxed its direct participation in educational work.

The lyceums and mechanics institutes, which developed during the early years of the nineteenth century, provided additional education for mechanics. The Gardiner Lyceum, founded in 1823, and the American Lyceum of Science and the Arts, proposed by Josiah Holbrook in 1826, were typical. The educational goals of such institutions were broad enough to include the cultural needs of the artist, the farmer, and the mechanic.

The mechanics institutes directed their attention primarily to the vocational needs of their members. Prominent among them were the Franklin Institute, Philadelphia, 1824; the Maryland Institute for the Promotion of the Mechanic Arts, Baltimore, 1826; the Ohio Mechanics Institute, Cincinnati, 1828; and the San Francisco Mechanics Institute, 1854. There were many others.

The demands of our national period, combined with the stirrings of the industrial revolution, were strange forces for the

American people to control. The factory system directed deadly blows toward apprenticeship; by trial and error, new institutions developed to provide the greatly needed industrial education. Technical institutes in tune with the new social system were founded. After the Civil War, a system of agricultural and mechanical colleges appeared in each of the states in response to the national interest in industrial education. Following closely behind were the private trade schools, corporation schools, and the "new education" which reflected the desire of the masses for things practical. At the same time, American public education struggled to provide educational opportunity for all the people.

Ancient Origins

The origin of industrial education is lost in antiquity, but ancient nations obviously depended upon forms of industry and upon craftsmanship for economic and civil survival. That craftmanship was highly developed can be inferred from the treasures that remain to indentify these early cultures. For thousands of years, the process of teaching and learning related to this industrial craftsmanship was a family affair, conducted largely through the father-son and master-apprentice relationships.

During the Renaissance and Reformation, something like formal industrial education came into being. The guilds had added a definite mark of respectability to craftsmanship, and craftsmanship itself had grown concurrently with geographical, economic, and scientific advancement.

Educational reforms of the sixteenth and seventeenth centuries provided for industrial education in theory and in some instances actually included industrial-related instruction in programs of formal education.

In the nineteenth century, positive gains of lasting significance were made in the utilization of the elements of industry in education. Pestalozzi, with his homespun philosophy and practical ideas about education, became a center of attraction for educators in Europe and America, and his ideas bore fruit in the United States. These influences supplemented the existing apprenticeship systems, the lyceums and mechanics institutes, and the numerous societies of craftsmen, and lent sustenance to the development of special schools in which industrial education was given new emphasis.

The Crucible, 1870-1906

Then a "new education" emerged in America in the late nineteenth century. Into the crucible went traditional educational ideas, social and economic needs, patterns of educational reform, and newer ideas from Russia and Scandinavian countries to form the beginnings of manual and trade education.

The awakening of educational consciousness in the United States occurred about 1820. General enthusiasm for public schools was slow to develop, but over the next fifty years the idea of the common school became woven unmistakably into the fabric of the American culture.

By 1870 the American people had accepted the concept of universal public elementary education, and progress in that direction tended generally to be satisfactory. Beginning with Massachusetts in 1851, state after state had enacted school laws requiring the attendance of youth at least through the eighth grade. This was the spirit of democracy at work. Its indomitable forces were behind a true free public education system within the reach of all.

The legal question of whether a people hold the right to tax themselves for whatever kind of educational system they desire was largely settled by the famous Kalamazoo Case in 1872. With that affirmative decision the way was reasonably clear for the high school to become the dominant educational institution in America. It was sometimes referred to as the "people's college," which indicated that courses must suit individual needs of students. This involved a vastly expanded curriculum and introduced many new practical subjects. Within the new environment of public secondary education, vocational education found its beginnings.

The Issues

Education needed by all men became the goal, and slowly but steadily more and more children were brought under the influence of the common school. A large percentage of the children were the sons and daughters or working men and laborers, and the common school would largely represent all of their formal educational experience. If the studies and methods of the common school were to be adapted to the needs of any class of people, then it ought to be the working class.

Upon the basis of the special needs of the working class the curriculum of the common school became the target for general criticism. Many critics felt that the curriculum was not appropriate for the special needs of the working class. School work was bookish. Words were taught instead of ideas. Too many things were taught, and they were taught because of fashion rather than fitness.

In order to correct the inadequacies of the common school program, various reforms were generously recommended. The school should concentrate on fewer subjects, should distinguish between knowledge and skill, and should recognize that skill cannot be obtained except by practice. The student should be tested by a call to demonstrate in practice what he had learned, not merely by having him tell about it. Only the useful and necessary parts of arithmetic should be taught and the curious or disciplinary elements should be avoided. And there were many other similar recommendations.

The constructive critics of the common school tended to live dangerously. They dared to cross or move up-stream relative to the prevailing educational current in their efforts to secure favorable attitudes toward introduction of new ideas into the curriculum. Education was supposed to be like the life to which students were being prepared.

Drawing had always been popular in classes conducted by the mechanics' institutes throughout the country. The influence of its success weighed heavily in the new curriculum. Drawing found many supporters because of its everyday uses on the farm, at home, and in the world of industry. Educators sensitive to community pressures were thinking of the expanded curriculum of the future and the additional responsibilities of the public schools. Certainly technical and industrial education must have a start in the public schools. The manual training movement had not yet begun, but the coming events were casting their shadows on the educational world.

No small part of this influence had come from the Morrill Act passed by Congress in 1862, which provided for the establishment of agricultural and mechanical colleges. An intense desire of the public for practical education had been developed. Although the Morrill Act was related to college-level programs, many discussions of it and the opinions expressed would have future value to other levels and kinds of industrial education.

Differences between skilled labor and educated labor were deemed to be largely differences of the degree and kind of education. The skills taught in the programs of the new colleges were supposed to have the character of genuine work, and students were not to be involved in play-work if the best ends of instruction were to be served. The need for competent instructors who were skilled in the various aspects of industry did not go unnoticed.

Much was said about the equal cultivation of the head, the heart, and the hand as representing a totality and completeness of instruction. Supplanting liberal education did not become a goal of industrial education. Instead, it was clearly the intent to provide a combination of liberal and practical education so that both areas would be enlarged and benefited; the so-called "industrial classes" were to have an education equivalent to that of the professional classes. The goal was—obviously—educated labor.

The idea of "educated labor" generally meant that the laborer, along with developing skill in his industrial pursuit, should also have instruction in liberal arts and in philosophy. The goal was to incorporate in the public schools an educational pattern in which general culture and hand culture could be carried on harmoniously.

There was agreement concerning the reasonableness of the demand for industrial training, for it was recognized that the decay of the apprenticeship system made industrial education a national necessity. One of the early educational developments in response to this need was the Manual Training Movement. The St. Louis Manual Training School is one of the more famous examples of what this movement accomplished. Its design was copied in other cities.

The Leaders

Into the crucible of manual and trade education came the theories, beliefs, and practices of the educational leaders of the time. Emergence of practical education as a consideration in the curriculum of the public school was much in the news, and the movement had its ardent proponents and its severe critics. The pages of educational literature between 1875 and 1900 record both sides of the argument in full.

The two principal personalities—judging from the quantity of their written views—were Calvin M. Woodward and William T. Harris. To a lesser extent E. E. White and John D. Runkle were involved in the discussions. The story of this educational battle of the century can be told in brief form by reference to these four persons, although occasional reference to others will serve to clarify some of the basic issues.

Events leading up to the establishment of the St. Louis Manual Training School began in 1855, when the trustees of Washington University established the O'Fallon Polytechnic Institute. For many years the Institute performed services similar to those of the mechanics' institutes, conducting evening schools for apprentices and journeymen, which included classes in mathematics and drawing. In 1865 Calvin M. Woodward began his teaching career at Washington University. In 1866 he became principal of the O'Fallon Polytechnic Institute, and two years later, when the Institute was organized as a part of the engineering department of Washington University, he was made dean of that department.

Sometime between 1868 and 1871 Woodward decided that the engineering students should construct models made of wood to illustrate certain mechanical principles. When he learned that the students had little aptitude in using hand tools, he asked the university carpenter, Noah Dean, to demonstrate their use. By 1871 a new workshop, modestly equipped, was placed at Dean's disposal. The work was carried out under Woodward's supervision.

These activities and Woodward's frequent discussions of manual education in the meetings of professional associations met with enthusiasm from the industrialists who offered financial assistance. Gradually a plan calling for the formulation of the ideas of manual training for the secondary school evolved. The Trustees of Washington University approved the plan and on September 6, 1880, the St. Louis Manual Training School went into operation with 50 boys enrolled in a program which consisted of two hours of woodshop and one hour each of mathematics, science, Latin or English, and drawing.

In the fall of 1880, President E. E. White of Purdue University entered this discussion of what the public schools should teach. He recognized that while the state had the right to teach any subject which might "promote the general welfare," it was not obligated to do so. He distinguished between general and special in education.

White was emphatic in his view that trades should not be taught in the public schools because this would direct public education away from its primary purpose. The guardians of liberal education considered technical education as a "deceptive farce," impractical, a potential threat to the intellect, and completely unacceptable in the public schools.

White did advocate a program of technical education that provided for half of each school day to be devoted to labor and the remaining spent in the regular school program. While he did want to cultivate respect for honest labor and a taste for industrial pursuits, he was firmly set against a "weak attempt to make artisans."

John Daniel Runkle, a graduate of the Lawrence Scientific School of Harvard University, was one of the first ten faculty members of the Massachusetts Institute of Technology (MIT). In 1868 he left his post as professor of mathematics to become the acting president of MIT. In 1870 he was made president.

In June 1876, Runkle and a large party of students and faculty members from MIT spent two weeks at the Centennial Exposition in Philadelphia, clearly bent on searching for things of value for their school. Runkle discovered the Russian exhibit sent by the Imperial Technical School of Moscow. The exhibit fired his imagination and provided an answer to one of his pressing problems, that of finding a method of giving practical training to engineering students. There was no question but that Runkle was inspired by what he saw in the Russian exhibit, and his quick mind immediately formulated plans for utilizing the ideas. He reported to the Corporation of the Massachusetts Institute of Technology and made recommendations concerning instruction shops for engineering students. The Corporation approved Runkle's plan.

Runkle's discovery excited many education-conscious groups. It was these groups which in turn discussed this idea and spread interest in this new direction in education. Runkle discussed the new system at the National Education Association (NEA) meeting in 1877, pointing out that American schools had been sending engineers into the field with their hands tied. Until then, engineers had had a good technical education, but they had little knowledge, and absolutely no skill, in connection with the practical aspects of construction.

Another prominent American educator who spoke with a loud

voice and whose ideas were heard by the masters of educational direction was William T. Harris. He was well informed concerning European educational ideas, and while serving as Superintendent of Schools in St. Louis he introduced kindergarten work and became one of the proponents and leaders of elementary work in science. From 1889 to 1906 he served as the U.S. Commissioner of Education.

Harris was ever the friendly enemy of manual training. He could support manual training, but only on his terms. His order of education was such that the first consideration was related to citizenship, the second "to the intellectual mastery of the scientific view of the world," and the third to education that pertains to the business of making a living.

Strong arguments in favor of industrial education and manual training could not shake Harris from his view that it was the function of education to cultivate the humanities as a first step, and then, perhaps, the industrial faculties. Manual training in its proper place was a good idea, but even good ideas could be recommended for the wrong reasons. He felt that manual training was "first defended on the preposterous ground that it is educative in the same sense that arithmetic, geography, grammar, and natural science are educative."

The Results

The rationale against manual training was harsh; but, undaunted, the proponents of manual training and industrial education struggled to maintain their position. They asserted that the lack of practical education in the public schools represented a deficiency in the school system. The aims of education proposed by the advocates of manual training amounted to a criticism of the established system of education, and it was natural to resent such criticism and to discourage efforts at reform of the curriculum. Points of view ranged from blind faith in manual training to bitterly obstinate opposition to its introduction in any form or at any place in the curriculum. Nor did one have to choose one extreme or the other, for there was a continuum of viewpoints, with many positions between the extremes.

Mechanics had customarily solved their own educational problems by establishing mechanics' institutes, mechanics' libraries, and professional associations. In the early years of the nineteenth century the workingman had battled to obtain equality of education for his children. Even his wildest dreams did not include the teaching of trades in the free public schools.

The idea of "educated labor" as opposed to merely "skilled labor" was gaining acceptance, but this differentiation was not followed by appropriate changes in the public school curriculum. However, lack of immediate action did not discourage the proponents of trade education. The necessity of providing a vast number of workers could not be overlooked by educators.

One of the first private trade schools was the Hampton Institute, organized by General Samuel Chapman Armstrong in 1868. Armstrong was convinced that if a free Negro race was to find adjustment in society, education would become a vital factor in that adjustment. Assistance from the American Missionary Society enabled the institute to become a reality. Trade training was combined with the elements of liberal education in order that the Negro might improve his character and social status. The Hampton Institute led the way in the education of Negroes. Booker T. Washington was one of its students.

The first school to offer specific trade training with supplementary studies directly related to each trade was the New York Trade School, founded by Colonel Richard Tylden Auchtmuty in 1881. As a result of his study of labor problems, Auchtmuty developed a pattern of trade training designed to give pre-employment instruction as well as supplementary instruction for employed workers. Although tuition was charged, much of Auchtmuty's personal fortune was used to support the school. Among the many benefactors of the school was J. Pierpont Morgan, who provided a generous endowment in 1892.

In contrast to the plan of instruction of the New York Trade School, the Hebrew Technical Institute, founded in New York City in November 1883, offered a greater range of subjects of a general nature. It may be classed more properly as a technical school rather than a trade school. The school required that an applicant be a resident of New York City, strong and healthy, of Jewish faith, and at least twelve and a half years of age. Each applicant was required also to supply letters of recommendation testifying to his scholarship and character.

Still another departure in trade training developed with the establishment of the Williamson Free School of Mechanical Trades in Philadelphia in 1891. The school was endowed by Isaiah V. Williamson, a merchant and philanthropist in that city, and was designed to take the place of the old apprenticeship training. Boys from 16 to 18 years of age were bound as indentured apprentices to the school trustees for three years. The school was entirely free—no charge was made for clothing, food, or instruction. Only the most worthy of all applicants were accepted by the board of trustees.

The Williamson School was founded at a time when the manual training movement was growing in popularity. The school subscribed to the nature of the movement and actually added work, preliminary to trade instruction, along the lines of manual training. It was felt that such instruction was necessary, and since manual training had not been widely established at that date, many of the pupils from the public schools would not have had such training.

The New York Trade School offered specific trade training with directly related scientific instruction. The Hebrew Technical Institute offered a limited amount of specific trade training, was organized in the manner of a technical institute, and combined trade training with the subject matter of general education. The Williamson school started with a program of manual training for all students, added some general education, and finally offered specific, intensive trade training. Other schools which developed during the early years of the trade school movement usually adopted one of these plans. The exceptions are found in the corporation schools, which attempted to revive the old type of apprenticeship to meet their particular needs.

Corporation Schools

As industrialization continued, many employers supported some form of industrial education. Those who could do so usually preferred to conduct their own systems of education. The others usually supported the plan of industrial training in the public schools.

In 1872 the firm of R. Hoe and Company, a New York manufacturer of printing presses, was confronted with a demand for improved machinery. This required a more intelligent class of workmen, and to obtain them the company established a school which met two evenings a week. Among the subjects studied were English, mechanical drawing, arithmetic, geometry, and algebra. The studies were directly related to the work of the firm.

In 1900 the General Electric Company of Lynn, Massachusetts, established an apprenticeship system which combined the activities of shop and classroom. Selected for study were academic courses which would develop for the apprentice a better understanding of machines and machine parts. Included in the studies were courses in interpretation of mechanical drawings, sketching, and design of auxiliary tools required for modern manufacture. The plan of combining apprenticeship with industrial science was evidently successful, since the company was satisfied with the results, and the system was widely copied.

In 1901 the Baldwin Locomotive Works of Philadelphia established school programs for three classes of their personnel. The first class was organized for those who had completed elementary school but who had not reached 16 years of age. They attended school three evenings a week for three years and studied arithmetic, geometry, mechanical drawing, and shop practice. The second class included those employees over 18 who had completed a more advanced educational program. This group attended school two evenings a week for two years and studied such subjects as chemistry, advanced mathematics, and mechanical drawing. The third group was composed of graduates of colleges and other advanced institutions. They were not required to attend classes but were required to read technical journals and turn in synopses of the various articles.

The Role of the Public School

By early this century, it was common knowledge that there was a need for trained mechanics in the United States and that the apprenticeship system was not able to cope with the situation. The idea that American youth had a right to expect some preparation for occupation as a part of his public school work was finding support among some educators. The fact that manual training groups had some responsibility or obligation in this regard was attracting the attention of many leaders of the manual training movement.

Charles H. Keyes, president of the NEA's Department of Manual Training, announced at the organization's Charleston convention in 1900 that he had received demands from various parts of the country for a consideration of the relation of manual training to trade training. The letters indicated interests in either one of two items: The first concerned the establishment of public trade schools; the second insisted that the public schools should include more work for business, vocation, or trade, "without sacrificing their general culture aims."

Charles F. Warner, principal of the Mechanic Arts High School of Springfield, Massachusetts, recognized the growing need for manual training to make some positive effort to contribute to the solution of this problem, which was then of national significance. Warner indicated that it was not possible for manual training to remain aloof. He took this stand knowing full well that, "One who advocates such a connection will probably be stigmatized as a deserter from the ranks of true educational manual training."

The four-year plan adopted by George A. Merrill, director of the California School of Mechanical Arts in San Francisco, began with two years of manual training during which the student had an opportunity to explore and discover which of the trades he wished to learn. During the last two years the student deepened his knowledge and skills in his chosen trade, and at the same time took an adequate amount of academic studies.

Because of the interest concerning the relationship of manual training to trade education, the NEA, at its convention in 1900, proposed that a committee of five be appointed to investigate the subject and report the next year. Although the discussions continued in other meetings, a formal written report of the committee may not have been prepared. Subsequent discussions and the writing of industrial educators suggest that the topic continued to be under investigation.

Arthur D. Dean proposed a program in trade education in which about half of the school day was to be given over to academic work and the other half to shop. This was almost identical to the plan which Merrill had found so successful in San Francisco. Dean felt that such a course would tempt many grammar-school boys to remain in school longer.

The growing interest among the proponents of manual training to do something specific about meeting the need for trade training did not include a desire to convert the manual training high school into a trade school. The existing program of manual training was intended to be left without change. The most complicating factor of all was that no one knew what kind of industrial training was really needed. If this could be determined, then finding the appropriate place for trade education in the public schools would be an easier task.

Despite the conflict of opinion concerning trade education, necessity ultimately forced the issue. There was a demand for attention and action. One of the most significant developments in the gathering forces for industrial education in the trades was the Douglas Commission in 1906. The Commission, which had been appointed in 1905 by Governor William L. Douglas of Massachusetts, reported on the need for public industrial education of a trade nature. This report caused influential industrial educators to think of manual training as only one aspect of a larger problem of industrial education.

Summary

Social need for industrial education developed in relationship to the economy of the nation. As industrial development proceeded to become the dominant factor in the economic life of America, its educational implications commanded attention. For a half-century a variety of forces—manual labor schools, lyceums, mechanics' institutes, and associations of craftsmen—placed an emphasis upon the need for industrial education.

These forces tended to operate outside the mainstream of public education. They were more a convenience to society than an integral part of general social development. About 1870, the situation had reached critical proportions in that the needs were great but the solutions were not adequate. From 1870 to 1906, concerted attention and action was focused upon the general problem of industrial education. Out of the crucible of discussion came the foundation for a new era in education.

The issues were clear. The common school was criticized because it failed to reflect the life for which it was supposed to prepare youth. On the other hand, there were arguments that the moral background of the school program was, in reality, the best preparation for life. And so the heated debate continued without clear evidence that either side was correct, but with a strong suspicion that both extremes were essential.

Though certain aspects of industrial education were regarded as anti-intellectual, drawing was not. Its educational values appeared to be sound, and its addition to the curriculum of the common school spread rapidly across the nation. Thus, one of the practical arts was established in high esteem as a vehicle of the total education of the individual.

Establishment of agricultural and mechanical colleges (Morrill Act of 1862) did much to clarify the image of industrial education in the public mind. Throughout the nation, the values of such instruction were proclaimed as an element of social progress. These colleges were a step toward the goal of educated labor, but a step which required much more attention to the development of industrial education in the public schools. The Morrill Act would greatly benefit those who were able to attend the colleges, but the vast majority of the public, who could profit from similar instruction, would be ignored unless some reflection of such educational purposes could develop also in the common schools.

Many prominent people participated in the discussion about industrial education in the late years of the nineteenth century. The proponents were enthusiastic about new educational values to be gained. The antagonists were fearful that existing values would be sacrificed for the sake of unproven theoretical considerations. But the viewpoint of society was changing and a new social spirit aided the development of attitudes in favor of the early manifestations (manual training) of industrial education.

From the standpoint of industrial education in the public schools, the two principal products of the crucible were: (1) development of a strong and expanded manual training program, and (2) the emergence of trade education.

Private trade schools set the pace in contributing to the development of an educated labor force. Corporation schools formed industrial education programs appropriate for their corporate objectives and found their efforts amply rewarded.

Pioneer work in establishing industrial education was developed on many fronts. Some states took action as states; individual initiative was apparent in other states. The NEA moved toward adopting industrial educators' points of view, and individuals offered their observations concerning the general development of industrial education. Finally, the greatest boost of all came from the report of the

Douglas Commission in Massachusetts in 1906, whose thorough investigation of the nature of, and the need for, industrial education served as a catalyst to increase enthusiasm for such education. The report was the opening wedge of the vocational drive to follow. ☐

References

Anderson, Lewis Flint (1926). *History of manual and industrial school education,* New York: D. Appleton-Century Company.

Bennett, Charles Alpheus (1926). *History of manual and industrial education up to 1870.* Peoria, Ill.: The Manual Arts Press.

──── . (1937). *History of manual and industrial education 1870-1917.* Peoria, Ill.: The Manual Arts Press.

Coates, Charles P. (1923). *History of the manual training school of Washington University.* U.S. Department of the Interior, Bureau of Education, Bulletin 1923, No. 3. Washington, D.C.: Government Printing Office.

Blake, James Vila (1886). *Manual training in education.* Chicago, Ill.: Charles H. Kerr and Company.

Eighth annual report of the Commissioner of Labor, 1892 (1893). *Industrial Education.* Washington, D.C.: Government Printing Office.

Manual training magazine, 1900-1906.

Massachusetts report of the Commission of Industrial and Technical Education, Senate Document No. 349 (April 1906). Boston, Mass.: Wright and Potter Printing Co.

National Education Association, 1870-1906.

Scott, Jonathan Frence (1914). *Historical essay on apprenticeship and vocational education.* Ann Arbor, Mich.: Ann Arbor Press.

Seybolt, Robert Francis (1917). *Apprenticeship and apprenticeship education in colonial New England and New York.* New York: Teachers College, Columbia University.

Smith, H. Ross (1914). *Development of manual training in the United States.* Lancaster, Pa.: The Intelligencer Print.

Woodward, Calvin, M. (1887). *The manual training school.* Boston, Mass.: D.C. Heath & Company.

CHAPTER 2

Policy Issue Perspectives

By Melvin D. Miller

POLICY issues in vocational education have been debated since the earliest attempts to establish vocational education as part of the nation's educational system. In fact, many policy issues have persisted in our attention; yet, although these issues may not have changed, positions have.

An examination of the legislative history for vocational education provides a basis for understanding how views regarding the implementation of vocational education have reflected the changing priorities and concerns of our nation. At the same time, societal changes have impacted on views held regarding a variety of other topics. Changes in federal legislation and societal views individually and collectively have influenced policy decisions regarding the practices of vocational education.

Policy serves to guide strategies for implementing educational programming at the local, state, and federal levels. In the latter case, it seems clear that federal legislation becomes the same as federal policy. Moreover, in spite of the constitutional view that education is a right of the states, when states accept federal monies for vocational education, the expenditure of those dollars must be in accordance with federal guidelines, and thus federal policy becomes the policy of the state. Similarly, state policy strongly influences local policy in many areas.

This chapter presents policy issues which have persisted over time and which have strongly influenced the direction and practice of vocational education. These issues, philosophy, legislation, schooling, work, participants, teachers, and leadership, are initially presented in an early historical context, and then developed to reflect major changes related to each policy area. Understanding the historical perspective within which past policy has been established most certainly should be useful in thinking about policy issues and questions that are presented in each section of this chapter.

Philosophy

There is little argument concerning the importance of philosophy. Questions concerning reality, truth, and value dominate the issues faced and problems to be solved in the business of living. In fact, it is not unreasonable to assert that declarations about reality, truth, and value say it all. At the same time, however, answers about the nature of reality, truth, and value, and the systematic way by which such answers are developed, are neither easily agreed to nor readily decided.

Arguments concerning reality, truth, and value are rooted in our earliest recorded history. Socrates and Plato, among the earliest philosophers, were the springboard from which Plato's student Aristotle advocated a different system of deciding issues pertaining to reality, truth, and value. A historical list of the world's greatest philosophers and their respective philosophic positions would reveal that there is a variety of systematic ways to describe a philosophic position. Furthermore, it would be apparent that consistency and coherence are hallmarks of each system. The decision is, then, which system or systems will be used to shape decisions while transacting life and thus shaping our future.

The future and philosophy are interactive both as process and product. The processes of philosophic thought influence today's events, which are a part of the process for determining the future. Similarly, the decisions or products of philosophic process help create the product labeled "the future." The critical nature of having a systematic way of viewing the world, in deciding answers to questions concerning reality, truth, and value, and conducting our affairs should give philosophy top priority as we think about the future. Clarifying one's philosophic position is important business. The demands and considerations involved in thinking about and selecting a philosophic position are multifaceted. Clearly, it is beyond the scope of this chapter to do more than call attention to the importance of philosophy as we think about the future and to hope that the reader has already embarked on the philosophic journey—a journey continuing throughout one's future.

Philosophy and Early Leaders

Accurately labeling the philosophic position of another is not easy. However, unless the individual is willing to take on a specific mantle or declare a philosophic identity, labeling is an alternative. Such is the case with two early leaders of vocational education, David Snedden and Charles A. Prosser. Neither evidenced concern for declaring a specific philosophic position. Rather, they sought to insure that "industrial education" would become available to the masses of youth not then being served by the nation's public schools.

The educational vision of Snedden and Prosser led them to argue for and debate the merits of their plan for public education. These debates, together with their writings and speeches, left a historic record for philosophers to examine. While a variety of philosophic indentities have been used to describe Snedden and Prosser, social efficiency is settled on by many (Wirth, 1983, p. 77).

In spite of whatever level of agreement reached regarding the appropriate philosophic label, it is arguable that philosophic considerations were not central to the formation of their educational position. A concern for the youth of our country became more important than philosophic discussion of what it means to be; the idea that the curriculum should have application in the workplace dominated other searches for knowledge; and the idea that schooling should prepare one to earn a living was advanced in preference to education designed to prepare the learner for learning for the sake of learning or more of the same. In short, the educational plan of Snedden and Prosser rested on society's sense of what we required to be successful in the workplace, whether it be the home, farm, business, or industry.

Philosophy Lacking

Successful practice has been the byword of vocational education in America. If it works, keep it. Vocational educators were exhorted to look at the world of work to see what change was necessary to insure continuing success in future practice—measure outcomes on job placement; model schools after the workplace. Each statement is an indicator of the strong tie to practice and the experience gained through successful practice. A record of success reinforced the usefulness of experience and practice. An analysis of why something worked was not nearly as important as the fact that it worked. There is little evidence to suggest that a philosophic examination of vocational education in relationship to the questions of reality, truth, and value commanded the attention of but a handful of vocational education's leaders.

The writing of vocational educators describing successful practice, however, allows the identification of a philosophic position using a deductive analysis of these writings. Such an analysis leads to the conclusion that the overriding philosophic position for the field of vocational education is pragmatism. Regardless of the apparent lack of philosophic examination and thinking by the practitioners of this field, a rather systematic and coherent pragmatic philosphic position is evident.

Pragmatism and Change

Philosophic pragmatists hold a strong orientation to change. According to this position, change is among the greatest of certainties. Change prevades the nature of being and describes what happens to learners. In like manner, change suggests appropriate roles for teachers. Change also indicates the nature of truth and predicts that future curriculum will be different from today's. Furthermore, change will be evident in the evolving purposes of schooling in our society.

Out of this milieu, it seems clear that vocational educators will serve their profession best by developing a strong understanding of the meaning of philosophy and its usefulness in shaping the practices of the future. The view that developing and using philosophy is an impractical exercise needs to be replaced with a view that the work of philosophy is the most practical of all activities. Philosophy is the major tool for analyzing the changing issues that will confront practitioners at all levels of vocational education. For the field to embrace this position will be a change itself.

Legislation

The history of federal legislation for vocational education is the history of public vocational education in America. Prior to the passage of the Smith-Huges Act in 1917, vocational education or industrial education as it was known had little presence in the public schools of our nation. The Smith-Hughes Act signaled the beginning of public vocational education and started a reformation of secondary education that is not yet complete.

The remarkable character of the first federal legislation for vocational education, and incidentally the first venture by Congress into the arena of public secondary education, is attested to by the enduring nature of that legislation. The Smith-Hughes Act remained virtually unchanged for almost a half century. While there were a number of amendments, none had the effect of redirecting the initial thrust, purposes, or intended outcomes of that legislation. The piecemeal add-ons did expand the scope of vocational programming and provide additional funding. Little else changed until 1963.

A New Pattern Emerges

The Vocational Education Act of 1963 set new directions and emphasis for vocational education. Categorical funding was provided for research, cooperative education, guidance, and disadvantaged and handicapped, together with set-asides for postsecondary vocational programs. All set specific, if not new, directions for the conduct of vocational education. Additionally, the declaration of purpose statement in the act directed that vocational education would be available to all people of all ages in the communities of our nation and provided additional emphasis for programming.

The expanded role set forth by the act affected virtually every program area encompassed under previous federal vocational education legislation. Subsequent amendments additionally influenced vocational programming without imposing any major limitations on the audience to be served or the programs to be delivered.

Changing Priorities

The expansion of vocational education emphasized by federal legislation in 1963 took on new meaning with the Carl Perkins Act of 1984. The wisdom of Congress deemed that previously unserved audiences would become beneficiaries of federal dollars for vocational education. It was not the intent of the act to redirect state funding for vocational education, but rather to hold the needs of various special populations as a national priority.

Clearly, the idea that vocational education could address the needs of special populations had to be accepted as a compliment by the field. Furthermore, to recognize that there were groups of individuals who were not being adequately served by the nation's schools was a harsh reminder of the early battles required to establish vocational education as a part of public education in America.

Responding to the new mandates for use of federal funds, however, posed important questions regarding the specific purposes of vocational education as well as creating uncertainty about how serving an even more diverse audience would impact on program enrollments. There was concern that the often expressed public view of vocational education as not being appropriate for able learners—that it was for somebody else's kids—would be further promoted.

The Future Role

The future role of federal legislation must be debated. Such legislation appropriately should be an expression of the nation's priorities. If there is to be a continuing presence in vocational education at the federal level, it is critical that the vocational education needs of our citizenry which remain unmet by individual states be addressed in federal legislation.

It is appropriate to question whether the need for such legislation continues to exist. Does the economic need for appropriate, quality education dictate the continuing promotion of vocational education as a national priority? Does the changing nature of the workforce and society demand specific education for work beyond that which is a part of the general education/college prep program that exists in public education today? With the mobility of our nation's people, are the states individually able to insure an adequate and skilled workforce? Should preparation for work be the responsibility of business and industry? What is the role of the military and the unions in insuring a supply of workers? Should vocational education be delayed until after the high school years? These questions must be debated as a part of our nation's agenda. Then, and perhaps only then, can a national policy on vocational education be reasonably developed.

Schooling

Schools at the turn of the twentieth century did not present a balanced view of either democracy or equality. Schooling at that time was based on preparation for college. Regardless of how liberal that education was declared to be, it was unappealing to youth of that day. And, if it was liberating, it was only in the sense that most of the secondary aged youth were liberated from continuing their formal education. More than 90 percent of such youth dropped out of the public education system before completing requirements for a high school diploma. Furthermore, the majority of those who did meet such requirements were women. Typically, both females and males left the public schools by the age of 14; the majority of these having not yet completed the sixth grade (U.S. Department of Labor, 1968).

Proponents of vocational education believed that by including vocational programs the schools would be more democractic for all. While the schools were freely open to every young person, the aims and purposes did not encourage offering preparation for the life's work that most youth would face. Vocational training was viewed as an alternative that would provide a reason for youth to continue in school beyond the age of 14, and thus extend their general education together with developing skills that would prepare them for roles as workers. Better citizens and better workers were among the outcomes sought (Prosser, 1913).

Separate School Systems Advocated

Vocational education was proposed as a separate system of education by Snedden. That vocational education might be controlled by the same men who then controlled the impractical education of the day was a major concern (Snedden, 1910). While some limited form of education involving shops existed in the schools, this education was not considered as "real" vocational education. What was being promoted was a practical education based on the requirements of the workplace, with the educational setting being as near a replication of that workplace as possible. Although those who argued for the separate school systems failed to achieve that goal, vocational education emerged as a result of their genuine concern for youth and the failure of the schools to provide an educational program not only attractive to young people, but also fitted to their needs.

John Dewey (1916) joined his voice with those who promoted vocational education. However, his goal was to bring about reformation of the schools. Vocational education was a means to induce changes that would improve all of education. The socialistic interests of Dewey were evident in many of his statements on vocational education. Regardless, it was clear that Dewey believed that occupations were central to life, and thus should be central to educational activity. In spite of points of agreement concerning the importance of vocational education, there was considerable argument between Dewey and the Snedden-Prosser camp.

Vocational Education—Method or Interest

Controversy centered in the how and why vocational education should be developed rather than whether it should be developed. On the one hand it was argued that vocational education, or occupations, should be the central theme around which education should be organized. Others argued that vocational education should not be restricted to the classroom; it needed to be expanded to the place where actual work was taking place. When that was not possible, the school should become a workplace and demonstrate the economics of industry by producing products and turning a profit.

For some, vocational education was a method to accomplish the purposes of education. For others, vocational education was a means to prepare youth for earning a living and making for an improved citizenry while at the same time improving the economic well-being of industry and consequently society itself.

A Plan for Redesigning Schools

Reformation in education continues. Many of the struggles of the past are the issues of the future. One school system exists as two and even three systems of education. College prepatory tracks are alive and well, existing for much the same purpose as they did at the turn of the twentieth century (Boyer, 1983). Education in this system is designed to prepare students for the rigors of a university education—an education which universities frequently claim is inappropriate for all but a small portion of the population. The end result is that a majority of those who enroll in four-year institutions of higher education fail to complete degree requirements at the end of four years.

General education exists for those who are not willing to undertake the rigors of the college prep program and/or who have not established an occupational direction for their lives (Parnell, 1985). Some critics of this system within the system have labeled it as goalless education. That label is fitting in the sense that many who wind up within this system have not set some clear, albeit temporary, direction for their lives. The real tragedy for these youth is that they leave school without possessing the skills important to competitiveness in the marketplace.

Vocational education continues to compete for students. While Gallup Poll results indicate that parents believe that preparation for work is an appropriate function of the schools, it appears that many do not encourage their offspring to enroll in programs designed to prepare youth for employment. At the same time, increases in entrance requirements for institutions of higher education cause secondary schools to raise graduation requirements. In turn, good students are directed away from vocational education in the belief that such courses will adversely influence their ability to enter a college or university. Regardless, states with high quality vocational education programs continue to experience growth in enrollments (Oklahoma State Department of Vocational and Technical Education, n.d.). In some instances, growing enrollments are based on adult participation in vocational education; in others, the growth pattern reflects secondary students or some combination of the two.

Reasons for this growth pattern are not clear. It may be an unanticipated response to increasing graduation and college entrance requirements, or it may reflect a variety of reasons such as unemployment, changing workplace demands, a desire for greater earning power, better publicity by vocational educators, or a plethora of other influences. Regardless, it seems clear that schooling and work are a part of life and living.

Educators, as they undertake the task of preparing youth for life and living in a world culture, need to critically examine the relationship of schooling and work. Is preparation for work appropriately served by a college prep or general curriculum? How are lifelong learning needs to be furthered by the schools? How critical is it that all learners be required to master the same liberal education? If learning is a lifelong experience, is it necessary that the same educational prescription be sequenced and followed by all? Is schooling largely a school-based experience, or should education be promoted as a community-based experience? Should the activities of schooling be organized with expectations similar to those of the workplace? Is education structured as a democractic experience? Should vocational education be job specific? Is vocational education a method of instruction more than an area of schooling? Without being redundant, it is appropriate to point out that these are not necessarily new questions. However, old answers to old questions are unlikely to provide appropriate direction for education, including vocational education, as society moves into the next century.

Work

At the beginning of this century, work was a more dominant feature for youth than schooling. Mandatory attendance beyond the age of fourteen was not common among the states. For the vast majority, if dropping out of the educational system had not occurred before that age, fourteen signaled the time to become employed or work full time on the farm.

Even for young women, work was a way of life. Commonly, girls joined the workforce after completing or leaving school and continued to work for five or more years preceding marriage. If that marriage was financially secure, it signaled the end of employment outside the home.

Changing Worker Patterns

The character of work underwent major changes at the time vocational education was being promoted. Small workshops and industries expanded into a national urban-industrial network having a few giant corporations controlling the country's corporate income. Increasing industrialization and mechanization changed handicafting into assembly line and mass production of goods. Worker discretion in the workplace gave way to management and supervisor control of worker behavior. Increasingly, the range of skills and processes of the work were reduced and specialized. Traditional apprenticeship programs lost their past basis for existence.

Moreover, the increasing economic strength of Germany drew attention to their vocational schools and by contrast the lack of vocational education for youth in America. A commonly held view is that work changes and the need for specialized workers to meet international competition together with the current failure of the schools to serve societal needs became the basis for a new vocationalism in education (Kanton, 1982).

Workplace Expectations

Changes in work and the workplace did not stop with the advent of vocational education as a part of American education. In fact, one of the challenges to vocational education has been in staying current with workplace change. The continuing automation of industry, specialization of tasks, increasing complexity of machines, tools, and processes, and a resultant dehumanization of work, have individually and collectively required adaptation by both vocational education and the worker.

The accumulating impact of change has influenced its own change. Productivity declined and worker interest in having more influence on the way work was accomplished refocused attention on the importance of the worker as a person. The work ethic, described by some as lost, was rekindled through encouraging worker input and direction. The Japanese system of Quality Circles, Volvo's model for team production of complete units, and various American productivity models have influenced the way work is performed.

Workers, too, have developed their own responses to change in the workplace. While change of occupation or major shifts in work-related activity were not common early in this century, many workers are experiencing at least two distinct careers during their working lives. These "second acts" reflect a desire to get away from a particular set of demands that frequently are based on economic need, and to move into a more satisfying producer role. To retire from one work life to begin a second more fulfilling one is likely to expand as a way of life. Changes in mandatory retirement, longer life expectancy, and a fundamental desire to be productive have also contributed to changing worker patterns.

Youth Return to Work

The youth of our nation also reflect a changing view of work. The participation of school-aged youth in the workforce is on a rising trend (William T. Grant Foundation, 1988). Regardless of whether or not this trend is stimulated by youth's desire to acquire material goods, or parental encouragement, or some combination of factors, many young men and women are learning about the requirements of the workplace while contributing to the nation's economy. The educative value of such experience is great.

Work is central to life itself. The work ethic which has been evident throughout America's history appears to be alive and well in spite of rumors to the contrary. The meaning of work to the individual is also important. Personal identity is frequently based on a person's occupational role. Our society also stresses the importance of work. Fundamental changes have recently occurred in the nation's welfare system that signal our society's concern for people as producers. These changes stress the importance of preparing people as workers and authorize several billion dollars for programs designed to move individuals from a consumer-only role to fuller participation as producers in the economic system of the country. This centrality of work in our society and the affairs of individuals should also be central in our educational system.

Developing a Vision

Education's leadership must participate in developing a vision of the future of work. Some argue that America will return to a goods-producing economy while others claim the future economy will be service-based. Others propose that in the world-based economy of the future, our nation will fill the information-producing niche. Current technological changes have stimulated a need for workers prepared to create, operate, and maintain new technology. However, the majority of workers in the technological workplace are not required to have high-level technological skills. Each scenario occasions a different configuration of workplace requirements. Yet, it seems obvious that we are going to need workers to participate in each—whether one or more—employment area of the future.

The time for the future is now. The majority of those who will be participating in the workforce during the first two decades of the next century are already in school. On the surface it appears that education has not changed, other than requiring more of the same, in response to workplace expectations of the future. A redesign and reformation of education must occur to give greater emphasis to the importance of work in our society. Education which focuses on preparation for more education is not an adequate provision for the future. Arguably, such education could be anticipating a lifetime of learning; however, the conditions that would promote that attitude are not a dominant feature of present education.

Vocational educators must display 20/20 vision regarding the future. Anticipating workplace needs for the year 2020 has to begin now. Without question, workers of that era must be thinkers and problem solvers. They will need to access knowledge and make application of information as a routine part of producing. Adapting to change and making application of technologies that are not now on the drawing boards of futurists will also be a routine part of the workplace. Designing a vocational education system that promotes the importance and excitement of learning as being more critical than what is learned has to become a prominent feature of education that is to serve the learning needs of both individuals and our society in the future. Acquiring 20/20 vision has to begin now.

Participants

Youth and their needs were central to the early efforts of the National Society for the Promotion of Industrial Education. High dropout rates and a lack of opportunity for a practical education dominated the concerns of early leaders of vocational education. Youth remain central to the efforts to maintain and expand educational opportunities today. With increases in dropouts, increasing teenage pregnancy and teenage suicide, increasing use of drugs, poorer achievement rates, higher illiteracy, and heightened social problems, the issues surrounding youth may have changed, but their need for vocational education as a part of their preparation for living has not.

Adults, like youth, traditionally have been included as a part of the audience to be served by vocational education. The Smith-Hughes Act was specific in providing for meeting both the civic and industrial "intelligence" of those who had left school to enter the workforce. Part-time vocational education for employed adults seeking to improve their opportunities through skill upgrading or preparation for a new role has largely been available through evening or short-term classes. Today adults are being integrated in regular daytime classes with younger learners, resulting in improved learning outcomes for both age groups.

Old Learners as New Learners

Educational activity conducted prior to the hiring of new employees has become a reality. Pre-hire education is designed to determine the adaptability and work-related learning capacity of prospective employees. In these same workplaces, those who demonstrate such capacities are then provided extended pre-job training while on the payroll. Furthermore, employers will continue to invest in the education of these same employees. Lifelong learning, as a requirement for maintaining a productive place in the workforce, is not only evident today but will be a standard in the workplace of the future. Vocational education will be an important way to meet these learning needs.

Expanding expectations of the school system have increased opportunities for vocational education to serve additional populations. The mainstreaming of all individuals in the public schools of our nation has brought a broader array of learners into the classroom of vocational educators. Serving the needs of learners with a variety of restrictions on their ability to compete with the larger population has deepened the responsibilities of preparing individuals for productive lives. At the same time, being able to serve those with special learning needs has created an image for some that this is the major role of vocational education.

Who then are the participants in vocational education of the future? First, it must be recognized that some are against having vocational education as a part of the public system of education, claiming that this is the responsibility of business and industry. Clearly, this issue must be reconciled before addressing other dimensions of the question. However, if workplace preparation remains as a part of our public education system, whether vocational education should be included as secondary or not must be determined. If it is not to be included as secondary education, how will the schools be reconfigured to meet the needs of the many youth already alienated by present day education? Or, should it be that vocational education should only serve the needs of special populations in their quest to be independent citizens? Should vocational education become the sole responsibility of postsecondary institutions—public and private— or should it be left to private educational agencies? And, how about those who are employed? Should their continuing workplace-related education be the primary responsibility of the employer, and does the size of the employer influence public response to this question? What is it that public tax monies should support in the way of vocational education?

Teachers

Vocational teachers, according to expectations set forth by the Smith-Hughes Act, need to be experienced in the occupational area to be taught. This commonly held belief reflected the idea that if you had not earned a living doing something, you probably would not be successful in helping others prepare to earn a living in that occupation. Having occupational experience was a prerequisite to be a vocational teacher. In fact, the requirement of occupational experience took priority over preparation to teach.

Teacher preparation programs were called for under the Smith-Hughes Act. To receive federal dollars for vocational education, states had to insure the presence of vocational teacher education programs. Such programs followed two basic models.

The first model, based on preservice preparation of teachers, was applicable to agriculture and home economics and paralleled other teacher preparation programs of the day. While the would-be teacher had to demonstrate experience in the area to be taught—for agriculture this meant having lived on a farm for two or more years after the age of fourteen—the professional courses generally followed the same pattern as for other secondary level teachers. Changes in vocational teacher education certification were like those of other secondary teachers, eventually requiring a baccalaureate degree as the standard. Significant changes in program design were nil.

The second model, based on inservice education, was characteristic to the teacher preparation of persons who taught the trade areas. Prospective teachers were selected from an appropriate area of the trades or industry prior to receiving any type of teacher education. While there might be some brief formal training before entering the classroom, most of the preparation to teach ocurred after the person was on the job as a vocational teacher. This model exists today as the dominant prototype for trade and industrial teachers.

A Call for Reform

Future expectations of vocational teachers set the stage for changes in the models for preparation of these teachers. While both systems have served the profession in the past, it is unlikely that either will survive without major redesign. The baccalaureate teacher education program is being assailed on several fronts. Critics charge that there is too much professional education and not enough subject matter content and insufficient preparation in the liberal arts. Some teacher educators advocate a liberal arts degree as the base for entry into teacher education, with the specialization and professional preparation occuring at the fifth and sixth year. Given these criticisms and, more importantly, recognizing the special needs of vocational teachers to be adaptive to the changing demands of the workplace, it is certain that new patterns for the preparation of vocational teachers will emerge.

The redesign of vocational teacher education is critical to future programs of vocational education. Emerging teacher education programs must be able to attract highly competent individuals with cognitive abilities that will allow them to conceptualize problems and propose workable alternatives. Future vocational teacher candidates additionally must have the personal communication skills and attributes that allow for group decision making and cooperation integral to the workplace. Furthermore, it is imperative that individuals be representative of persons from non-traditional roles as well as ethnic minorities. The realization of these outcomes is a challenge yet to be met by the profession. It is, however, a challenge that cannot be avoided.

Leadership

Leadership for vocational education has historically emerged from the teaching ranks. Teachers became department heads or local directors of vocational programs. State agency supervisors came from local schools and state directors of vocational education were selected from local schools or promoted from within the state agency itself. The tradition of having been a vocational teacher is a strong thread of continuity that has constituted the warp and woof of leadership for vocational education. That tradition also relates to the two major service areas identified by the Smith-Hughes Act, agricultural education and trade and industrial education.

Agricultural education has a strong basis for leadership based on the requirements of Smith-Hughes. The act required states to designate state level supervisors for these programs. Additionally, the requirement that teacher education programs be created for this field added impetus to leadership emerging from this area.

Trade and industrial education (T&I), while established as an area by Smith-Hughes, depended on workers from the trade areas together with industrial workers to supply teachers for programs in this area. The antecedents for leadership were not necessarily a part of these teachers' experience. Yet, in many of the states which were heavily industrialized in 1917, it was teachers from T&I who emerged as state leaders.

Creating a Leadership Pool

With the changes in vocational education that were created with the passage of the Vocational Education Act of 1963, the visionary leadership of the day saw a need for leadership to be prepared for the expanding programs of vocational education that were on the horizon. Funding for a leadership development program in vocational education was approved as a part of the 1968 Amendments to the 1963 Vocational Education Act. Commonly referred to as the EPDA 552 program, it was out of this effort that a sizeable pool of leaders was prepared for leadership roles that rapidly emerged during the seventies. It was this effort that helped universities unify programs to better meet the personnel needs of vocational education during the next two decades.

Leadership during the decade of the nineties will certainly demand responses differing from those in the past. Expanding and changing roles for vocational education together with a more diversified and varying audience will require new strategies for delivery of services. Workplace changes will further impact on the place where schooling occurs and in part will stimulate the empowerment of teachers. Even the graying of America will impact the need for additional leaders as retirements allow for upward career opportunities within the profession. And how will the profession respond?

Whatever the response, planning and preparation will be keys. It is not adequate to believe that appropriate leadership will simply emerge from the ranks. Workplace demands of today's professionals do not allow adequate time for major professional studies nor the concomitant time for reflective thinking. Resources at both the federal and state level need to be focused on developing leadership for the future. A plan for attracting highly qualified individuals into graduate programs must be instituted. At the same time, graduate programs must reflect change and increasing flexibility required to be adaptive for the future. Identifying research needs, using research findings to propose alternatives to emerging problems, developing a better knowledge base about learners and learning, developing skills in the area of metacognition, opting for decision making involvement at all levels, adapting to new management strategies, being able to ascertain the right things to do and then doing the things right, and expanding linkages with a broad variety of audiences are all candidates vying for attention in the reformation of graduate programs seeking to prepare future leaders for vocational education. How to stimulate the magnitude of effort demanded in preparation of leaders for the future must be resolved by those with a 20/20 vision.

Experience and Philosophy

Experience has been the measure for decision making in vocational education for more than the last half century. Experience has been a central theme in preparation for work; it has been a prerequisite for vocational teachers; and it has guided the practices of the profession. In short, experience has been "king of the hill" in vocational education.

As the "king of the hill" it has too frequently substituted for philosophy. Unfortunately, while it can be useful in deriving and verifying a philosophic position, it is not a substitute for philosophy. Experience alone fails to provide a way of answering, "What is it that we ought to ought?" Philosophy as an area of concern, a way of thinking, a way of knowing the important questions, and a way of viewing the world is the experience yet to be touted by the profession. The exercise of philosophic thinking is the experience base that will complement past accomplishments while at the same time aiding advances in the quest for even greater excellence. That philosophic journey is now. □

References

Boyer, E. L. (1983). *High school: A report on secondary education in America.* New York: Harper and Row.
Dewey, J. (1916). *Democracy and education.* New York: Macmillan.
Kanton, H. (1982). Vocationalism in American education: The economic and political context, 1890-1930. In H. Kanton and D. B. Tyack (Eds.), *Work, youth and schooling* (pp. 14-44). Stanford, Calif.: Stanford University Press.
Oklahoma State Department of Vocational and Technical Education (1988). *In search of excellence: 1988 annual report.* Stillwater, Okla.
Parnell, D. (1985). *The neglected majority.* Washington, D.C.: Community College Press.
Prosser, C. A. (1913). The meaning of industrial education. *Vocational Education,* May.
Snedden, D. (1910). *The problem of vocational education.* Boston, Mass.: Houghton Mifflin.

U.S. Department of Labor (1968). *Trends in the educational attainment of women.* Washington, D.C.: U.S. Government Printing Office.

William T. Grant Foundation Commission on Work, Family and Citizenship (1988). *The forgotten half: Pathways to success for America's youth and young families.* Final Report: Youth and America's Future. Washington, D.C.

Wirth, A. G. (1983). *Productive work: On industry and school, becoming persons again.* Lanham, Md.: University Press of America.

CHAPTER 3

The Secondary Vocational Program

By Gerald D. Cheek

VOCATIONAL education, like any other discipline, wants to provide the finest for its clientele. As a profession, it should set its own direction and not allow others to determine its future. However, recent attacks on education, with emphasis on achieving excellence, have once again put secondary vocational education on the defensive. As a result, many in the profession are perplexed and uncertain of the future.

Considerable numbers of influential people view secondary vocational education as less than excellent. In fact, many outsiders would like to see secondary vocational education eliminated. This is not going to happen, but what does the future hold for secondary vocational education? More importantly: How can the profession take charge, plot its own course, and be in control of its own destiny? Since we have no way of knowing the future, we can only raise questions and look at trends that may provide insights of what will come.

Secondary vocational education has undergone numerous changes during the past decade. These changes have come about because of pressures from both outside and inside the profession. Some believe that certain changes are being implemented too quickly, without supporting evidence or adequate citizen involvement. Others want to throw away all of the old and start over immediately. Needless to say, secondary education in the United States is in a period of rapid transition.

Recent national studies that assesed the quality of secondary education failed to mention vocational programs in their final reports: *A Nation at Risk; Action for Excellence; Report of Twentieth Century Fund Task Force on Federal Elementary and Secondary Educational Policy:* and *High School: A Report on Secondary Education in America.* This was not surprising, since none of the blue ribbon panels included members knowledgeable in vocational education. These groups were largely composed of the academic elite, representatives from large corporations, and politicians. However, the composition of the panels and the fact that they ignored vocational education provide a mirror of their priorities for secondary education. For example, vocational education did not even register when issues of economic development were considered. If nothing else changes in the future, the image of vocational education and its perceived importance must be improved. It must be perceived as being a critically important part of the secondary curriculum.

With all of the emphasis in education being placed upon achieving excellence, vocational education is once again under a microscope. Its worthiness and even its continuance are being closely examined. Many of the proposed changes have come about because general education is under attack. The trend to achieve excellence in education by returning to the "basics" has resulted in a reform movement that is having a negative impact on the secondary vocational curriculum.

Before projections are made for the future, one should examine the axioms of secondary vocational education. These axioms are offered because they have guided the development and continuance of its programs and have been used to evaluate its effectiveness. An examination of these axioms, in light of present circumstances, can provide clarification of where secondary vocational education should and can be directed. If cures are mandated, the profession can formulate convalescent strategies and take positive and deliberate actions to ensure a healthy and viable place for secondary vocational education. The basic question remains: What will secondary vocational education be in the future?

Axiom #1: Secondary Schools Can Prepare Students For Work

Secondary vocational education has held a prominent position in the past, principally because it has attempted to serve youth by preparing them to enter the workforce. National problems associated with high youth unemployment, changing technologies, and poor economic conditions have contributed to a changing emphasis in high school preparatory programs. These problems are real today and will undoubtedly be with us in the foreseeable future.

Some of the social issues that receive daily attention are unacceptably high illiteracy and dropout rates, the increasingly high incidence of drug abuse and violent crimes, and low academic achievement by many students. With all of these issues, along with an increasing population of underachievers, vocational education has come under attack for not attaining the goals that others have in mind for our profession. Vocational education has been viewed by some as being a "dead end" that will lead to despair for anyone who pursues it. This critical view might be justifiable if secondary vocational education was terminal and graduates could not pursue further education or training. Such criticism might also be justifiable if vocational education prepared students for a single job and failed to educate them in the affective and cognitive aspects of the working world environment.

Secondary vocational education continues to prepare students with average and lower-than-average abilities and motivation so that they can become contributing members of society. With assistance from the private sector, programs in agriculture, business, health, home economics, marketing, and industrial education continue to be successful in preparing students for the workforce. However, it has become increasingly more difficult to "squeeze" sufficient time from the secondary curriculum for this important effort. Increased graduation requirements have resulted in fewer elective hours and students are having difficulty finding time in their schedules for either exploratory or preparatory programs. Vocational programs are being reorganized into one hour classes that more easily fit into the regular school schedules, regardless of the programmatic consequences. Increasingly, attention is diverted to teaching basic skills and providing a familiarization with technology rather than preparing students for the next level of vocational or technical education. Additionally, several states have already conducted studies and are now exploring options to have related content substitute for general academic graduation requirements. Some vocational courses have been found to offer sufficient content in communications, science, mathematics, health, and economics and have been approved to grant general education credits. Efforts to assist students in attaining job requirements have been switched to helping them meet graduation requirements. Courses in health occupations have turned toward nutrition, AIDS prevention, sex education, and personal health in order to be approved as a substitute for general education credits. Business subjects have eliminated three-hour blocks and focused on personal bookkeeping, written communications, general computer skills, and general typing instead of offering sufficient time and practice for job entry requirements. Trade and industrial education (T&I) programs are becoming difficult to distinguish from technology education programs. They are assuming an exploratory role and teaching "clustered" occupational areas in communications, power and energy, transportation, electro-mechanics, graphic arts, manufacturing, and construction. Additionally, agriculture education programs have, in many instances, changed to exploratory programs in gardening, horticulture, mechanics, science, and agribusiness. These and other changes have been made with a focus on new graduation requirements, notwithstanding their negative impact on preparation for work.

Secondary home economics programs probably have been the least affected area of vocational education. Consumer home economics, which constitutes the majority of such programs, never was designed to prepare graduates for wage earning occupations. However, during this transition, many programs which prepared students for jobs in child care and commercial food production have been changed to consumer education programs.

Even with all of the changes, placing students in related jobs for which they were prepared is still considered the standard for assessing the effectiveness of programs in secondary vocational education.

However, this standard does not take into account the background and capabilities of students, their past educational experiences, and the design of the program offering. Furthermore, the criterion of assessing program effectiveness solely on related job placements does not even consider the economic conditions at the time of graduation. Additionally, it doesn't take into account the fact that many occupations have become so technical that the secondary school effort is designed to prepare students for postsecondary programs where they will complete their technical training.

If the nature of the clients served and time available for training have changed, the criterion for assessing program effectiveness must also change. Accountability should be based on the goals of all secondary vocational programs and not just those preparing students to enter work.

Axiom #2:
There Is Permanence
in Job Skill Requirements

According to several reports, many of the low level skilled jobs are disappearing from the work place. Critics who have a negative opinion of vocational education voice their skepticism about preparing students for such low level and assembly line jobs. However, secondary vocational education has never attempted to prepare minimally skilled workers for service and manufacturing. Such workers are customarily trained on the job, since little time is needed and such training requires specialized equipment.

Historically, vocational education has provided training in recognized semi-skilled occupations that require considerable time to learn. While most entry level semi-skilled jobs are low on the occupational ladder, they do lead to promotion as a result of experience and success on the job. Like others in the work force, vocational graduates will change jobs, receive different titles, and may even change their occupations. This is not to be considered unfortunate or harmful, it is just the normal procedure for workers as they progress through their careers.

Contrary to the thinking of many, the "basics" of semi-skilled occupations have not changed drastically over the years. Today, a machinist, secretary, carpenter, auto mechanic, drafter, salesperson, cook, electrician, mason, broadcaster, welder, etc., is expected to perform his/her duties utilizing new technologies, materials, and equipment. While new technology has had an impact on how the worker performs the basics and reduced the amount of physical labor, the basic tasks have continued to be a part of the job and still remain.

Semi-skilled jobs constitute a large percentage of today's work force. However, it is projected that new jobs in this category will decrease from the present 40 percent to approximately 27 percent by the year 2000. This is a complicated projection because many job titles rather than jobs are being eliminated. This is being done by "clustering" jobs with different titles and giving the resulting job a new a broad, vague, and often meaningless title.

An example of this happening is with the job titled "maintenance mechanic." Work traditionally done by a team of specialists such as electricians, welders, machinists, mechanics, mill wrights, etc., is being combined into the job of one individual. Industries are usually accomplishing this by cross-training incumbent workers. However, this new job is an extremely difficult one to train, even when the incumbent worker is proficient in one or more of the specialties. In the future, if four jobs are combined into one, and the entry level loses its title, is the entry level job itself lost? The answer is no, but statistically yes! In fact, few jobs are actually lost because of new technologies.

Without permanence, there will be no need to purchase expensive equipment and build or renovate laboratories. However, a large investment in equipment may be questionable for developing a preparatory program in an occupational area that is experiencing rapid and dramatic changes. However, the basics of these occupational areas may be taught and articulated with a postsecondary institution.

Additionally, secondary vocational education contributes more to its students than just developing the manipulative skills required in jobs. Skills and knowledge associated with work attitudes, socialization, safety, health, hygiene, and ethics are also taught, and these applied skills will never become absolute. Students are taught good work habits and often they develop a sincere desire to become a productive worker in a society which is increasingly complex occupationally. Through vocational youth clubs, students are given oportunities to learn leadership skills. They are given responsibilities and provided activities that help students develop socially.

These important qualities are difficult to accomplish in other school programs that are normally regimented and lack the proper social environment. Additionally, and to some more importantly, students learn to apply math, science, and other basics that provide relevance to otherwise abstract subject matter. Many vocational students are classified as not being able to learn, but some students learn differently and vocational education provides a mode that facilitates their cognitive development.

Changes are occurring so rapidly, and jobs are becoming so sophisticated, that some contend that technical skills are not as important as they once were. Critics argue that vocational education should be providing experiences that assist students to "learn how to learn" instead of teaching technical skills. They advocate an education that goes beyond the use of tools and equipment and includes the ability to communicate, make decisions, solve problems, analyze and evaluate tasks and situations, and most importantly, enable one to learn continuously. However, if students don't get their first job, it will be difficult to determine whether they are able to perform and learn.

The challenge for secondary vocational education is to provide preparatory programs in occupations that have permanence in basic job skill requirements and provide separate exploratory programs in occupational areas that are more sophisticated and require postsecondary training. Exploratory programs of this nature should teach generic work and employability skills rather than job-specific skills.

Axiom #3:
Career Decisions and Choices
Can Be Made Early

Guidance counselors and other academics continue to argue that career choices should be delayed until after high school is completed. This is understandable, since these very people were privileged to delay their decision while attending college—something not all secondary graduates can afford or want to do. Little attention is given to the motivational value of early career choices and the part vocational education plays in career guidance.

Counselors discernibly believe that the ladder concept that

involves moving a person up through the organization can only happen in the private sector and not in education. They don't seem to believe that orientation and vocational programs can be arranged in a fashion that would enable students initially to be exposed to broad occupational clusters and later to specialize in a job within an occupational cluster. The assumption continues that employers will provide all of the necessary skill training or that the preparation of individuals for jobs should only take place in postsecondary institutions.

The broad concept of career education was to start during the early years in school, with awareness programs, and continue throughout postsecondary education. Since many of the awareness and exploration programs have disappeared, vocational education has had to assume these responsibilities so that students can make more informed career choices.

The importance of making early career choices cannot be overemphasized. The school should assist and encourage early career choices rather than trying to prevent students from making them. Making a career choice early does not mean that students enrolled in secondary vocational programs have made their final choice and that they are not allowed to change.

Outside of vocational education, little practical help is provided in the school setting to assist students with career exploration and decision making. This responsibility should not be solely borne by vocational education. Helping students choose careers is a responsibility that must be shared by all elements of the community and its educational system.

School officials have not been supportive of students making early career choices. Career education's attempts during the 1970s seem to have failed to make a lasting impact. General education and vocational education have not formed a lasting pact to educate all children. Their roles were not solidified and many career education programs vanished after funding disappeared. General and vocational education remain separate because they are fearful of the outcomes. Vocational educators are fearful of becoming more general and general educators are fearful of being required to teach about occupations.

Generally, counselors are not equipped to provide students with sufficient information on what is required to be successful in occupations that do not require college degrees. However, this doesn't mean that students who enter vocational programs are less informed than their counterparts who enter college. A sad indictment of their lack of effectiveness is that 50 percent of entering college freshmen do not have a declared major.

Little attention has been given in the orientation of school counselors and administrators to the world of work. All too often counselors and administrators have no work experience other than in the field of education. They know little about technical occupations and are not prepared to work with representatives from the private sector when they are asked to assist students in making the transition from education to work. Additionally, in most cases, counselors are not able to assist students in attaining employment.

Even though it is well documented that the school provides little assistance with the school-to-work transition, large numbers of students do decide to go to work and not to go on to postsecondary education. When some argue that students are not prepared to go to work and should delay this decision, they ignore the social and economic realities which necessitate "getting a job."

Axiom #4:
Vocational Education Is Different from General Education

In the eyes of most, vocational education remains separate from and different from general education. This must be true since vocational education was not mentioned during national studies assessing the quality of education in the nation's secondary schools. This separatism persists even though some have observed that vocational education is becoming more like general education. Certain specialized applied math, science, communications, and literacy courses are being called "vocational education." In several states, students are granted general education credits for content learned in vocational subjects. The "return-to-the-basics reform movement" may succeed where career education failed in uniting vocational and general education.

In some instances, secondary vocational education is becoming an appendage of general education. In the future, it may become a part of education that supplements and enhances general education rather than focusing on the preparation of students for the world of work. As vocational education becomes more closely identified with the imparting of basic skills, it will stray away from the association it has had with the economy and the labor market. Moreover, it will no longer be appropriate to use the evaluation criterion of job placement when assessing the effectiveness of vocational education. Both general and vocational programs should then be evaluated upon how well they have prepared students for the next level of education. For many, vocational programs will become exploratory rather than preparatory.

The question of whether vocational and general education are different is now increasingly difficult to answer. Some projects have been implemented that have a vocational/career curriculum. These projects may start as early as the first grade and continue on through high school. Courses have been suggested that focus on personal development, social systems, information skills, resource management, technology, and career opportunities, as well as occupational preparation in cluster programs. Additionally, programs are expected to be adapted to meet the needs of special populations.

Exploratory programs in agriculture, business, health, home economics, marketing, and technology education have provided bridges between general education and vocational education. However, at the time vocational education becomes preparatory, it is separated from its exploratory counterparts. In fact, this apparent family remains at odds and continues to incite confrontation on differences instead of suporting each other's position. Proclamations for unanimity seem to fall on deaf ears. How can vocational education become an integral constituent of general education when this feud continues within the family? Few would argue that separatism has been harmful to students. Both should stand ready to defend the education of the individual and contribute to the needs of society. However, separatism of academic and vocational students must continue to occur if secondary education is to remain committed to serving students who do not plan to attend postsecondary education. It also is necessary if vocational education's identity is to continue.

Axiom #5:
It Is Possible to Remain Current with New Technologies

The workplace is becoming increasingly complicated, and for the most part, highly technical. Our nation is entering into a new cycle of development which many refer to as the "information age." More jobs are requiring the handling of information, and from all projections this will increase in the future. Flexible manufacturing, robots, computers, and information handling systems will impact heavily on traditional occupations. As a result, longer and more sophisticated preparation will be required. Vocational and technical education are having difficulty keeping pace with these trends. The private sector is also having trouble transferring these new technologies into the work place, since many workers lack the knowledge and skills on which to build new learning experiences.

Today, few can find jobs which don't require a minimum command of communications, mathematics, scientific principles, and technical literacy. With the emphasis being placed on quality and higher productivity, more paperwork and reasoning skills are required in what once were unskilled jobs. Continuing education has become a way of life in order to maintain one's position. Semi-skilled jobs are rapidly becoming classified as technician level jobs and the need for applied science and mathematics is increasing.

Keeping current with new technologies has been a problem which will escalate in the future. The workplace of the future will be more complicated, and many manufacturing companies will no longer have long production runs that provide stable job requirements; they will instead have short duration production runs that are market driven. Instead of production driven manufacturing, it will be product driven, which will require a more sophisticated and flexible worker. Workers will be required to make numerous machine adjustments, enabling the company to change from mass production to flexible production. The production process will become more responsive to the demands of a changing market.

Occupations in agriculture, manufacturing, construction, and service that require lower-level basic academic and technical skills are fewer in number, while the number of youngsters needing special assistance in preparing for work is increasing. A paradox exists with this dilemma. For example, (a) students graduating from public schools have lower achievement levels than in the past, (b) the percentage of adult illiterates is increasing, (c) funding levels for vocational education have decreased, (d) vocational education now serves a higher percentage of low achievers and unmotivated students, and (e) dropout rates are increasing. Even with these discrepancies, it is projected that by the year 2000, the United States may not have the entry level work force needed to maintain a healthy economy.

Vocational education must solicit and obtain the support of the private sector to remain current and expand to meet future demands. This is paramount since neither the federal government nor the local education administration has the will or the resources to solve these problems.

Every preparatory program should terminate by providing a capstone internship experience in the real world of work. The best place to learn many aspects of a job is on the job. Students must be provided on-the-job supervised experience using the latest technologies and equipment. This is not to be confused with work-study that merely provides students with a job so they can financially afford to stay in school. Cooperative education, utilizing proper placements, will keep instructors informed of how current their programs are with the new technologies. Without assistance from corporate America, secondary vocational education will have a difficult time meeting the requirements of this axiom.

Axiom #6:
Vocational Education Can Provide Programs for All Levels of Students

Today, vocational education in high schools is being asked to provide quality programs for those students who can benefit from the experience as well as for those with lesser abilities and motivation. The total educational delivery system has essentially failed students who are less able and less motivated. Alternatives are constantly being sought to assist with this dilemma. Adding to the problem are the legislative mandates to "mainstream" handicapped students and eliminate separate special education programs.

Vocational education has borne the brunt of this movement.

However, few states and communities have allocated sufficient funds to properly implement these mandates. Federal vocational funds, even though in short supply, have been diverted for this purpose at the expense of other established directions. Students are placed into programs and exposed to technical concepts, machinery, processes, materials, and techniques used in business and industry. Little attention is given to instructional strategies for delivering education for such diverse student populations at the same time. It should not be surprising to find that vocational education has not been much more successful in providing education for the handicapped and special needs students than the other education programs from which they are transferred. Individualized approaches have been attempted, but they have little chance of succeeding if students are not motivated or do not have sufficient academic skills.

Some educational planners have designed and implemented programs for special populations to learn basic academic skills and have tried to call it "vocational education." The difference seems to be the offering of an alternative learning environment for achievement in the "basics." Application of theory to real-life situations (learning by doing) has long been the forte of vocational education.

Today, many argue that so much attention has been given to special needs students that vocational education of the future will be restricted to serving only that population. If this is the future direction, can vocational education prepare the lesser qualified and unmotivated students with employability skills for the future? Hardly! Can vocational education improve its image? No!

With so much attention given to special needs students, little has been given to students who are highly motivated, average, and above average. Their needs in technological education are not being met. Secondary vocational education has an established responsibility to these students as well as the below average students. Few if any objections are heard when programs are established to accommodate the gifted student. In fact, concepts such as the magnet school may be a socially acceptable form of discrimination and elitism.

The schools of the future may include three levels or tracks; one for the gifted, one for the average, and one for the low achiever. Can and will vocational education be expected to serve all three populations? Not effectively, unless they can be separated.

New Directions: Keeping Perspectives in Focus

The United States does not have a national work force policy or any central planning agency. As a result, there is disorientation and confusion among the many organizations attempting to forecast needs that will facilitate better development and utilization of our human resources. It creates waste, competition, and duplication among agencies attempting to prepare people for the world of work. Because of these problems, the forces demanding changes to eliminate waste and become more productive in educating our work force come from a variety of sources.

Public and private agencies are not financially able to do all that is needed in developing our human capital and are constantly competing for limited funds. Some claim that the Jobs Training Partnership Act (JTPA) will become our nation's work force policy. This is very meager, indeed, since JTPA focuses on those who haven't benefited from our free enterprise system. Placing our priorities on those who have failed should not take the place of programs designed to prevent failure.

Secondary vocational education is often criticized by those in postsecondary technical education, government, JTPA, community colleges, organized labor, the private sector, and professional organizations. It is a visible source of work force education toward which frustrations can be vented. Secondary vocational education has not even been accepted by the Department of Labor, as well as others, as a player in the important game of preparing our nation's work force. Others involved in work force education criticize secondary programs by interpreting their own positions and informing the public on how they can perform this task better, instead of becoming a partner in this effort. Decision makers often ask outsiders: What should be the direction of vocational education? Even when they are not qualified to respond, or have ulterior motives, they are widely quoted as the authority that should be followed. As a profession, those in it should listen to *what* is being said, but they must also know *who* is saying it, and *why*. It is easy to criticize, but it is very difficult to offer solutions to education problems. Under the best of conditions, education is a complex and difficult process. Simplistic and naive approaches will not resolve its problems, as leaders in the United States and abroad have learned.

Economic Considerations

Secondary vocational-technical education has in the past and should continue to remain closely associated with the demands of labor and the economy. Recent developments in education have attempted to remove this critically important obligation of reacting to labor demands by preparing and placing skilled workers. Notwithstanding all the criticism, the affinity between vocational education, labor demands, and the economy must remain.

Some of the problems that are linked to vocational education are problems of management, labor, and the national and international marketplace. They are problems with the economic structure of the country. It must be remembered that education does not create jobs, businesses do. Their requirements are those of today, but vocational education should not be found guilty of preparing students for jobs that may or may not exist in the future. With the recent emphasis upon increased productivity, and jobs becoming more technical, businesses are looking toward education to help solve the problem of foreign competition. Foreign competition will continue to intensify as countries such as Japan, Singapore, Mexico, Korea, Brazil, and Taiwan continue to develop economically. Additionally, if the European Economic Commission is successful in uniting Europe into one economic community, it will be the strongest competitor to the U.S. economy. Some warn that the most critical issue facing our nation today is international economic competitiveness.

Economic planners interested in developing communities are constantly looking for ways to improve the labor force in order to attract new businesses. In doing so, they have provided numerous opportunities to form linkages and partnerships between vocational education and the private sector. Vocational education is indeed an important asset in community economic development.

Vocational education has traditionally prepared students for employment with small and medium-sized businesses. These are establishments that cannot afford to provide their employees the needed training. This is still true today. Big businesses, with training departments and sufficient budgets, can and do train their own employees. As a result, they advocate more academic preparation in the basics. Moreover, they generally do not support vocational education at the secondary level. Why should they? They don't hire its graduates. Additionally, vocational education is viewed by some big businesses as preparing workers for their competitors. Future employers of secondary vocational education graduates will continue to be small companies that need ready-trained personnel. They will have most of the future opportunities and will continue to employ most of the semi-skilled workers.

Education for the improvement of economic conditions for individuals makes more sense than education to solve social problems. Social problems seem to be out of control, and without solutions that can be resolved by secondary vocational education. However, high youth unemployment is an economic problem that could be resolved. This problem cannot be ignored by secondary vocational education.

Impact of Social Problems

The Vocational Education Act of 1963 placed emphasis upon sociological and humanitarian goals. This trend-setting legislation has significantly changed the direction of secondary vocational education. The social benefits of vocational education may have placed a banner into the hands of vocational education which is fast becoming a noose around its neck. It is becoming increasingly evident that social problems associated with discrimination, learning disabilities, disadvantaged, handicapped, illiteracy, dropouts, drug abuse, and AIDS cannot be solved in the schoolhouse. Additionally, problems associated with the decline in the family structure, such as high divorce rates, teenage pregnancy, and latchkey children, cannot be solved by vocational education. Education in general has been assigned these responsibilities, and they are passed on to vocational education because to many, there seems no better place to dump them.

The reform movement in education has not been compatible with social reform. Many fear that a push for academic excellence will result in higher dropout rates, which are naturally associated with numerous social problems.

A basic question must be asked: Is it more important to try and fail with too many goals or to succeed with a few? Vocational education must find a way to purge itself of unattainable goals and redefine and clarify its mission. It must focus on what can be accomplished and not attempt to be "everything for everybody"!

Man and education were not created equal in the eyes of society. Vocational education and its students do not share an equal status and position in education. In many ways, vocational education shares a common concern with the minorities and women in that it must "be better to be equal." Change is not good if it does harm to the employability of people. It is true that those in the profession need to be informed about the social and psychological implications of its form of education. However, outspoken sociologists and psychologists should not be allowed to control vocational education. Vocational educators understand people better because they have worked with them, not because they have studied them in the abstract.

Political Interference

A massive reform movement is also occurring within the federal government. This reform movement is known as the "New Federalism." The federal government is shifting traditional responsibilities to the state and local governments. While doing this, most of the responsibilities for training the nation's workforce have been further decentralized.

It is difficult to separate political forces from all others. Politics involves politicians and, if elected, politicians become government officials. Idealistically, they represent the people and carry out their wishes. However, lately it seems that public officials have their own agendas and government is involved in everything.

Many of the political forces that have impacted on secondary vocational education have done so in a negative fashion. Politicians wishing to be reelected have used vocational education as "political honey" to attract votes. They use it to help satisfy special interest pressure groups demanding social reform. They want to please everyone and, above all, be reelected.

Instead of being concerned with the employment needs of the people and the skills they need to be employable, politicians have emphasized the evils of the welfare system and promised vocational training for anyone needing or wishing to have it. In doing so, vocational education has become associated with the welfare system and the education of the disadvantaged. Vocational education has redirected its attention away from high quality programs toward the special needs of the disadvantaged and the handicapped. Secondary vocational education, if run as advocated by the federal government, would be like the seriously ill patient who is brain dead and has been put on a life support system. However, federal legislation is not the life support system keeping the brain dead patient alive. Federal funds only provide about 10 percent of the monies spent on vocational education. Since it is the states and the local communities that are keeping the seriously ill patient alive, why is so much effort expended catering to politicians who pass federal legislation that degrades quality vocational programs?

Return To Vocational's Basics

Presently, many vocational educators are willing to (a) increase the academic rigor, (b) start programs that prepare those entering new technologies, (c) provide for the development of higher-order skills, (d) obtain general education credits, and (e) propose changing programs so students can receive transferable credits or advanced standing. New efforts are attempting to address and give attention to basic skills, study of self and the world of work, modes of communications, decision making and problem solving, and career choices. Many are attempting to find ways to integrate vocational and general education programs. They are trying to find avenues to achieve excellence by creating a curriculum that will be common for all students and eliminate the stigma of being called "vocational education." Students are exposed to the basics as well as exploring occupations. Additional attention is given to employability skills and general preparation for employment. Most certainly, secondary vocational education is trying to do too much for too many with one program.

Are these changes better for students, or are these changes an attempt to gain respectability by trying to teach the basics better than general education has in the past? It is dangerous to become merely an alternative to *how* the basics will be taught. If general educators eventually accept and implement the methodology and content we use, why should vocational education continue, since it would be a duplication of effort?

A key strategy for secondary vocational education is to provide a variety of educational choices and levels of education within itself for the development of human capital. Secondary vocational education should have its focus squarely on economic considerations, since most social problems disappear when economic conditions improve. Sound educational decisions must be made instead of political ones. In plotting its future, secondary vocational education must solicit support from the private sector. Strength and power for vocational education can only come from the private sector. If asked, small, medium, and even some large businesses and industry will support the efforts of secondary vocational education. It is good for their businesses and good for the economic and social climate of the communities in which they reside.

Forming joint-venture partnerships between companies and vocational programs has been highly successful in improving the relationships between education and the private sector. It has also changed the passive nature of advisory groups to an active one. However, this relationship must be beneficial to both parties and the private sector must be encouraged to take a proactive role in the affairs of the school. Advisory groups, in name only, may do more harm than good. When asked, representatives from the private sector expect to become actively involved. Lack of active participation will form bad perceptions that vocational education doesn't need support or assistance. This virtually untapped resource should and must be developed for secondary vocational education to survive and flourish.

Additional support should be solicited from the various branches of the military, organized labor, and postsecondary education. All are dependent upon qualified personnel entering their organizations, and they are interested in quality vocational program graduates.

Most vocational educators have sought support from education, professional organizations, teacher education, and political associations. All have provided only minimal support in comparison to what is needed. Additionally, support cannot be expected from these groups since general educators, teacher educators, and politicians are presently under seige themselves.

Even before the reform movement began in general education, there were many attempts to improve the quality of vocational education. While the reform movement has escalated these efforts, Table 1 shows the trends that have developed.

Secondary vocational education must have a flexible delivery system that will serve a diversity of clients. This doesn't mean that it should happen in the same classroom or be restricted to the senior

Table I

Trends of Secondary Vocational Education

PAST	PRESENT-FUTURE
Goals	
Job Preparation	Prepare for Postsecondary
Vocational Education	General & Technology Education
Separate Education	Combined With General Education
Work Force Needs	Societal Needs
Considerations	
Economic	Social & Political
Curriculum	
Use of Job Analysis	Conceptual
Specific	Generic
Psychomotor Development	Cognitive & Affective Development
Job Related	Basic Education
Medium Level Skills	Low Level Skills
Transferable Skills	Adaptability Skills
3 Hour Blocks	1 & 2 Hour Blocks
Out of School Experience	In-School Experience
Separate Programs	Clustered
Rigorous	Less Demanding
Real-World/Hands-on	Simulations/Observations
Shops/Laboratories	Classrooms

high level of secondary education. Four separate and distinct programs should exist in secondary vocational-technical education. They should be separate and distinct so they will have an opportunity to be appropriately planned, implemented, and evaluated. No one should be better than any other, just different from the rest. They will require different (a) curricula, (b) time allocations, (c) facilities, (d) instructor qualifications, (e) student entry requirements, and (f) funding levels—because they *are* different. However, they can offer articulation between the two levels of secondary education and between secondary and postsecondary. They will carry the theme of occupational/career education which is paramount to preeminence.

One: Exploratory and Orientation Programs

Secondary vocational education should and must support orientation programs because *all* students need to become aware of the world of work. Much of the career guidance responsibility rightfully belongs to vocational education, and it should be accepted. These programs should be designed to enable students to explore as many occupational areas as possible. They should be hands-on occupationally oriented experiences that will motivate students to apply abstract academic content. Learning should not be confined to the classroom. It should involve the home, the community, and especially establishments where people work.

Exploratory programs in agriculture, business, home economics, and technology education should be available for every student in secondary education. These are general education subjects and all students will benefit by completing these subject areas. Without these exploratory programs, there is little hope for developing focused quality programs designed for later school years.

Two: Basic Skills Programs

Vocational education should offer programs in basic skills education for students with special needs. These programs can provide meaningful educational experiences to students who have difficulty with the symbol-based content taught in general education. The "learn-by-doing" methodology, using real-life activities, does not detach meaningful content from activities. Therefore, it simplifies the learning process by connecting things and events together. However, this methodology is not just for the low-achiever and handicapped. It is primary to the very nature of vocational education and must not be eliminated for any reason.

To accomplish what is intended, programs must be organized and conducted separately. Some will criticize this approach and say that the law mandates that handicapped students be maintreamed into regular programs. However, the present homogenized programs are not working. Are math and science teachers being forced to handle mixed student populations in advanced courses? Hardly! These subjects have prerequisites and entry requirements and students must be qualified before enrolling. Most secondary vocational programs are not permitted to impose admission requirements and teachers are expected to adjust the curriculum to fit every individual student. This tragedy is primarily happening in vocational education and not in other subject areas.

Vocational education has adjusted its expectations downward and in many cases now has little to offer those who seriously want and need to prepare for a job or go on to postsecondary education. Its attempts to serve all have resulted in serving none well. It has succumbed to outside pressures and eliminated the idea that students should be qualified prior to entering a program. In doing so, articulation and career guidance have been eliminated. Vocational education has become the dumping ground for students who pose problems for the educational system that are too difficult to handle. This is not a solution that treats the illness; it merely masks the symptoms of an educational system that is ill.

Vocational education should not be a part of a system that "institutionalizes" its clients. All students, not just the academically inclined, should be provided an education and "not just training." Instead of just knowing the correct answers, students must be taught how to obtain answers. Instead of just knowing how to do something, they should also know why.

Three: Technology Transfer Programs

Secondary vocational education must offer educational programs in applied technology for students pursuing technical careers that will require postsecondary preparation. Vocational education should also serve the average student as well as those that are above average. This will be difficult to implement successfully, given the present stigma that is associated with serving special needs students. Postsecondary vocational education is dependent upon receiving students with a background and the basics in technology. Yet it is impossible to offer high quality technical programs that are restricted to two years of preparation in courses organized to attract all "comers," without prerequisites.

Technical education should not be a different division of vocational education, i.e., agriculture, business, marketing, home economics, trade and industrial. It is merely a different level. Secondary vocational education is the foundation for successful postsecondary technical education. Without its presence, postsecondary programs must allocate time to teaching the basics, and this time will be taken away from teaching the advanced technologies that are presently required of entering technicians. There are many successful 2+2 "tech-prep" articulated programs and they should be used as models for this type of delivery system.

Students take advanced mathematics, science, principles of technology, manufacturing and construction technology, computer applications, etc., that prepare them for the next level. Preparatory programs cannot continue to prepare students for entry levels in occupations that have become technologies. Technological education, striving to prepare technicians, is synonymous with postsecondary education, not secondary education.

Four: Occupational Preparation Programs

Preparatory programs must be designed to remain relevant to the needs of a technological society. The curriculum should reflect the manipulative, cognitive, and affective skills required to be employable in recognized occupations. Resulting jobs should offer advancement to a higher stratum than just entry levels. Programs should be adequately funded, equipped, and designed to provide real-life experiences that are compatible with present occupational standards.

The program must have strong ties with the private sector that will evlauate, guide, and assist its continued development. The program must have a capstone experience which involves an internship with close supervision and related studies. Teachers of these programs should be routinely given up-dating experiences in the occupational area they teach.

Students who pursue these programs must have an employment objective, but they should be first exposed to a wide range of occupations. Prior to entering, they should understand where they are going and why. More importantly, students should not be cut off from attending postsecondary education at a later time if they wish. Preparatory programs should remain separate from general education, but have strong interdisciplinary connections to academic study. Even though a student has chosen an occupation, this should be accomplished without neglecting the indispensable elements of general education. Secondary vocational education should offer education in today's cognitive knowledge and job skills, not yesterday's or those needed in the distant future.

Summary

The problems facing secondary vocational education are many. It must have a partner to help find solutions. This can only be accomplished by developing linkages with the private sector so it can survive and accomplish its intended goals.

The fundamental and time-honored reason for the existence of secondary vocational education is the preparation of students to enter the work force. However, it is not the only reason for its continuance. Additionally, secondary vocational-technical education must provide orientation/exploratory programs as early in education as feasible. Vocational education must strive to force orientation and exploratory programs into the lower grades so that students will be able to make better career choices before leaving secondary education.

It must continue to conduct educational programs for special needs students who want and can benefit from what vocational education has to offer. However, it is not fair for them and other students just to reduce the difficulty so they may succeed in an integrated classroom. Secondary vocational education must continue to offer separate programs that prepare its graduates for work. Finally, secondary vocational education must become "vocational-technical" education by forming an articulated alliance with postsecondary education for preparing students for technical careers. ☐

References

Barnow, Burt S. (March 1986). *Labor market changes in the next ten years*. Washington, DC: Department of Labor.

Boyer, E. L. (1983). *High school: A report on secondary education in America*. (The Carnegie Foundation for Advancement of Teaching) New York: Harper and Row.

Gonzalez, Ed (January/February 1985). Voc ed: Does it have a future? *NEA Today*.

Guiton, Bonnie (January/February, 1988). Reflections of a 1950s youth at risk. *Vocational Education Journal*, 20-21.

Hoyt, Kenneth B.; Evans, Rupert N.; Mackin, Edward F.; and Mangum, Garth L. (1972). *Career education: What it is and how to do it*. Salt Lake City, UT: Olympus Publishing Company.

Hughes, Ruth (1984). *Secondary vocational education: Imperative for excellence*. Columbus, OH: The National Center for Research in Vocational Education, Information Series No. 277.

Hunter, Beverly and Aiken, Robert (March 1987). The evolution of computer courses in vocational education: Perspectives and directions. *T.H.E. Journal*, 54-57.

Johnston, William, (1987). *Workforce 2000: Work and workers for the 21st century*. Alexandria, VA: Hudson Institute.

Mertens, Donna M.; McElwain, Douglas; Garcia, Gonzalo; and Whitmore, Mark (1980). *The effects of participating in vocational education: Summary of studies reported since 1968*. Columbus, OH: The National Center for Research in Vocational Education.

National Alliance of Business (1987). *The fourth R: Workforce readiness*.

National Commission on Excellence in Education (April 1983). *A nation at risk: The imperative for educational reform*. Washington, DC: Department of Education.

Somers, Gerald G. and Little, J. Kenneth, eds. (1971). *Vocational education: Today and tomorrow*. Madison, WI: The University of Wisconsin, Center for Studies in Vocational and Technical Education.

Swanson, Gordon E., ed. (1981). *The Future of vocational education*. Arlington, VA: The American Vocational Association, Inc.

Task Force on Education for Economic Growth. (1983). *Action for Excellence: A comprehensive plan to improve our nation's schools*. Washington, DC: Education Commission of the States.

Warmbrod, Catharine and Long, James (October/November 1986). College bound or bust: Ten principles for articulation. *AACJC Journal*, Vol. 57, No. 2, 29-31.

Weir, Douglas (December 9, 1985). Vocational education in the 1990's—more or less? Presentation to AVA Convention.

William T. Grant Foundation (1988). *The forgotten half*. Washington, DC: Commission on Youth and America's Future.

CHAPTER 4

Postsecondary Occupational Education

By Charles R. Doty

THIS chapter is designed to give a brief history of occupational education in community, junior, and technical colleges in the United States; guiding principles of these institutions; issues concerning these and related institutions; an in-depth discussion of one of these issues with predictions of future trends; questions to be answered; major resources and suggested readings to provide information for future planning of occupational education; and associations that have an emphasis on postsecondary occupational education.

History

Historically, the two-year college/institute development can be divided into four eras: prior to 1900, the preparatory years; from 1900 to 1920, the formative years; the diversification years from 1920 to 1948; and the community college era from 1948 to the present. A philosophy developed among leaders in the late 1800s that led to the formulation of ideas for the separation of the lower years of study from the upper years in a university. In 1892, William R. Harper, president of the University of Chicago, created two divisions of the

University: The Academic College, to include the first two years of college, and the University College, to include the upper years. In 1896, the names of the divisions were changed to Junior and Senior College, thus the term "junior college" was created.

Movement during the first years of junior colleges coincided with the reformation of the American university, and yet another force was in effect, i.e., many secondary school graduates were not adequately prepared for the demands of college study. University leaders encouraged the junior college curriculum to be college preparatory, i.e., transfer oriented, and in some cases the laws of a state dictated that the junior college curriculum be transfer oriented as much as possible. By the 1930s, there were about 280 junior colleges. Some of these junior colleges by the end of the 1930s began to respond to the needs of their local communities by developing curricula for agricultural interests, the oil industry, etc.

In 1947, President Harry S Truman charged a President's Commission on Higher Education with the responsibility of evaluating and recommending areas of development for higher education. The report (1948) recommended establishing tuition-free public two-year colleges to provide youth the opportunity to continue their education and suggested the name "community college" be used for these institutions. The goals of these colleges were to provide educational service to the entire community, serve as a center for adult education, and meet the total needs of the post high school community. The two-year community colleges were to be locally controlled and financed, as contrasted with junior colleges that are private institutions dependent on tuition and philanthropy.

In July 1972, the American Association of Junior Colleges, organized in 1921, changed its name to the American Association of Community and Junior Colleges (AACJC). By 1978, AACJC had renamed its journal the *Community, Technical and Junior College Journal.* According to the AACJC's *Building Communities* (1988), there are 1,224 regionally accredited community, technical, and junior colleges with 5,000,000 college credit students and 4,000,000 non-credit and continuing education students. These students comprise approximately 43 percent of the nation's undergraduates and 51 percent of all first-time freshmen *(Building Communities,* 1988, p. 6). Various reports indicate that the majority of enrollment in community colleges is in occupational programs or in courses where persons have the goal to retrain themselves for the job market or to gain promotion in their jobs (Stacey et al., 1988, p. 6; Harris & Grede, 1977). During the development of junior and community colleges, the technical institute came into being. In 1751, Benjamin Franklin advocated a change in curriculum from the traditional to a more applied curriculum. In 1822, the first technical instutute in America was established in Gardiner, Maine. Technical institutes have generally been postsecondary institutions with a curriculum based on scientific applications. Many two-year institutes evolved into four-year/university technical institutes. However, there are approximately 644 technical institutes in the nation that have expanding enrollments and curricula.

The private junior colleges in the nation quickly converted into community colleges during the early 1970s in order to survive. Those that remain, about 154, offer transfer and liberal arts instruction.

To summarize, three types of postsecondary institutions evolved in America that offer occupational curricula. The *1986 Technician Education Directory* reports sending a survey to over 3,000 institutions that offer such education. This *Directory* has a listing of 2,103 community, technical, and junior colleges offering occupational education in 170 different categories such as industrial, agricultural, business, civil, electronic, medical, consumer science, environmental, etc. In addition to the community, technical, and junior colleges, over 100 private, profit trade schools exist that offer occupational education.

Guiding Principles

The first recommendations for community colleges were developed by the Truman Commission on Higher Education in 1948 as previously described. At that time, 640 private junior colleges existed. By 1970, most junior colleges had converted to community colleges and the Carnegie Commission on Higher Education had published the landmark *Open Door Colleges*. The Carnegie Commission's twelve guiding principles were:
 1. Community colleges should be within commuting distance of all persons except in sparsely populated areas.
 2. The Commission favors comprehensive colleges rather

than more specialized colleges.
3. Community colleges should remain community colleges because they have an important role that should not be abandoned.
4. Full transfer rights to 4-year colleges and universities should be established.
5. Occupational programs should be given the fullest status and support within the colleges.
6. The Commission supports open access for all high school graduates and other qualified individuals.
7. There should be low or no tutition.
8. Occupational and personal guidance should be provided.
9. The colleges should be community cultural centers.
10. Optimum college size should be 2,000 to 5,000 students.
11. A local advisory board should govern each college.
12. Financing should be equitably shared by federal, state, and local sources. (pp. 1-2)

Because of tremendous social and economic changes within and outside the United States, the guiding principles for community colleges have been constantly questioned. Parnell (1982) wrote *Some Tough Questions About Community Colleges* and *The Neglected Majority* and as president of AACJC with the AACJC Board of Directors appointed an AACJC Commission on the Future of the Community Colleges. The Commission, headed by Ernest L. Boyer, produced a planning document titled *Building Communities: A Vision for a New Century* (1988).

The AACJC Commission report, while not mentioning the *Open Door College,* did not repudiate any of the twelve principles. Instead the Commission expanded on areas of concern and gave detailed recommendations. concerning "The Essentialness of Work," the Commission concluded that community colleges should have first-rate technical and career-related programs in order to prepare students for the "Information Age." This conclusion was based on information from the U.S. Department of Labor, which has estimated that 75 percent of all job classifications will require postsecondary education for entry by 1995.

The Commission stated that comprehensive high schools do not have the personnel or equipment to provide comprehensive technical

education programs. Shared-time and full-time vocational schools are not metioned. The Commission, to solve this problem, proposed a 2+2 articulation program in which students in grades 11 and 12 could begin a technical program with a community college. In addition to the above recommendation, the Commission made six more suggestions:
1. Articulation agreements, e.g., 2+2 or 2+1, should be established with high schools so high school students can complete a certificate or associate degree.
2. Inverted models should be used in every state, i.e., the first two years in the community college should be specialized education in four-year colleges.
3. Faculty should assist students in "closing the gap" between "liberal" and "useful" arts.
4. Agreement on general education should be reached for the associate degree.
5. Administrators and faculty should be carefully selected to keep technical programs up to date.
6. The associate of applied science degree should emphasize knowledge and skills for the Information Age.

Thus, the community colleges have had several commissions giving guiding principles which imply the purpose to provide leadership in social and economic education. The private junior colleges have transfer and liberal arts education as their goal. Technical institutes' main purpose is technical education with the provision for further education. The term "terminal education" should never be used when referring to either technical or vocational education, because such education provides a basis for an individual desiring higher education. Private, profit trade schools have the role of providing education not offered by the public institutions, as well as often being able to initiate programs more rapidly than public institutions.

Issues

In an era of world-based economic structures and intense economic competition among nations, probably the most crucial concern of political leaders, business leaders, educators, etc., is structuring education, both public and private, to ensure national survival. Stacey et al. (April 1988), in the paper *Education and Training of*

16- to 19-Year Olds after Compulsory Schooling in the United States, identify three national and state level issues. Which delivery system(s) will best increase retention of at-risk youth? Which will best solve the illiteracy problem of the United States? And how can education and training be structured to ensure economic development?

Opposing views for the solution of these issues have resulted in national and state legislation to fund education. As stated by Stacey et al., the federal level initiative has been to pass legislation such as the Jobs Partnership Act of 1982 to stress training by private employers. Federal policy has been to limit funds for public vocational education.

Perhaps the biggest problem or issue with secondary vocational education is that planning documents such as the *Open Door Policy* or *Building Communities* produced for postsecondary institutions have not been written for secondary vocational education and are not generally accepted by secondary vocational educators. In addition, state and national evaluations of secondary vocational education have been conducted by persons without vocational background or secondary teaching experience who are perceived by secondary vocational educators as being biased against vocational education. Therefore, planning documents for secondary vocational education have reactionary themes rather than future goals as their emphasis. They fail to ask such questions as: How can education and training be structured to ensure economic development as well as provide fulfillment for each student? To answer this question, the issue of the placement of vocational education arises.

Vocational Education Placement

Beginning in 1980 with President Reagan's administration, the issue of the placement of vocational education became a critical question. Anyone who has followed the history of vocational education knows that this issue has existed for a long time in terms of many academicians seeing no value in vocational education being offered in public secondary education and by the U.S. Bureau of Labor proposing that the administration of vocational education be within that bureau. The discussion of this issue will proceed from a review of two historic views of vocational education to viewpoints given from 1982 to the present, followed by a summary and predictions of trends.

It is ironic that academicians seem to have ignored H.W. Holmes's (1914) essay on education for the Harvard Classics in which he expressed that vocational education is a "mighty" advance in education because it will offer inspiring opportunities for extending general education. Prophetically Holmes stated that the problem of vocational education is not a problem of justification, but one of organization and extension. Holmes further stated that it is the persistent problem of general education that complicates the issue.

In *General Education in a Free Society: Report of the Harvard Committee* (1962), general education is described as that education which prepares a person for life and change and is the sole means for communities to protect themselves from rapid change (p. 266). Within general education is the component of vocation. Further, general education should not be placed artificially in competition with specializing education because general education encompasses specialized education. The Committee even points out that persons preparing for college have an almost wholly cognitive education without direct manipulation of objects, which was judged as being a serious mistake. Holmes, in summarizing his view on the issue of vocational education, concludes that educators can only emphasize the value of liberal studies and resist the tendency to specialize too soon. Within the views of Holmes and the Committee lies the crux of the issue of the placement of vocational education: At what point in a person's education has the person learned enough to be flexible to meet life's demands, at what point should specialized education occur, and to what extent should specialization occur?

Before reviewing various positions on this issue, one must realize that historically vocational education has drawn its content from the trades, whereas the curriculum offered in postsecondary institutions has been based on the sciences. In addition to content source is the national movement to structure the secondary curriculum to an almost exculsively academic curriculum via increasing high school graduation requirements to the point that traditional vocational education cannot be accomplished, i.e., job-entry level competency.

Swanson (1982) asked if vocational preparation belonged in secondary schools at all. In his essay, he identified critics with three points of view: those who want any work preparation programs separated from school because of the image of charity and indentification with disadvantaged persons; critics who argue that the time available to students at the secondary level is too valuable; and critics who state that vocational education should be done at the postsecondary level. His conclusion is that the American secondary school system is not structured for such education and should, therefore, be redesigned so vocational education might be properly offered. Unfortunately, he is not clear on restructuring, but his identification of problems concerning governance, testing that equates to "tracking," and only one of five high schools offering any opportunity for vocational education is notable.

Bell (1984) asked if a consensus of opinion had occurred that vocational education at the postsecondary level showed the best return on investment. He further pondered that even if such opinion were true, what would be the effects of deemphasis or elimination of vocational education on the millions of students who go directly to work and "never see a postsecondary institution." He worried about the career education aspect and the loss of leadership education accomplished by student organizations. He viewed any attempt to separate vocational education from other education in master planning as a "mockery." He saw no conflict between advocacy of excellence for academic education and a commitment to a strong system of vocational education in the secondary and postsecondary schools. He saw vocational education as a major supplier of skilled workers that must change to respond to business and industrial needs.

Feldman (1985) in "The Ambush of Vocational Education" summed up the goal of two reports—*A Nation at Risk* and *Education's Involvement in Learning*—as being a declaration of war on vocational education at the secondary and postsecondary level respectively. Neither of these commissions had representatives from vocational education. He concluded that any efforts of academic educators to solve the problems of American education alone as would be "grotesque." His plea was not to seek "separate but equal" emphasis on vocational education but to seek full integration of thought and practice about education, a new vision of excellence that integrates the thoughts of all educators.

Bennett (1986) addressed the 1985 national convention of the American Vocational Association in a carefully prepared political statement that might be interpreted to mean that he advocated vocational education at the postsecondary level. His definitive statements in that speech leave no doubt that he viewed a broad education as being the best education, especially at the secondary level.

Parnell (1987), the president of AACJC, advocated the idea of the high school/community college connection as noted in *The Neglected Majority*, a 1986 AACJC publication. This connection is a vertical articulation of the curriculum beginning in the junior high school years. Parnell wants close communication between secondary schools and the colleges to achieve structure and substance in the curriculum to help students function as independent and productive citizens. His conclusion from reviewing National Center for Education Statistics in *High School and Beyond* concerning the 11 million who will not complete high school out of 40 million who began elementary school is that many of these persons will get to the community colleges and technical institutes five years later. He does not advocate moving vocational education to the colleges, but does ask for a review of the curriculum.

Smith (1987) summarized the testimony of the New Jersey Vocational Education Association given to the New Jersey Panel on Secondary Vocational Education. This testimony supported vocational education at the secondary level based on such reports as the *Unfinished Agenda* and recent national publications such as the *Wall Street Journal, Newsweek, Gallup Poll, Phi Delta Kappan,* and *AVA Update*. His conclusion was that the recent shift of occupationally specific education to the postsecondary level may not be totally justified when employment opportunities are examined and the aspirations of people are considered.

Weir (1987), in *Vocational Education in the 1990's—More or Less?*, while not advocating where vocational education should be offered, advocated a more liberalizing direction within that education, i.e., more human and interpersonal skills and adaptability skills, because changes in labor markets and life styles will require more breadth and flexibility. He concludes that vocational education as shown in the 1984 Carl D. Perkins Act is out of date.

In the AACJC Commission report *Building Communities: A Vision for a New Century*, headed by Boyer (1988), heavy emphasis was placed on work. Community college faculty are urged to close the gap between "liberal" and "useful" arts. Students in technical studies should be helped to discover the meaning of work, and students in arts and sciences should understand the value of work. Clear statements of core curriculum for technical programs should be agreed upon by students, faculty, and administrators. Special attention should be given to employing technical education faculty and administrators to ensure up-to-date programs and balanced curriculum. Each college should work with employers to develop programs to keep the work force up to date. Economic development should be a major goal of the community, junior, and technical colleges. Regional clearinghouses to study emerging work force needs should be established. Partnerships between employers and colleges should be formed for training and retraining programs and to provide continuing education for faculty upgrading.

To summarize, the impetus for vocational education came from educational leaders who saw great value in vocational education for the general education of all persons, i.e., vocational education is a part of one's general education and should not be considered "apart" from general education. Yet there has been a persistent separating in word and deed such that the *Report of the Harvard Committee* (1962) includes criticism of such separation in secondary schools, the AACJC Commission (1988) recommends closing the gap between "liberal" and "useful" arts in postsecondary schools, and Feldman pleaded that there not be a "separate but equal" emphasis on vocational education but an integration of all education. Bell (1984) even called such separatism a "mockery."

Those persons who have written about vocational education being or not being in the secondary level have questioned the value of such education, asked what effects might be on students who are unable or unwilling to go to postsecondary institutions, questioned what is going to happen to those who do not graduate from elementary or high school, and examined the data on labor demand. None of these persons answered definitively whether vocational education should be offered at the postsecondary level. But they did pose such questions and cite data that indicate a lack of wisdom in eliminating vocational education at the secondary level. The proposal by the AACJC (Boyer, 1988) to articulate with secondary schools and Parnell's (1987) request for a review of secondary vocational curricula might be interpreted to mean community college/technical institute staff believe secondary vocational education is and can be valuable.

Trends

A review of the literature revealed many sources concerning the future of vocational and technical education. The following are selected as representative, although the reader is encouraged to examine the listing under "Major Resources and Readings" at the end of this chapter.

The Carnegie Council on Policy Studies in Higher Education (1980) saw the beginning of signs of a struggle for survival by many higher education institutions. One of those signs was the turn toward vocational and professional studies based on student demand.

Abram et al. (1983) stated that both secondary and postsecondary vocational education levels are facing the challenge of educating workers who will be able to manufacture, test, design, program, install, maintain, and repair high technology equipment.

The Iowa Industrial Jobs Training Act that became law in 1983 offers incentives to businesses that use community colleges to train employees for newly created jobs. This law encouraged partnerships between schools and industry *(The Chronicle of Higher Education*, Jan. 30, 1985, p. 3).

Levin (1984) examined employment projections between 1978 and 1990 and found the 20 occupations expected to have the largest growth were not high-tech occupations, e.g., janitors, salesclerks, general office clerks, food service, secretaries, trades helpers, blue collar workers, etc. Only about 7 percent of all new jobs will be high technology jobs.

The Task Force on the Role of Community Colleges in Economic Development (1986) surveyed 1,144 colleges and received replies from 442. Fifty-two percent of the respondents had revised their mission statements to include economic development. Seventy-seven percent encouraged faculty involvement in economic development. The Task Force concluded that economic development innovation appears to be in the early stages but the diffusion of these projects will increase. Economic development activities include supporting the establishment of new and expanding business and industry, technical assistance in managerial functions, delivery of job specific entry level and customized training. Some colleges even secure loans for the companies.

Cohen et al. (1986) stated in *Key Resources on Community*

Colleges that vocational programs have become the mainstay of two-year college curriculum with enrollment in occupational programs outstripping enrollment in transfer programs (p. 322).

Frantz et al. (1987) conducted a nationwide survey to determine vocational education enrollments in secondary schools that might have been affected by increasing high school graduation requirements. They found that most states and territories have increased such requirements. One third of the states included some vocational education as part of the requirements for general education. For years 1984-85, graduation requirement increases had not negatively affected enrollment. However, they stated these new requirements will not be observable until the 1986-87 and 1987-88 school years.

Norris and Townsend (1987) report that vocational agriculture now faces reduction of multi-teacher departments with FFA membership dropping over 100,000. They recommend implementing nontraditional courses as entrepreneurship; fruit, nut, and vegetable production; forestry; and cooperative education. They advocate dropping the term "vocational" and refer to subjects as courses in agriculture science. Science credit for these courses should be given for graduation credit and meeting the "basics" requirements. If changes are not made, secondary agriculture may be gone by the end of the 1990s.

Dr. Ray Ryan, director, National Center for Researching Vocational Education, in a speech at Rutgers University, April 1988, stated that vocational education will be transformed in the future, i.e., that the model from the Smith-Hughes 1918 federal legislation is not always appropriate in today's environment. He believes a new vision of education for a "knowledgeable worker" must be developed. Among the abilities of this worker are those of being able to adapt to group work settings, problem solving, innovating, being self-motivating, etc. This person will, because of a better education, have good self esteem. His model for employment education would include leadership education, multi-job skills, specific job skills, team work skills, and employer work expectations.

Pucel et al. (1988), in a study to assist in policy determination for postsecondary vocational education curriculum in the year 2000, for Wisconsin, found a 21 percent disagreement between instructors/employers and technical institute directors/state board members. In addition, concerning program needs assessment, national or international data would probably not be used to plan curriculum offerings. Such findings seem frightening in terms of linking education to the reality of the economy of a state and nation. Concerning international trends, from June 22 to July 1, 1987 the first International Congress on the Development and Improvement of Technical and Vocational Education was organized by UNESCO and held in Berlin, German Democratic Republic. Major international trends included a greater enrollment in technical and vocational education than general education, progress in overcoming low status and insufficient training facilities as a result of policy statements and reforms suggested in *UNESCO's Revised Recommendation Concerning Technical and Vocational Education*, and an increased emphasis on linking general education to working life, especially for persons 12 to 15 years old. The Congress recommended that technical and vocational education be given an important place in national development plans.

Predictions

There are 44 states in America in which either higher high school graduation requirements have been implemented or university/college entrance requirements have been increased. The result is a reduction in enrollment in vocational education at the secondary level. Shared-time vocational schools, where students are transported from sending comprehensive high schools, may be eliminated within three to four years. Full-time vocational schools will continue to exist; however, the length of the school day will be increased to allow tutoring in English, math, science, foreign language, etc., or the amount of laboratory time will be reduced to allow remedial instruction. Vocational education students will be predominantly those who are educationally, economically, and/or mentally and physically handicapped. In effect, the secondary vocational education system, being examined and duplicated throughout the world, is being systematically dismantled in America. This situation violates several principles upon which American education is built, i.e., flexibility in education among states, freedom of choice of education, and the opportunity for a second or third chance provided in America's schools.

Assuming that enrollment in vocational education and other applied arts at the high school level continues to decrease, by 1994 the nation will begin graduating students who have few psychomotor skills and little knowledge of tools, equipment, materials or processes. The meaning of the high school diploma will be solely that of an entrance requirement for college rather than that graduates have some ability to be self-sufficient.

The effect of having persons without knowledge of tools, etc., will be noticed by employers prior to 1990, which may cause the employers to pressure school boards to reexamine the curriculum. However, the school boards will be powerless to make adequate changes because of the restructuring or elimination of teacher education programs (agriculture teachers, trade and industrial teachers, etc., will not be available), existing graduation requirements, and political positions.

Most community colleges will continue to prosper but will struggle internally to define institutional goals. Students will decide the struggle by enrolling and paying tuition for those courses and programs which they need and want.

Junior colleges will increase offerings in occupational education or be eliminated; i.e., junior colleges will continue to become comprehensive community colleges even if the name junior college is not changed.

Technical institutes will continue to prosper even more than community colleges because of students' view of the relevance of the curricula to "making a living." These institutions as well as the community collges will promote school-industry partnerships to keep up to date. The community colleges and junior colleges will have problems with "academic freedom." Technical education staff, because of the universality of technical content, will not be as bothered by this factor.

Private, profit trade school enrollment will increase dramatically. The 1988 expenditure (Jaschik, 1988) in which $3.34 billion is authorized nationally for education and training in community colleges, private trade schools, etc., will aid in this increase. Students will enroll in private trade schools to avoid further general education courses which they have experienced during elementary, middle, and high school and for which they would have to pay tuition in community colleges and some technical institutes.

Questions for Thought

As one reads the literature and attends conventions, it seems that while the community college/technical institute leaders are concerned with technical education, little or no mention is made of those areas in which secondary vocational education has served, i.e., trades such as plumbing, electrician, etc. If vocational education is eliminated at the secondary level will these "trades" be acceptable curricula for the community colleges and technical institutes? Or does public education need to provide for such "trade" education? Will trade schools/unions/industry undertake such education? What will be the consequences for the individual if trade schools/unions/industry control occupational education?

Assuming that vocational education is retained at the secondary level, how or should the curricula be changed?

Several writers have suggested changes in the vocational curricula at the secondary level. Much of this change seems to be content covered by other existing curricula. Will vocational eduction lose its identity if the focus is moved from "job entry level" preparation?

How can community colleges and technical institutes keep a balance between the technical requirements and general education requirements so the students are prepared for life after graduation?

Can an economy be self-sustaining based on a labor force having little or no early education in the psychomotor domain?

Can an economy be self-sustaining based on a labor force that provides basic services, that only has persons who are educationally, economically, and/or mentally and physically handicapped?

Can a nation survive that makes using one's hands socially unacceptable? □

Major Resources and Suggested Readings

The following documents are selected from hundreds of sources. These documents were selected because they provide a description of the historical and philosophical thinking upon which the present vocational and technical education is based. Many are documents which represent studies that were designed to give educational planners some view of the future.

Arns, K.F. (Ed.) (1981). *Occupational education today: New direc-

tions for community colleges. San Francisco, CA: Jossey-Bass, Inc., (ERIC Document Reproduction Service No. ED 200 286). Chapter titles in this monograph include, e.g., the "Changing Focus of Occupational Education," "Challenges Facing Community Colleges for the 1980's," "Survival in a Different Future and Program Reassessment," and "Reduction and Redirection."

Boyer, E. L. (Commission Head of Carnegie Foundation for the Advancement for Teaching) (1988). *Building communities: A vision for a new century.* Alexandria, VA: American Association of Community and Junior Colleges. This wide-ranging study on community, junior, and vocational and technical institutions was conducted by the Carnegie Foundation for AACJC. Key recommendations for the future of these institutions include "The Essentials of Work." This is the first major study of these institutions by the Carnegie Foundation since the 1970 study titled *The Open Door Colleges.* (Available from AACJC.)

Charner, I., and Rolzinski, C. A. (Eds.) (1987). *Responding to the needs of today's workplace: New directions for continuing education.* San Francisco, CA: Jossey-Bass, Inc. This book concentrates on problems and issues of integrating education and work for adult workers to assist postsecondary educators' ability to respond to changes in the economy. Chapters titled "English-Language Training for the Workplace," "Developing a Computer Integrated Manufacturing Education Center," "The Business Development and Training Center," "Worker Education for a Changing Economy," "Critical Questions and Issues for Integrating Education and Work" illustrate some of the important topics in this report.

Cohen, A. M., and Brawer, F. B. (1982). *The American community college.* San Francisco, CA: Jossey-Bass, Inc. (ERIC Document Reproduction Service No. ED 213 469). This text is a comprehensive study of the social and historical background of community colleges—their purposes, development, and changing patterns. The collegiate function is a primary topic throughout the text with a heavy emphasis on questioning new direction for the colleges.

Cohen, A. M.; Palmer, J. C.; and Zwemer, K. D. (1986). *Key resources on community colleges: A guide to the field and its literature.* San Francisco, CA: Jossey-Bass Inc. This document contains an annotated bibliography of 650 items representative of the ideas that have shaped two-year colleges. Chapter 8 is titled "Occupational Education." Other chapters cover the many areas one needs to gain an overview of the complexity of two year colleges, e.g., "Faculty," "Financing and Budgeting," and "Remedial and Developmental Education."

Committee on Education and Labor (1982). *New technology in the American workplace.* Washington, DC: U.S. Government Printing Office (ERIC Document Reproduction Service No. ED 230 708). This congressional report contains testimony given at the first of a series of comprehensive hearings on the impact of automation on employment and the workplace. Such agencies and organizations as the following testified: International Association of Machinists and Aerospace Workers, A.F. of L., C.I.O.; the Working Women Education Fund; Unimation, Inc.; Chase Manhattan Bank; National Productivity Group; Advanced Office Concepts; GCA Corporation; and the U.S. General Accounting Office.

Committee of Science, Engineering, and Public Policy: Joint Committee of the National Academy of Science, National Academy of Engineering, and the Institute of Medicine (1986). *Scientific futures.* Washington, DC: National Academy Press (ERIC Document Reproduction Service No. ED 277 582). This is fifth in a series to anticipate new avenues for research. This volume focuses on applications of science technology which could have economic and social benefits, e.g., decision making and problem solving or microelectronics in communications.

Council on Competitiveness (April 1987). *America's competitiveness crisis: Confronting the new reality.* Washington, DC: Council on Competitiveness, 1331 Pennsylvania Ave., N.W., Suite 905-North Lobby, Washington, DC 20004. This is a comprehensive study of the national and international economic conditions existing and predicted to exist. The council states that all Americans' personal and professional lives will undergo fundamental changes. Americans must mobilize and "sustain the political will to solve the competitiveness problem at its roots" (p. 39).

Doty, C. R., and DeCastro, C. (1984). *Decision making systems and data sources for technical education in community colleges/technical institutes.* New Brunswick, NJ: Rutgers-State University of New Jersey (ERIC Document Reproduction Service No. ED 258 607). This annotated bibliography cites sources dealing with two problems: (1) deciding which curriculum should be developed and

(2) developing curriculum efficiently. The sources cited were selected on the basis of ease of availability, applicability to automated technologies, practical usefulness, and generalizability. Thirty-six documents are cited covering areas such as automation technologies, changing occupations, computer applications, curriculum development, job markets future, and preparing for high technology.

Doty, C. R. (Ed.) (1987). *Developing occupational programs. New direction for community colleges.* San Francisco, CA: Jossey-Bass, Inc. The goal of this monograph is to provide the reader a conceptual framework for the process of occupational curriculum development. To achieve that goal, the text examines decision making policies at the federal level, presents a flow chart for curriculum development, and gives practical information concerning accreditation, needs analysis, licensing and certification testing, articulation, evaluation, and an extensive annotated bibliography of sources.

Doty, C. R. (1985). *Technical upgrading.* Arlington, VA: American Vocational Association, Inc. (ERIC Document Reproduction Service No. ED 262 829). This paper reviews information and resources on technical upgrading for faculty and offers recommendations for the implementation of a staff development program.

Doty, C. R.; Tornell, H.; and Wenzel, W. (1980). *Review and synthesis of research and development in technical education.* Columbus, OH: National Center for Research in Vocational Education. (ERIC Document Reproduction Service No. ED 193 526, also see ED 214 568). These two documents contain a comprehensive review of representative literature concerning postsecondary technical education spanning the years 1968 to 1980.

Galambos, E. C. (1984). *Issues in vocational education.* Atlanta, GA: Southern Regional Education Board (ERIC Document Reproduction Service No. ED 240 312). The report contains questions, issues, and problems concerning the 14 states of the SREB. Policy issues concerning the purpose of secondary vocational education, feasibility of achieving the purpose stated for secondary vocational education, articulation between secondary and postsecondary institutions, and realities of vocational programs at secondary and postsecondary levels considering labor market demands.

Grapevine. Published by the Center for Higher Education, College of Education, Illinois State University, Normal, Illinois 61761-6901, (309) 438-7655. Provides data on higher education finance, appropriations, and trends in funding.

Harris, N. C., and Grede, J. F. (1977). *Career education in colleges.* San Francisco, CA: Jossey-Bass, Inc. A classic work because of its comprehensive discussions of the biases concerning vocational education in higher education and the basic principles of the economic institution that colleges must recognize in developing programs.

Hollenbeck, K. M., and Dean, G. D. (1987). *Understanding the dynamics of postsecondary education: A design study. Final report.* Columbus, OH: National Center for Research in Vocational Education (ERIC Document Reproduction Service No. ED 284 976). This is a progress report of the first year of a national two-year study to conduct a study concerning postsecondary occupational education delivery. The study will concentrate on two areas: curriculum and instruction decision making processes and student motivation and choice behavior.

Holmes, H. W. (1914). *Education I. General introduction.* In W. A. Neilson (Ed.), *Lectures on the Harvard classics,* (pp. 287-303). New York: P. F. Collier & Son Company. In planning for the future, it is sometimes wise to read those essays which clearly defined the philosophy and principles upon which a field of endeavor was initiated. This is one of those essays, particularly on the topic of vocational education.

House Committee on Education and Labor (1986). *Education and training for the American Competitiveness Act.* House-R-99-597. Washington, DC: U.S. Government Printing Office. (ERIC Document Reproduction Service No. ED 271 628). The research findings and recommendations of the House Committee are given as rationale for establishing programs of education and training designed to improve the competitiveness of American workers in international trade.

Katsinas, S. G., and Vincent, A. L. (1988). *Economic development and community college models of institutional effectiveness.* San Francisco, CA: Jossey-Bass, Inc. This document contains a thorough explanation of federal policymakers seeing a much more active role for institutions of higher education in economic development. Six existing models of two-year college economic development programs are described.

Kolberg, W. H. (1986). *Employment policies: Looking to the year 2000.* National Alliance of Business. The report is a statement of the Alliance's philosophy for providing education for present and future workers and suggestions for funding such education.

Kopecek, R. J., and Clarke, R. S. (Eds.) (1984). *Customized job training for business and industry. New directions for community colleges, number 48.* Los Angeles, CA: ERIC Clearinghouse for Junior Colleges (ERIC Document Reproduction Service No. ED 252 267). This is a source book that describes and analyzes contracted customized training for business and industry provided by community colleges. Contracted customized training for business and industry is a significant new program focus.

Long, J. F. et al. (1984). *Economic development and the community college. Research and development series no. 251.* Columbus, OH: National Center for Research in Vocational Education. (ERIC Document Reproduction Service No. ED 256 932). The text explains what two year postsecondary institutions can do as participants in economic development at the local, state, and national levels. Issues, definitions, approaches, and case studies provide guiding principles for economic development programs.

Ochoa, A. M., and Hurtado, J. (Eds.) (1984). *Educational and societal futures: Meeting the technological demands of the 1990's. Proceedings of a conference at Anaheim, CA, April 28, 1983.* San Diego, CA.: National Origin Desegregation Assistance Center (ERIC Document Reproduction Service No. ED 272 584). Papers within this document discuss the steps that might be taken to prepare students and teachers for the future or speculate on what schooling, curriculum, and educational needs might be like in the next century.

Office of Technology Assessment (1988). *Technology and the American economic transition: Choices for the future.* Washington, DC: Congress of the United States. Congress assigned the OTA the task of giving Congress perspectives for economic development within the United States. Documents such as this are prepared to guide Congress in preparing legislation. (ERIC Document Reproduction Service No. ED _____ [to be assigned].)

Office of Technology Assessment (1983). *Automation and the workplace. Selected labor, education, and training issues.* Washington, DC: U.S. Government Printing Office (ERIC Document Reproduction Service No. ED 230 701). Procedures for evaluating potential employment change associated with automation are in this publication. Modes of delivery of education, training, and retraining for persons holding or seeking employment in manufacturing industries are described. Methodology for a survey to identify education and training requirements is given.

Stacey, N.; Alsalam, N.; Gilmore, J.; and To, Duc-To (April 1988). *Education and training of 16- to 19-year-olds after compulsory schooling in the United States.* Washington, DC: Higher Education and Adult Learning Division, Office of Research, Office of Educational Research and Improvement, U.S. Department of Education. This paper describes the education and training investments of 16- to 19-year olds with emphasis on state and national issues and policies that influence the nature of transition from compulsory schooling to further education, training, and work. Discussion is documented by research.

Task Force on the Role of Community Colleges in Economic Development (1986). *Community colleges and economic development.* The National Council for Occupational Education. The results of a national survey by NCOE to examine the nature and scope of economic development, in community, technical, and junior colleges are given. Note: economic development is a new innovation not yet clearly defined.

The Fund for the Improvement of Postsecondary Education: Comprehensive Program. Office of Postsecondary Education. Attn: 84. 116A, U.S. Dept. of Education, Application Control Center, Room 3633, Washington, DC 20202, (202) 245-8091 or (202) 245-8100. This fund is authorized by Title X of the Higher Education Act as amended in 1986. The main goal is to encourage the reform, innovation, and improvement of postsecondary education and provide equal education opportunity by finding projects designed to reform curriculum, provide education for a changing economy, use new technology, and improve undergraduate education.

THE Journal: Technological Horizons in Education. Reader Service Department, P.O. Box 15126, Santa Ana, CA 92705-0126. This publication offers free one-year subscriptions to qualified individuals in education institutions and training departments in the U.S. and Canada. The goal of the journal is to inform the reader concerning education and technological advances. Each issue is on one topic, e.g., Emerging Technologies (Aug. 1987), Skills for a Technological World (Mar. 1988), Computers in Education Worldwide (Dec./Jan. 1987-88).

Associations

Persons attempting to gain future perspectives for planning vocational and technical programs should seek information from associations other than vocational technical specialty groups. The following associations have national and international perspectives that will be useful.

American Vocational Association Technical Education Division: The goals of the Division are to identify professional standards, provide professional upgrading activities, identify the functions of technical education in preparing people to work, promote the offerings of technical education programs, and encourage communication of industry and business with technical educators. Members receive the *American Education Journal* and *Update*. Information is available from Janice Van Dyke, Director of Development, State Technical Institute, Memphis, TN 38134.

American Society for Engineering Education: ASEE has two divisions, the Engineering Technical College Council that conducts studies of technician-technology education, e.g., manpower studies, curriculum needs, etc., and communicates with the Accreditation Board for Engineering and Technology that accredits associate degree programs; and the Engineering Technology Division which oversees the Council and provides ASEE vision for future work. The address is ASEE, Eleven Dupont Circle, Suite 200, Washington, DC 20036.

National Alliance of Community and Technical Colleges: The Alliance is a nonprofit consortium of community, technical and junior colleges that promote excellence in postsecondary occupational education by sharing resources, networking, studying common problems, conducting professional development activities, and securing funding. Each year a theme is studied, e.g., 2 + 2 articulation, economic development, etc. The Alliance is located at the National Center for Research in Vocational Education, 1900 Kenny Rd., Columbus, Ohio. 43210.

National Association of Industrial Technology: NAIT is an organization of educators, industrialists, and employers concerned with technological and managerial sciences. The purpose of NAIT is to improve baccalaureate degree programs; however, many two year college faculty are members to facilitate the 2 + 2 concept. The *Journal of Industrial Technology* is published quarterly. The address is NAIT, Eastern Michigan Univerity, Ypsilanti, MI, Alvin E. Rudisill, Ex. Dir.

National Association of Trade and Technical Schools: NATTS's accrediting purpose is to initiate and maintain high education standards and ethical practices in private trade and technical schools. Eight hundred accredited schools are listed in its annually published *Handbook of Trade and Technical Careers and Training*. NATTS, Educ. Dept., 2251 Wisconsin Ave., Washington, DC 20007.

National Institute for Certification in Engineering Technologies: NICET's function is to evaluate the programs of those who voluntarily apply for certification. It was founded to assist institutions educating technicians as a part of the engineering team. Certification programs are being developed that have national use, are job-competency based, and are non-discriminatory. National Institute for Certification in Engineering Technologies, 1420 King St., Alexandria, VA: 22314.

National Council for Occupational Education: NCOE is a private non-profit organization affiliated with the American Association of Community and Junior Colleges. NCOE endeavors to unify all areas of occupation, support favorable legislation, provide an advisory council to AACJC, and develop national leadership. It has established task forces to study, associate degrees, humanities in technical education, economic development, verticle articulation, productivity, etc. The *NCOE Newsletter* is published quarterly. Write Dr. Russell C. Paulsen, North Central Technical Institute, 1000 Campus Dr., Wausau, WI 54401.

The American Association of Community and Junior Colleges: AACJC's mission is to provide leadership and services for community technical and junior colleges. A majority of the 1,222 two-year colleges in the U.S. with a total enrollment of 5 million students, are institutional members. AACJC's "Keep America Working" program is one effort to help the nation compete in the world economy. AACJC publishes a *Directory, AACJC Letter,* and the *Community, Technical, and Junior College Journal.* AACJC, Suite 410, One Dupont Circle, N. W., Washington, DC 20036.

The American Technical Education Association: ATEA differs from other organizations for technical education in that its focus is on improving the expertise of instructors and administrators and forming cooperative agreement with industry rather than legislative lobbying. A refereed journal is published four times a year, *ATEA Journal.* Write Betty Krump, ATEA Ex. Dir., North Dakota State School of Science, 800 College St., Wahpeton, ND 58075.

The National Association of Industrial and Technical Teacher Educators: NAITTE was formed to help persons preparing trade and industrial and technical teachers. Information is available from Nelson A. Foell, Dept. of Occupational Education, Box 7801, North Carolina State University, Raleigh, NC 27695-7801.

References

AACJC Commission on the Future of Community Colleges (1988). *Building communities: A vision for a new century.* Alexandria, VA: American Association of Community and Junior Colleges.

Abram, R.; Rose, B.; and Landrum, B. (1983). *Preparing for high technology: 30 steps to implementation.* Columbus, OH: National Center for Research in Vocational Education (ERIC Document Reproduction Service No. ED 228 471).

Bell, T. H. (1984). Vocational education and the education reform movement. *Voc Ed, 59* (7), 33-34.

Bennett, W. J. (1986). Forum: Vocational education in the high school. *Vocational Education Journal, 61* (2), 13-15.

Bureau of Labor Statistics (1988-89). *Occupational outlook handbook.* Washington, DC: U.S. Labor Department, Bureau of Labor Statistics.

Carnegie Commission on Higher Education (1970). *The open door colleges: Policies for community colleges.* San Francisco, CA: McGraw Hill Book Company.

Carnegie Council on Policy Studies in Higher Education (1980). *Three thousand futures: The next 20 years for higher education.* San Francisco, CA: Jossey-Bass, Inc.

Education reform in Minnesota (1988). *PEI Quarterly,* 3-4.

ERIC Clearinghouse for Junior Colleges (January 1987). *Information sheet.* Los Angeles, CA: University of California.

Feldman, M. (1985). In the name of excellence: The ambush of vocational education. *Community, Technical, and Junior College Journal, 56* (2), 16-20.

Frantz, N. R., Jr., Strickland, D. C.; and Elson, D. E. (1987). High school graduation requirements and vocational education enrollment patterns in 1984-85. *Journal of Vocational and Technical Education,* 3(2), 3-12.

Galambos, E. C. (1984). *Issues in vocational education.* Atlanta, GA: Southern Regional Education Board (ERIC Document Reproduction Service No. ED. 240 312).

Graney, M. R. (1964). *The technical institute.* New York: The Center for Applied Research in Education, Inc.

Grubb, W. N. (1984). The bandwagon once more: Vocational preparation for high tech occupations. *Harvard Educational Review, 54* (4), 429-451.

Indiana Association of Area Vocational Districts, Inc. (January 21, 1987). *Why should we provide secondary vocational education in Indiana?* Speedway, IN.

Jaschik, S. (October 9, 1988). Welfare-reform agreement creates a new role and problems for colleges and trade schools. *The Chronicle of Higher Education, 35* (6), 1 & A30.

Jones, A. H. (1988). Viewing the field again. *School Shop, 47* (8), 2.

Lemons, C. D. (1984). *Education and training for a technological world.* Columbus, OH: National Center for Research in Vocational Education (ERIC Document Reproduction Service No. ED 240 383).

Lewis, A. C. (1987). From Washington. *School Shop, 47* (2), 77-79.

_____ (1987). From Washington. *School Shop, (4)* 40, 36-37.

National Alliance of Business (1986). *Employment policies: Looking to the year 2000.* Washington, D.C.

National Governors' Association: Center for Policy Research and The Conference Board (1987). *The role of science and technology in economic competitiveness. Final report.* Washington, DC: The

National Science Foundation.
N. J. Department of Higher Education (Feburary 20, 1987). *Chancellor's report to the board of higher education.* Trenton, NJ.
Norris, R. J., and Townsend, J. (1987). Coping with declining enrollment. *Agriculture Education Magazine, 60* (1), 7-8.
Parnell, D. (1982). *Some tough questions about community colleges, AACJC pocket reader, 3.* Washington, DC: AACJC, (ERIC Document Reproduction Services NO ED 220 139).
_____ (1987). The high school/community college connection has opened the door for millions of Americans. *ATEA Journal, 14* (3), 10-11.
Prakken, L. W. (Ed. & Publisher) (1986). *Technician education directory.* Ann Arbor, MI: Prakken Publications, Inc.
Pucel, D. et al. (1988). *Visions for change: The control and characteristics of postsecondary vocational education curriculum in the year 2000: Implications for policy.* St. Paul, MN: University of Minnesota (ERIC Document Reproduction Service NO. ED 290 954, also see ED 288 086)
Report of the Harvard Committee (1962). *General education in a free society.* Cambridge, MA: Harvard University Press.
Smith, W. G. (1987). Testimony: Executive summary recommendation. *VEANJ Newsletter,* No. 1, 3.
Swanson, G. I. (1982). Is high school the place for vocational education? *VocEd: Journal of the American Vocational Association, 57* (2), 30-32.
Task Force on the Role of Community Colleges in Economic Development (1986). *Community colleges and economic development.* Wausau, WI: National Council for Occupational Education.
The Carnegie Commission on Higher Education (1970). *The open door colleges.* New York: The Carnegie Foundation for the Advancement of Teaching.
Two-year colleges in Iowa benefit from law designed to lure 4000 jobs to state (1985). *The Chronicle of Higher Education, 29* (20), 3.
UNESCO. Division of Science, Technical, and Environmental Education (1988). *Technical and vocational education: International congress on the development and improvement of technical and vocational education.* Paris, France. (Available from UNESCO, 7 Place de Fontenoy, 75700, Paris, France.)
U.S. Department of Education (1987). *Postsecondary vocational*

education: Fact sheet. Washington, D.C. U.S. Department of Labor (June 25, 1987). BLS previews the economy of the year 2000. *News.*

Weir, D. (1987). Vocational education in the 1990s. *Journal of Vocational and Technical Education, 4* (1), 39-47.

Welsh, F. G. (March, 30, 1988). The continuing need for vocational education. *Education Week.*

CHAPTER 5

Vocational Teacher Preparation

By John W. Glenn, Jr., and Richard A. Walter

THE content and scope of vocational teacher preparation programs are largely a function of the role, expectations, and requirements placed upon the graduates of the programs. As those expectations evolve, so too must the teacher education programs evolve.

The primary role of the vocational teacher as the deliverer of occupationally specific skill training was formalized by the provisions of the Smith-Hughes Act in 1917. The effect of that perception on teacher education was clearly spelled out by the Federal Board for Vocational Education, which emphasized that it was of much greater importance that the vocational instructor be competent in the trade being taught, rather than whether the individual qualified as a professional teacher, or in some cases, even a high school graduate (Fogan, 1968).

That philosophy was short lived because of the growing recognition that knowing how to perform a skill did not predispose one's ability to transfer that skill to the student. No longer was occupational competency acceptable as the sole definer of the instructor's role. It was expected that the individual also would master and use instructional techniques similar to those utilized by the graduates of normal schools. In fact, as early as 1936, the Industrial Education Subcommittee of the Association of Liberal Arts Colleges of Pennsylvania for the Advancement of Teaching was advocating a requirement that all vocational industrial teachers be college graduates, in addition to possessing adequate trade experience. Now, as then, changes in the expectations of the teacher dictate changes in the vocational teacher preparation programs.

Current and Projected Expectations

Educational reformers of the 1980s have produced changes that will continue to influence vocational education well into the next century. These, coupled with technological advancements, legislated mandates, population demographics, and parental expectations have expanded the role of the vocational teacher.

One of the reformers' strongest rallying cries has been an emphasis upon basic academic skills. The increased graduation requirements created as a result of this concern have placed demands on the vocational teacher in two major areas: marketing the program and the provision of basic skills instruction.

Marketing secondary vocational programs often was not of primary concern to the teacher in the past. There was an adequate supply of traditional students who had sufficient time in the class schedules to accommodate the large time commitment vocational classes required. The back-to-basics movement has changed that situation. Now the teacher is called upon to tailor the program to accommodate shorter time frames of instruction and be attractive to both traditional and non-traditional students.

Basic academic skills are an integral component of all vocational programs. However, teachers are now expected to identify those skill areas and provide specific instruction and remediation for all students.

The reform movement also has focused attention on the practice of providing an alternative route to certification for many vocational teachers. Proposals to require subject matter specialization at the undergraduate level, and postpone teacher preparation until the graduate level, have been introduced in many states. If the proposals are enacted, the practice of permitting vocational instructors to become permanently certified at less than the baccalaureate level is not likely to be continued.

Vocational teachers have always been expected to provide their students with accurate, up-to-date instruction. Granted, not all occupations have been equally affected, but the pace of technological advancement has made that expectation increasingly difficult for many teachers to fulfill.

The 1963 Vocational Education Act signaled a change in the scope of vocational education programming and the clientele that was to be served through those programs. Each subsequent piece of legislation has served to increase the emphasis on those changes, as well as the need for the teacher to provide appropriate learning experiences for a broader spectrum of students.

Both secondary and postsecondary vocational instructors have had traditional student cohorts to draw upon as the major providers of enrollees for their classes. Declining numbers in those cohorts, coupled with the effects of advanced technology upon the workforce, have produced a demand that vocational teachers provide instruction to classes composed of students with a much broader range of ages and experiences.

Secondary vocational education programs have experienced both positive and negative impacts from parental expectations. The seventeenth annual Gallup Poll reported growth in the acceptance of vocational education as a requirement for those not planning to attend college, as indicated by the change from 64 percent in 1981 to 75 percent in 1985. However, the acceptance of vocational education as a requirement for those planning to attend college declined during the same period, from 34 percent in 1981 to 27 percent in 1985. The latter change takes on additional significance when considered in combination with the shift in importance placed upon a college education. In the 1978 Gallup Poll, 36 percent of the respondents felt that a college education was very important, as compared with 64 percent in 1985 (Gallup, 1985).

The level and category of skills with which vocational teachers are expected to equip their students to satisfy business and industry demands often depend upon the type and size of the company providing the information. Survey responses range from an emphasis on job keeping skills and corresponding deemphasis on specific job skills, to an emphasis on customized training for a specific job and an accompanying deemphasis on job keeping skills.

Taken together, these factors all indicate a broadening of what constitutes vocational education, the age and ability range of the students enrolled, and the role that the teacher is expected to fulfill. Each of them also translates into an issue which impacts the content, requirements, and delivery of teacher education programs.

Goals and Delivery Models for Preparing Teachers

The goals of vocational teacher preparation are to equip a prospective teacher with state-of-the-art technical knowledge, a sound background in general education, and pedagogical competencies that will facilitate student learning in the classroom/laboratory setting. The delivery methodologies employed to achieve these goals reflect the dynamics of vocational education as a component of secondary and postsecondary educational programs.

The delivery models through which vocational teachers are prepared also reflect each state's certification regulations, the location of vocational teacher preparation institutions, and the geography of each state. Trade, technical, and health occupations, and specific agricultural subjects areas have historically stressed significant work experience as a major prerequisite to employment as a teacher, while technology (industrial arts), business/distributive, general agriculture, and home economics education have required a baccalaureate degree in the respective discipline as the major requisite. The differences in entry level requirements have a definite bearing on the manner in which vocational teacher preparation programs are organized and delivered.

Work Experience Requirement

With work experience being a primary requisite to becoming a vocational teacher, program applicants are typically required to verify their work experience and/or other occupational preparation related to the specialization area in which they desire to become certified to teach.

Many states and vocational teacher preparation programs require prospective teachers to complete an occupational competency examination, or its equivalency, in their specialization area. Others will waive the examination requirement if the candidate has completed a sufficient number of college level courses related to the occupation.

Teacher Education Program Components

The educational reform movement has increased academic requirements in most states, which has forced the vocational teacher education community to focus greater attention on the general education component of their teacher education programs. Anderson and Wiersteiner (1987) reported that most states now require teacher candidates to pass a standardized test of basic academic skills as part of the certification process.

The professional education component of a vocational teacher education program must now include competencies related to special needs students, computer literacy, adult learners, and students with multicultural backgrounds, as well as the traditional areas of instructional development, laboratory organization, instructional delivery, and assessment of student achievement. This expansion of the needed competencies has presented vocational teacher educators with a challenge to design and deliver an all-inclusive curriculum, which meets overall degree requirements without exceeding specific credit hour limitations.

The delivery of quality vocational teacher preparation programs which include the general education, occupational specialization, and professional education components is largely a function of each state's policies regarding the preparation of teachers, the academic program mission of the college or university, and the financial commitment to deliver such programs. Reform must be followed by the involvement and financial commitment of all agencies with a role in the preparation of teachers.

Delivery Modes

Vocational teacher preparation programs are delivered through campus-based programs with a field-based component, an entirely field-based program, and/or a combination of both delivery modes. The program delivery mode selected is dependent upon whether the students are preparing to be a teacher or have obtained a teaching position based on their prior work experiences and are now in need of vocational teacher certification to maintain employment.

The field-based delivery mode is a unique characteristic of vocational teacher education programs. It was created because of the emphasis placed upon recruiting highly competent technical specialists as teachers. Many adults who are potential vocational teachers are already established in their respective communities, with families and other responsibilities that limit their mobility, and thus require delivery of vocational teacher education programs in more than one geographic locale. The core competencies also may be organized in an individualized performance-based delivery mode with observations and assessments made by school personnel and representatives of the teacher education program.

The preservice, traditional, undergraduate vocational teacher education programs are primarily delivered through on-campus course work with specific field-based (school setting) experiences designed to provide students with in-school experiences prior to their supervised student teaching. These programs face a challenge in recruiting highly competent students who have related work experience and/or an associate degree in an occupational specialization area, since they must compete for students with business and industry. Programs with larger concentrations of students in a specific area, such as agriculture, home econmics, business/distributive, and technology (industrial arts) education, offer the technical specialization areas as a component of the program and recruit prospective teachers as college freshmen. These programs face competition from industry for graduating students. If education is going to attract the brightest and retain them as teachers, public policy must be amended so that teachers' salaries are comparable to industry.

Diversity of Population Served

The spectrum of constituencies that vocational teacher education serves dictates that the program delivery system be responsive and reflect the professional development goals of both potential teachers and inservice teachers. The programs must offer the latest technology while upholding sound educational philosophy, principles, and research.

Vocational teacher education programs provide preparation for classroom, supervisory, and administrative positions. The area/regional occupational center, vocational/technical high schools, and comprehensive high schools provide vocational and technical programs at the secondary level. At the postsecondary and adult level, occupational programs are offered at area/regional occupational centers, technical institutes/colleges, community colleges, job training programs, and proprietary schools. In addition, there are a number of occupational programs run by state agencies working with youthful offenders, mental health clients, and convicted felons. Instructional planning, delivery, and evaluation strategies that meet the needs of individual program users is a key to successful teacher education program delivery.

General Education Versus Professional Education

The increased emphasis on general education has forced teacher education programs to examine their degree requirements as they relate to the specialization area, general education, and professional education portions. There is much discussion as to whether the professional education experience should be at the master's degree level. Many baccaleaureate degree advocates believe that well educated students can be prepared for teaching at the baccalaureate degree level and have broad and enriching general education experiences along with their specialization and professional education courses.

As the debate ensues as to what level professional education program should be offered, the vocational teacher education community needs to address the general education needs of its students if they are to be effective in the classroom. Historically, work experience has been a major prerequisite to teach a vocational subject, followed by professional education courses and general education. The importance of general education in a technologically sophisticated work environment forces a reexamination of the manner in which program requirements are structured. A major challenge in completing this process is the firm belief in the need for significant work experience in the occupational specialization area to be taught.

Occupational Experience—How Much is Enough?

Relevant and current work experience in the occupational area for which certification is sought has been a primary requirement for entry into a vocational teacher preparation program. The exact number of years of work experience required for individuals with a high school education and work experience in their occupational area varies among the states from two to seven years. Individuals with an associate degree or its equivalency are generally required to have from two to five years. Those with a baccalaureate degree are typically required to verify one to three years of work experience (Mastain, 1988).

As the role of vocational education at the secondary level is examined, there are proponents who believe that students should receive a global orientation to vocational education at this level and learn specific occupational skills at the postsecondary level. Those adopting this position point to a reduced need for skill development and a corresponding deemphasis on work experience.

Objections to this premise are based upon the 50 percent of high school students who do not attend postsecondary institutions and therefore need entry level occupational skills, and the many potential dropouts who may be motivated to complete high school through vocational education. Additionally, students planning to go on to college directly after high school benefit from having occupational skills which they can use to earn money to pay part of their college expenses. Those arguing from this position maintain the necessity of both skill development and related work experience.

The vocational education community has generally agreed to the guidelines mentioned above, but constantly needs to reinforce its beliefs, mission, and program objectives to school boards, the community, and legislative bodies that determine the destiny of vocational programs. The greatest challenge is communicating to parents and the general public that vocational skill development is an integral part of the secondary curriculum and is needed by all students as a part of their total educational experience.

Cooperation with General Education

The planning, design, and implementation of a vocational teacher education program requires ongoing dialogue and cooperation with departments and faculty offering the general education component of the program. This will develop the knowledge base, competencies, and skills that will facilitate both personal and professional growth.

The economic interdependence of nations emphasizes the need for interdisciplinary experiences within the vocational teacher education program that expand the students' awareness of cultures. These future teachers are going to be preparing students to live and work in a society which must compete with other nations for consumers of the goods and services they produce and market.

Increased Teacher Certification Requirements

The reform movement's emphasis on math, science, and communication skills has resulted in a strengthening of teacher certification requirements in all discipline areas and the addition of national or state teacher examinations. In vocational education, the tenet that work experience in the area to be taught is a primary requisite of teaching has resulted in many teachers entering the profession with strong vocational and pedagogical skills and limited general education experiences.

The challenge to vocational teacher educators is to integrate general education skills into all student assignments, and to advise students to work simultaneously on professional and general education courses as they work toward initial certification.

Control Over Teacher Education Programs

Colleges and universities have specific program guidelines that are followed in the development and operation of programs. In addition, program operation is influenced by state education department regulations, regional accreditation bodies, and professional associations. Vocational teacher educators provide valuable input into the content of the baccalaureate degree programs and must balance the requirements, trends, and perceived needs of society. Local education agencies complicate the situation by circumventing program and state certification requirements in their efforts to fill vacancies. The vocational teacher education community is thus challenged to be responsive and at the same time achieve specific program goals.

The issues of shared governance in the preparation of teachers, whether initial teacher education preparation should be provided at the undergraduate or graduate level, and the number of field-based preparatory experiences in the program have become the subject of much debate in the educational community. Resolution of these issues usually ends up being implemented through changes in certification regulations. This in turn puts the entire process into the political arena, where state boards of regents are lobbied by representative groups to enact changes. Thus, teachers, teacher educators, and other education groups are challenged to organize in order to be heard.

Recruitment Efforts

As Ascher and Birchenall (1987) point out, increasing degree requirements will limit the supply of vocational teachers. Therefore, recruitment efforts must focus on a variety of employment pools, such as: secondary vocational school graduates; skilled craftsmen and technicians; two-year vocational, technical, and proprietary school graduates; adults who have decided on a mid-life career change; and non-traditional individuals entering the work force.

Another resource that vocational teacher education needs to cultivate is individuals with a baccalaureate degree and significant work experience in a technical area, who would like to move from business/industry into education. Graduate level programs need to be available to provide these individuals with an opportunity to prepare for the transition in a manner that allows them to continue employment in their current job.

Women and minorities constitute a growing percentage of today's work force. A key recruitment challenge is increasing the number of women and minority vocational teachers.

Image Building

Strategies must be developed to improve the image of vocational education through increased public relations and knowledge of what programs are, specific entry requirements, and employment oportunities upon completion of vocational programs.

Erickson (1985) notes that this lack of understanding has resulted in vocational teacher education remaining a low priority in higher education with much needed resources often diverted to higher profile departments.

Increased Funding

As Anderson and Wiersteiner (1987) reported, more than 60 percent of the vocational state directors and college department chairs share the opinion that present levels of funding are insufficient to prepare enough vocational teachers to fill anticipated openings. But the recent pattern indicates that vocational teacher education is not a high priority on college campuses.

In fact, a study conducted by the University Council for Vocational Education found that a majority of programs had reduced their full-time faculty and support staff at the same time that state education departments were reducing their funding for vocational teacher education activities (Adams, Pratzner, Anderson, and Zimmerer, 1987).

Publish or Perish

Vocational teacher education has historically been a labor intensive program involving teaching, service, and research. The teaching and service components have required major emphasis in order to deliver programs where inservice teachers work and live. With vocational education faculty working to meet delivery needs at off-campus locations, their time for personal research and writing often is spent commuting. Unfortunately, many colleges do not acknowledge this dilemma through reduced teaching loads, but have the same expectations for research by the vocational education faculty as they do for faculty involved in on-campus programs.

The challenge for vocational educators is to receive recognition for program delivery requirements as part of their work load and within promotion and tenure criteria. Houston (1987) suggests that colleges address the issues as industry would, by creating differentiated assignments such as curriculum development, research, instruction, evaluation, and community service.

Distance Learning

The development of telecommunication and satellite transmission of video and voice has brought a new opportunity to the delivery of vocational teacher preparation programs. Vocational teacher preparation programs can use the new technology to simultaneously deliver courses to multiple off-campus delivery sites. Such efforts would reduce the number of human resource hours currently required to deliver the certification program, and augment opportunities for meeting the growing professional development needs of inservice teachers. The challenge posed to vocational teacher educators is to secure the resources to purchase the necessary equipment, design the curriculum, and to develop telecommunications-based delivery strategies.

Collaboration Efforts

Technological advances in the work place emphasize the need for business, industry, and government to work more closely with colleges and universities in sharing equipment and human resources. The number of entirely new jobs that are created yearly requires worker updating and retraining at an unparalleled rate.

The educational community cannot afford to purchase the latest equipment and change personnel to keep pace with state-of-the-art technology. Collaborative working relationships that provide opportunities for college and university faculty to work with members of business, industry, and government must be developed. Such efforts are going to be a key to high quality programs in vocational education and will prove to be mutually beneficial to all involved.

Summary

As we move into the 1990s, changes in the role and function of vocational education at both the secondary and postsecondary levels impact the organization and delivery of teacher preparation programs. The philosophical tenet that vocational education prepares people for entry level employment will continue to be key, but vocational education also must reflect its expanding role in the integration of basic academic skills, transferable job skills, and specific job skills.

Special populations (minorities, adults, women, special needs, etc.) will continue to influence the experiences selected for inclusion in teacher preparation programs. Likewise, technological developments will dictate requirements for continuous updating of inservice teachers. Vocational education is a key to the nation's economic health, and teacher education programs are a vital component. But, if teacher education is to fulfill that role, then continuous program development, public awareness efforts, and political action activities will be essential.

References

Adams, D. A., Pratzner, F. C., Anderson, B. H., and Zimmerer, M. E. (1987). Vocational teacher education in an era of change. *Vocational Education Journal*, *62* (4). 24-27.

Anderson, L. D., and Wiersteiner, S. (1987). *A national survey report on the current status and direction of vocational trade and industrial teacher education programs as reported by state vocational directors and university department chairpersons.* Unpublished manuscript, Indiana State University, Terre Haute, Indiana.

Ascher, G. A., and Birchenall, J. M. (1987). Raising standards and increasing access. *Vocational Education Journal*, *62* (4), 33-34.

Association of Liberal Arts Colleges of Pennsylvania for the Advancement of Teaching (1936). *Suggested certification requirements in secondary education.* Industrial Education Subcommittee. Harrisburg, PA: Author.

Bell, T. H. (1988). Parting words of the 13th man. *Phi Delta Kappan*, *69* (6), 400-407.

Berliner, D. C. (1985). Critical needs in teacher education. *Journal of Industrial Teacher Education*, *22* (4), 5-11.

Committee for Economic Development (1985). *Investing in our children: Business and the public schools.* New York: Author.

Cooke, G. C. (1985). *Toward excellence in secondary vocational education: Improving teaching.* (Information Series No. 293). Columbus, OH: National Center for Research in Vocational Education. (ERIC Document Reproduction Service No. ED 254652)

Doty, C. (1986). Political, research, and curriculum consideration. *NAITTE Professional Monograph Series*, *2*, 12-13.

Erickson, R. C. (1985). Challenges to vocational teacher education. *Vocational Education Journal*, *60* (6), 28-31.

Finch, C. R. (1987). The commission reports on education: Implications for improving vocational education. *Occupational Educa-*

tion Forum, 16 (1), 3-8.

Fogan, B. J. (1968). *Basic certification requirements for trade and industrial education teachers.* Columbus, OH: Ohio State University.

Gallup, A. M. (1985). The 17th annual Gallup poll of public's attitudes toward the public schools. *Phi Delta Kappan, 67* (1), 53-47.

Hall, C. L. (1984). *Preparing teachers for the future: Gazing into the vdt.* Ruidoso, NM; Paper presented at the Vocational-Technical Teacher Education Conference. (ERIC Document Reproduction Service No. ED 256756).

Herr, E. L. (1987). The unfinished agenda: The state of the nation in vocational education. *Journal of Industrial Teacher Education, 23* (1), 49-58.

Houston, W. R. (1987). Lessons for teacher education from corporate practice. *Phi Delta Kappan, 68* (5), 388-392.

Mastain, R. K. (Ed.) (1988). *Manual on certification and preparation of educational personnel in the United States.* Sacramento, CA: National Association of State Directors of Teacher Education and Certification.

Parks, D. L., and Henderson, G. H. (1985). Strengthening the academic foundations of vocational education. *VOCED, 60* (4), 34-36.

Pritz, S. G. (1988). Basic skills: The new imperative. *Vocational Education Journal, 63* (2), 24-26.

Sherman, S. W. (Ed.), (1983). *Education for tomorrow's jobs.* Washington, DC: National Academy Press.

Stein, M. B. (1986). Preservice and inservice needs. *Vocational Education Journal, 61* (2), 37-38.

The National Commission on Secondary Vocational Education. (1985). *The unfinished agenda: The role of vocational education in the high school.* Columbus, OH: The National Center for Research in Vocational Education.

The William T. Grant Foundation Commission on Work, Family, and Citizenship (1988). *The forgotten half: Non-college youth in America.* Washington, DC: Author.

Zellner, R. D., and Parrish, L. H. (1986). Critical issues in vocational teacher education. *Vocational Education Journal, 61* (2), 39-40.

CHAPTER 6

Organizational Structure of Vocational Education

By James P. Greenan

THE field of vocational education has continued to evolve and change, especially its organizational structure, throughout its history. Philosophical, economical, political, and social influences have contributed to its evolution. This has been particularly true of the "first" 100 years of "modern" vocational education legislation (Wenrich, 1970). The organization and advancement of vocational education at the federal, state, and local levels from the Morrill Act of 1862, Smith-Hughes Act of 1917, the Vocational Education Act (VEA) of 1963, the Vocation Education Amendments of 1968, the Education Amendments of 1976: Title II—Vocational Education, and the Carl D. Perkins Vocational Education Act of 1984 have been characterized by diversity and continuous change. Subsequent amendments to the Perkins Act are likely to produce similar changes. Several national commissions and reports (National Commission on Secondary Education, 1983; Parnell, 1986; National Commission on Secondary Vocational Education, 1984; Boyer, 1983) have expanded directly or indirectly, validly or invalidly the purposes, curriculum, delivery systems, and organization of vocational education in the United States.

The organizational structure of vocational education has involved three levels or delivery systems in which most social service agencies function: (a) federal, (b) state and regional, and (c) local. This is especially the case for the education enterprise. Past and existing organizational structures of vocational education have been and continue to be shaped by historical reflections, philosophic perspectives, economic necessities, political persuasions, and social needs (Greenan, 1988).

The purpose of this chapter is to provide a reflection of the past and existing organizational structures of vocational education, and to present a perspective for a future structure of vocational education. This chapter is organized around federal/national, state and regional, and local structures. The discussion regarding federal/national organizational structure examines the federal role in vocational education, legislative needs and intiatives, agency relationships, and leadership functions. The state and regional discussion focuses upon governance structures, state planning, program delivery, evaluation, and interagency collaboration. The discussion of local organizational structure includes a conceptual program model, program levels, program or service areas, programs, support services, general and vocational education, and interdisciplinary programming. Historical, philosophical, economical, political, and social perspectives are related to each structure.

The goal of this chapter, therefore, is to provide an examination and reflection of the past and present, and a perspective of the future organizational structure of vocational education. It is hoped that persons in the field can use this information in the guidance and direction of vocational education over the next decade and beyond.

Federal/National Role in Vocational Education

The federal or national role in vocational education has been, and continues to be, characterized by a variety of institutions with roots in legislation, departments of government, and professional associations. The Morrill Act of 1862, the Smith-Hughes Act of 1917, the Vocational Education Act (VEA) of 1963, the Vocational Education Amendments of 1968, the Education Amendments of 1976: Title II—Vocational Education, and the Carl D. Perkins Vocational Education Act of 1984 have been the major pieces of federal legislation that have identified the federal role and guided and driven federal policy for over 100 years. In addition, federal legislation relating to vocational education emanating from other fields such as labor, health and human services, rehabilitation, and special education has contributed significantly to the federal structure and policy of vocational education. Over the years, the legislation has created initiatives focusing on creating state universities for the agricultural and mechanical arts, job training, area vocational schools, services for special populations, national advisory committees, equity, and research and development. Accordingly, the organizational structure has changed at the national level to accommodate these evolving initiatives.

The United States Department of Education (USDE), formerly the United States Office of Education (USOE), created in 1978 by Congress, is the major governmental body within which vocational education legislation and policy is implemented at the federal level. The USDE (see Figure 1) is composed of several offices, one of which is the Office of Vocational and Adult Education (OVAE) led by the assistant secretary for vocational and adult education. The OVAE (see Figure 2) is composed of 3 major divisions: (a) Division of National Programs, (b) Division of Adult Education, and (c) Division of Vocational-Technical Education. These divisions are responsible for providing leadership and implementing national policy in areas relating to finance, administration, program improvement, and vocational program implementation. The VEA of 1963 required a sole state agency to administer and supervise the operation of vocational education in each state.

A third force that has shaped and continues to shape the national organizational structure of vocational education is the presence of professional associations, such as the American Vocation Association (AVA). A major emphasis of AVA is to influence legislative development and policy, and proact and lobby on behalf of the vocational education profession in matters of major importance. Over the years, the AVA and its membership have had a significant impact upon vocational education programming and its structure at the national level. Other related professional assocations, lobbies, and special interest groups have also had an impact upon vocational education at the national level.

Figure 1

Organizational Structure of the United States Department of Education

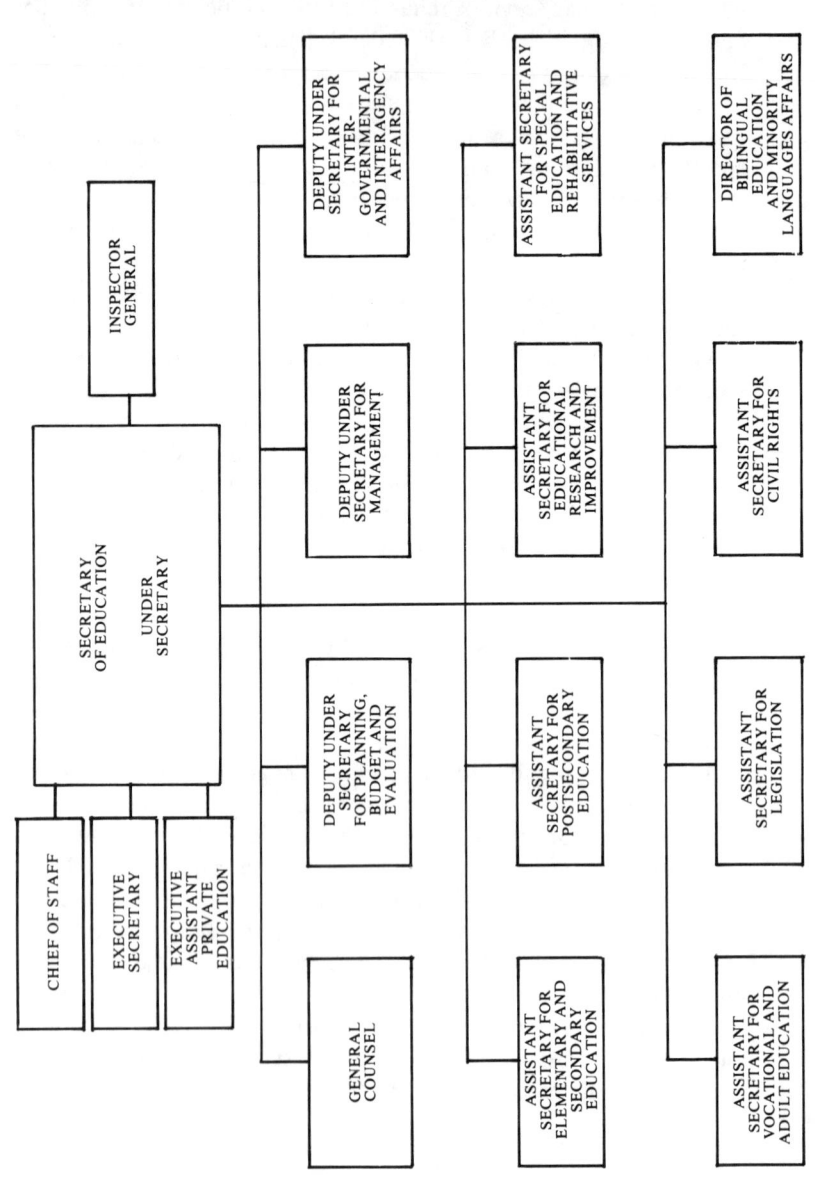

Figure 2

Organizational Structure of the
United States Department of Education

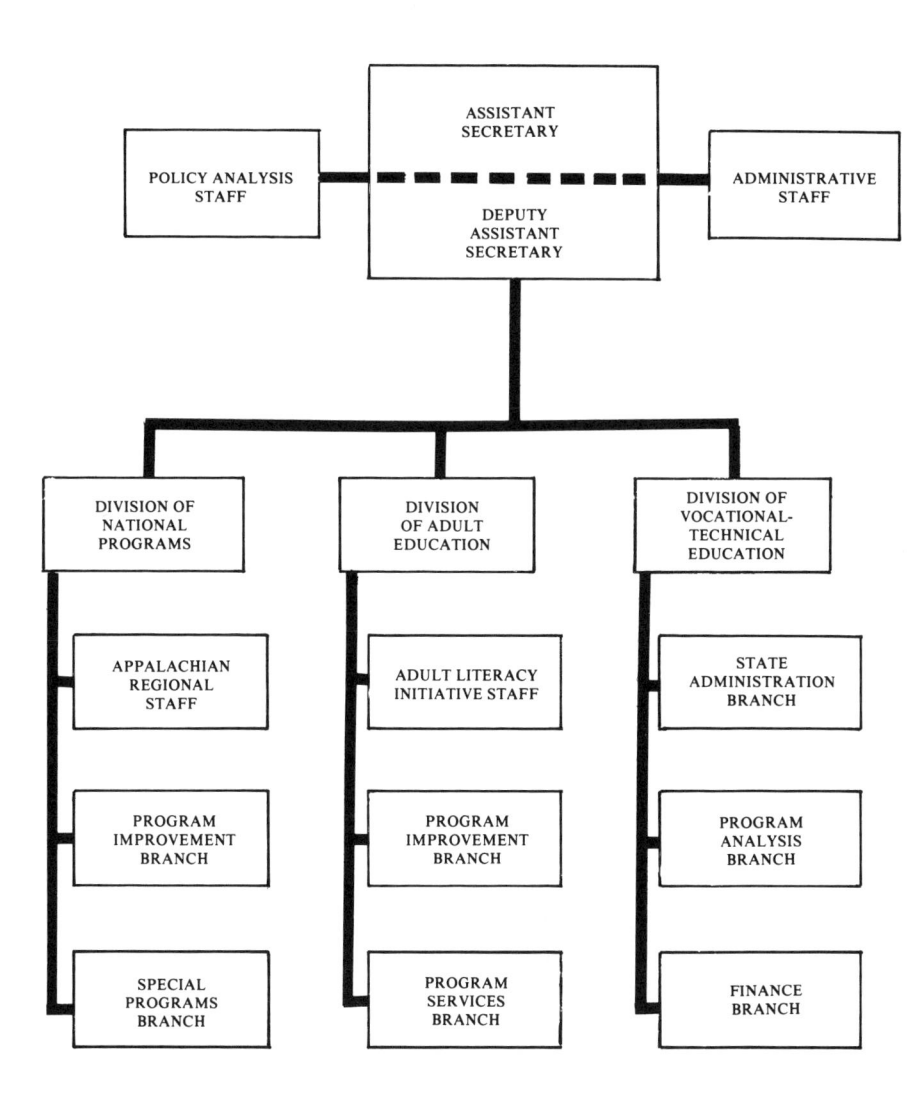

```
                    ┌─────────────────┐
                    │    ASSISTANT    │
┌──────────────┐    │    SECRETARY    │    ┌──────────────┐
│    POLICY    │----│                 │----│ADMINISTRATIVE│
│   ANALYSIS   │    │     DEPUTY      │    │    STAFF     │
│    STAFF     │    │    ASSISTANT    │    │              │
└──────────────┘    │    SECRETARY    │    └──────────────┘
                    └─────────────────┘
                             │
        ┌────────────────────┼────────────────────┐
┌───────────────┐   ┌───────────────┐   ┌───────────────┐
│  DIVISION OF  │   │   DIVISION    │   │  DIVISION OF  │
│   NATIONAL    │   │   OF ADULT    │   │ VOCATIONAL-   │
│   PROGRAMS    │   │  EDUCATION    │   │   TECHNICAL   │
│               │   │               │   │   EDUCATION   │
└───────────────┘   └───────────────┘   └───────────────┘
        │                   │                   │
┌───────────────┐   ┌───────────────┐   ┌───────────────┐
│  APPALACHIAN  │   │ ADULT LITERACY│   │     STATE     │
│   REGIONAL    │   │ INITIATIVE    │   │ADMINISTRATION │
│     STAFF     │   │    STAFF      │   │    BRANCH     │
└───────────────┘   └───────────────┘   └───────────────┘
        │                   │                   │
┌───────────────┐   ┌───────────────┐   ┌───────────────┐
│    PROGRAM    │   │    PROGRAM    │   │    PROGRAM    │
│  IMPROVEMENT  │   │  IMPROVEMENT  │   │   ANALYSIS    │
│    BRANCH     │   │    BRANCH     │   │    BRANCH     │
└───────────────┘   └───────────────┘   └───────────────┘
        │                   │                   │
┌───────────────┐   ┌───────────────┐   ┌───────────────┐
│    SPECIAL    │   │    PROGRAM    │   │    FINANCE    │
│   PROGRAMS    │   │   SERVICES    │   │    BRANCH     │
│    BRANCH     │   │    BRANCH     │   │               │
└───────────────┘   └───────────────┘   └───────────────┘
```

Legislative Needs and Initiatives

The history of vocational education is characterized by a considerable amount of involvement in federal legislation and public laws that have improved the field's capacity to serve all persons, including those who may have a disadvantage or who have been disenfranchised from the educational and employment systems. For example, the Perkins Act has focused organizationally upon (a) Title IIA—handicapped, disadvantaged, single parents and homemakers, adults in need of training and retraining, incarcerated, criminal offenders, sex bias/stereotyping in vocational education, services; (b) Title IIB—research, curriculum, personnel development, evaluation, local program improvement, statewide program improvement; and (c) Title III—consumer homemaker education statewide, home economics for the economically disadvantaged, and state program administration (Illinois Commission on Intergovernmental Cooperation, 1987). However, as vocational education proceeds into the 1990s, legislation must be increasingly sensitive to the needs of the unserved and underserved. Existing and proposed legislation in other related fields also should consider adopting new vocational initiatives. Coordination between and among legislation initiatives must be encouraged to eliminate, or at least minimize, duplication of effort. Legislation should strive to promote and create workable partnerships of employment and training in traditional vocational settings. The decade of the 1990s should break down the barriers that inhibit organizational coordination in programmatic areas such as vocational and special education, vocational education and employment and training programs, and vocational education and other federal job training programs. Progress has been made in the last decade, but many more improvements and initiatives need to occur.

Agency Relationships

The USDE/OVAE must continue to provide leadership at the national level and more clearly convey the roles and responsibilities it has in carrying out the federal mission. Worthington (1979) has said that the federal role of vocational education should not be one of operational authority of educational services but rather that of program support services and facilitation. He maintains that operational authority should continue to be returned (deregulated) to state and local authorities. Further, the federal role should go from a compliance monitoring role to a facilitator's role. In addition, Worthington has suggested that future foci should be upon program quality and scope, retraining of adults, and improved collaboration with business, industry, and labor.

State and local programs are confirming or redefining their places within the educational enterprise—that is, defining the programmatic, political, economic, and social place of vocational education within (general) education and among employment and training programs. This also needs to be done at the federal level. The future organization and structure of vocational education will be determined, in large measure, by the way in which the purposes and curriculum of vocational education are perceived (Copa, Plihal, Scholl, Ernst, Rehm, and Copa, 1985; Pucel, DeVogel, and Persico, 1988; Oakes, 1986). For example, redefining roles and coordination with agencies advocating for special populations (e.g., handicapped, disadvantaged) is a crucial need. Legislation in both vocational education and special education addresses handicapped learners in secondary and postsecondary settings. Agencies must work together to ultimately achieve significant measures of success.

Professional associations that directly and indirectly relate to vocational education must enhance their capacity to advocate effectively for their constituents. As in other areas of public service, coordination is essential to eliminate, or at least greatly reduce, duplicative activities. Joint planning, agenda writing, and promotional activities are areas of mutual benefit and concern.

Leadership Functions

The organizational structure of vocational education at the national level should include a clear vision of leadership functions. Gentry (1978) has noted the need for four main leadership functions in vocational education: (a) planning, (b) coordination, (c) need identification, and (d) equitable distribution of funds. In addition, legislation, governmental agencies, and professional associations need to place more emphasis on leadership functions relating to policy development serving special populations, curriculum program evaluation, advocacy, and interagency coordination.

State and Regional Levels

The VEA of 1963 called for the creation of a sole state agency to administer and supervise the operation of vocational education at the state level. Since that time the governance structures of the 50 states, District of Columbia, and surrounding territories which submit and have approved state plans for vocational education, and which receive Perkins funds have been characterized by their diversity. Gentry (1978) identified five basic governance structures adopted in the 50 states: Type A (n=6)—states with one agency for all levels of education; Type B (n=31)—states with an agency for elementary and secondary schools including vocational education and a state coordinating or governing agency for higher education; Type C (n=8)—states with an agency for elementary and secondary schools, an agency for vocational education, and a state coordinating or governing agency for higher education; Type D (n=3)—states with an agency for elementary and secondary schools including vocational education and governing boards for individual institutions of higher education with no statewide governing agency; and Type E (n=2)—states with other governing structure types: e.g., Hawaii—a state department of education, a board of regents for the university system including all vocational education; South Carolina—a state board of education for elementary and secondary education which is responsible for vocational education at the secondary and adult levels, a postsecondary and technical education board which is responsible for postsecondary vocational education, and a higher education board. Type B was the most common governance structure, respresented in approximately 60 percent of the states. A sample structure is provided in Figure 3.

Similarly, Hodes (1979) noted different governance structures, compositions, and levels of authority within states. Some states have interagency agreements and coordination emanating from state legislatures. Hodes further stated that "differences that exist in the organization, governance, and financing of vocational education systems of the 56 states and territories are likely to have a significant impact on the manner in which federal policies are implemented in these different states and territories and on the effect of those policies in achieving the objective established by the federal government" (p. 10).

Figure 3

Organizational Structure of a State Education Agency

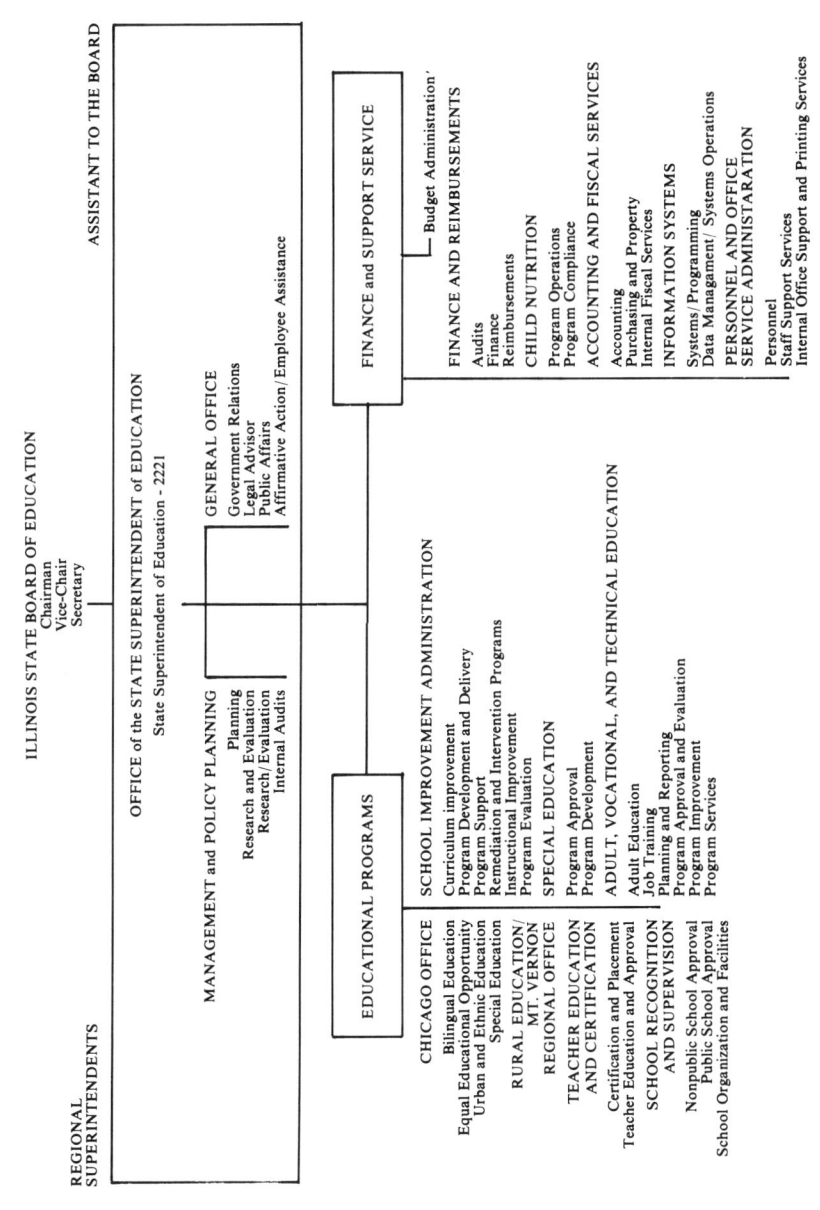

ILLINOIS STATE BOARD OF EDUCATION
Chairman
Vice-Chair
Secretary

REGIONAL SUPERINTENDENTS

ASSISTANT TO THE BOARD

OFFICE of the STATE SUPERINTENDENT of EDUCATION
State Superintendent of Education - 2221

GENERAL OFFICE
Government Relations
Legal Advisor
Public Affairs
Affirmative Action/Employee Assistance

MANAGEMENT and POLICY PLANNING
Planning
Research and Evaluation
Research/Evaluation
Internal Audits

FINANCE and SUPPORT SERVICE

- Budget Administration

FINANCE AND REIMBURSEMENTS
Audits
Finance
Reimbursements

CHILD NUTRITION
Program Operations
Program Compliance

ACCOUNTING AND FISCAL SERVICES
Accounting
Purchasing and Property
Internal Fiscal Services

INFORMATION SYSTEMS
Systems/Programming
Data Management/Systems Operations

PERSONNEL AND OFFICE
SERVICE ADMINISTARATION
Personnel
Staff Support Services
Internal Office Support and Printing Services

EDUCATIONAL PROGRAMS

SCHOOL IMPROVEMENT ADMINISTRATION
Curriculum improvement
Program Development and Delivery
Program Support
Remediation and Intervention Programs
Instructional Improvement
Program Evaluation

SPECIAL EDUCATION
Program Approval
Program Development

ADULT, VOCATIONAL, AND TECHNICAL EDUCATION
Adult Education
Job Training
Planning and Reporting
Program Approval and Evaluation
Program Improvement
Program Services

CHICAGO OFFICE
Bilingual Education
Equal Educational Opportunity
Urban and Ethnic Education
Special Education

RURAL EDUCATION/
MT. VERNON
REGIONAL OFFICE

TEACHER EDUCATION
AND CERTIFICATION
Certification and Placement
Teacher Education and Approval

SCHOOL RECOGNITION
AND SUPERVISION
Nonpublic School Approval
Public School Approval
School Organization and Facilities

Seckendorf (1981) further delineated 10 different state government structures, five different types of state administrative agencies with major responsiblities for vocational education, and five different levels of state authority over institutions that provide vocational education programs. At the regional level, he identified eight types of agencies, five kinds of local boards, and six different arrangements for fiscal response. Seckendorf claims the primary similarities among state governance structures lie within objectives and program classification.

Clearly, several models of state governance structure have emerged over the past 25 years for administering and supervising the operation of vocational education in states. The delivery of education programs, and vocational education programs in particular, has been and continues to be viewed within the purview of the individual states. Various arguments can be supported to advocate the effectiveness of a specific model for a particular state. For example, there are advantages for all state education functions being governed under one education agency or for vocational education being governed separately. Similarly, disadvantages can be enumerated. Governance issues continue to confront state agencies (Gentry, 1983; Dunham, 1980; Florida Council on Vocational Education, 1986). However, vocational education cannot afford to be alienated from the educational enterprise and lose its identity as an educational discipline. Future state governance structures should be sensitive to this concern. Likewise, general education must recognize vocational education as a discipline fully embodied in statewide planning, administration, and evaluation activities. Artificial distinctions need to be removed. Problems and issues related to basic skills, equity, special populations, and youth unemployment will require solutions and input from all areas of education. Governance structures should seek to identify commonalities, reduce duplication, encourage collaboration, and eliminate counterproductive programmatic alienation. This is perhaps exemplified by the need for vocational and special educators to work together to serve the needs of handicapped learners or for vocational educators to work with mathematics, reading, and writing teachers to enhance students' functional skills necessary for employment. Also, state and regional governance structures in the next decade should be concerned with improving intra- and intervocational program relationships and articulation between delivery levels (e.g., secondary, postsecondary). Relationships between general and occupational programs must be more clearly identified and recognized within governance structures. More emphasis should be placed upon programmatic rather than economic and political models of governance and programming.

Planning and Interagency Collaboration

Planning efforts that reflect interagency involvements with vocational education will become increasingly important in the next decade, especially as they relate to programming, funding, resource allocation, and legislation. A formal vehicle to coordinate planning should be the state plans of these agencies. Articulation and coordination among public and private sector agencies is necessary to achieve excellence (National Commission on Secondary Vocational Education, 1984). Pucel, DeVogel, and Persico (1988) cite the importance for cooperation and planning among business and industry, state vocational and technical education agencies, vocational programs, labor union, professional associations, state employment and training departments, community colleges, and federal and state agencies.

The National Commission on Secondary Vocational Education in its report *The Unfinished Agenda* stated that, "within state policy guidelines, each secondary school should formulate or contribute to a meaningful and cost-effective regional plan for providing employment-related education. Such plans should include policies and formal arrangements among elementary and junior high schools, community colleges, and other employment and training related organizations" (p. 27). The commission further stressed the importance of business, labor, and the community in cooperative arrangements and the development of vocational education, and they "must seek each other out." These activities should include new approaches for executing arrangements, and the development of new types of arrangements for achieving goals, given the diversity of state and local level agencies (Ruff, 1981). Planning activities should consider such factors as: declining enrollments in secondary programs; enrollment increases in postsecondary, adult, and continuing education; critical needs for upgrading and retraining of workers; services for special populations; relationships with other content educators within areas such as basic skills; and other influences external to vocational education. Funding increases or shifts are unlikely to increase proportionately to needs. For example, funds that support vocational education are typically derived from the federal vocational education act, state dollars, state general education dollars, and local dollars derived from property tax revenues. The major sources, therefore, are federal, state, and local tax dollars. As monetary resources become increasingly tighter and demands for resources become greater, the need for efficient planning and use of funds will also increase. Methods for distribution of these funds may differ according to the source of funds. The state agency responsible for the administration and supervision of vocational education, however, usually does not posses and allocate the major amount of funds required to support vocational education. Therefore, collaboration among agencies in program planning activities is essential.

Program Delivery and Evaluation

The manner in which states deliver and evaluate programs differ in relation to their planning and interagency activities. Hodes (1979) identified seven types of institutions, 13 different types of program administrative structures, and four different types of single- and multi-district services plus regional programs that deliver resources. Seckendorf (1981) identified six types of institutions, 13 kinds of program administrative structures, and four different types of single- and multi-district services. He claims that there is a greater need for instrastate consistency rather than for interstate consistency with respect to program delivery and evaluation. In all states, however, a state advisory council for vocational education (SACVE) provides input and guidance, and the state plan provides the requirements and guidelines for delivering vocational programs.

The requirement for evaluation is clear in the federal legislation. States are required to evaluate local programs on an ongoing basis. Commonly, evaluations may reflect a "three-phase" approach that includes local plan development, approval, and evaluation or a locally directed evaluation in which local program developers and implementers conduct ongoing, formative evaluations of their programs. Self-study and consultant evaluation teams are typical evaluation techniques used. States are also required to produce and submit an annual accountability report documenting the extent to which and how successfully their state and local plans have been implemented. Program evaluation will be increasingly important in program improvement, planning, and meeting accountability demands. Future evaluations should be formative, summative, and practical, and should produce results that can and will be used.

It is quite clear that in the next decade the field of vocational education must consider a number of factors that will influence the extent to which program delivery will have meaningful effects. State leadership personnel will need to consider content in regard to organizing and structuring vocational programs. Technology will continue to change rapidly. State program functions will need to be more clearly delineated from federal or national functions. States must assume more of a role in conducting needs assessments, identifying personnel training needs, and serving business and industry needs. States will also need to assume a more active role in tracking demographic shifts and changes and identifying changes in employment patterns. For example, structural and demographic shifts in terms of age, geographic location, and declining youth population will be especially visible for the next ten years. Seckendorf (1981) notes the need for states to pay particular attention to "outside influences" affecting vocational education. For example, economic, social, demographic, political, and philosophical influences must be considered along with programmatic influences. Persons external to vocational education need to be involved in program delivery and evaluation of vocational education. Their involvement will be necessary to find workable and effective solutions to problems related to youth and older worker unemployment, minorities, special needs populations, women, labor, worker and occupational requirement changes, basic skills of students (and workers), adult retraining and continuing education, and immigration of higher numbers of persons into the United States. In part, states will need to increasingly make data-based decisions in future program planning and delivery activities.

Local Level

The delivery, organization, and structure of vocational education programs at the local level, in large measure, are a function of the organization and structure of vocational education at the state level.

In some states, the state vocational agency maintains maximum autonomy over local programs. In other states, local level programs maintain maximum autonomy over most phases of vocational programming. However, the traditional organization and structure of vocational education at the local level (and the state level) have frequently been complex. For example, there has been interprogram disjointedness (e.g., industrial, agricultural, health, home economics, business) and intraprogram separateness (e.g., general education, industrial arts; occupational, trade-industrial education). Technological content differences among programs or service areas are usually obvious, but not always. Student educational goals (e.g., general education and occupational) are also usually obvious. However, the education discipline of vocational education which includes a variety of programs, delivery systems, and program phases is sometimes fractionated. The programs have several commonalties, a major one being that each relates to employment related education. The field of vocational education, therefore, should have an essence; and its organization and structure should have internal consistency.

Vocational education has become increasingly involved in dealing with problems pervasive to all its programs. Problems and issues related to equity, special populations, basic skills, and curriculum have major implications for the different levels upon which vocational education is currently practiced and should be practiced. Vocational education, therefore, should be viewed as a discipline, in much the same way as the educational disciplines of science and mathematics are. For example, science includes programs such as earth science, biology, chemistry, and physics. All these programs have an essence which binds professionals—the study of knowledge and observation and understanding of the principles and laws of the natural and physical world. Similarly, the vocational education field should strive for an essence, internal consistency, and an operational structure which encourage programmatic relationships rather than dependence on external influences. Further, local programming, organization, and structure should, therefore, focus upon programmatic priorities and consumer needs rather than upon traditional social, political, and economic structures. These structures often serve to separate and confuse, and communicate neither within the field nor to the public what vocational education is about.

Conceptual Program Model

The conceptual program model in Figure 4 illustrates the relationship among vocational program phases and delivery systems, program or service areas, and programs. The model conveys the need for the field of vocational education to become more well defined and internally consistent, and reflect an educational discipline with an essence. The model, of course, can be operationalized to reflect nuances among different states and local programs.

The model and future vocational programs should relate and interrelate the programs comprising vocational education, as in the educational disciplines of science, mathematics, music, art, and history. The unique differences among program areas are in technical skill knowledge or requirements, although there are often similarities among programs. Curriculum initiatives, recent studies, and research have frequently cited the commonalities among programs with respect to the cognitive and affective knowledge and skills needed in different vocational programs and work settings (Greenan, 1983), and the commonality of problems and issues facing professionals in these program areas. In summary, agricultural, business and marketing, health, home economics, and industrial educators should identify their similarities, understand their nuances, and plan, deliver, and advocate for all vocational programs.

In the decade ahead, vocational educators should view the field beyond the political and economical confines—existing only for some students, at a very specific time, and for which federal funds are the main concern. Vocational educators should view their discipline as do professionals in other educational disciplines. For example, vocational education should be conceived as having a place in the K-12 curriculum. Vocational education is the only discipline without a K-12 curriculum or program in the public schools. Perhaps, in part, this explains many of the problems students, parents, and vocational educators encounter as students first enter the ninth or tenth grade. Students have not had opportunities for career/vocational awareness, orientation, and exploration experiences necessary for making career/educational decisions at the secondary level. Vocational education should be promoted as a discipline and as having a place in the elementary school program—not as training as the public often perceives, but, as awareness as in the example of infused activities

Figure 4

Organizational Structure of a State Vocational Education Agency

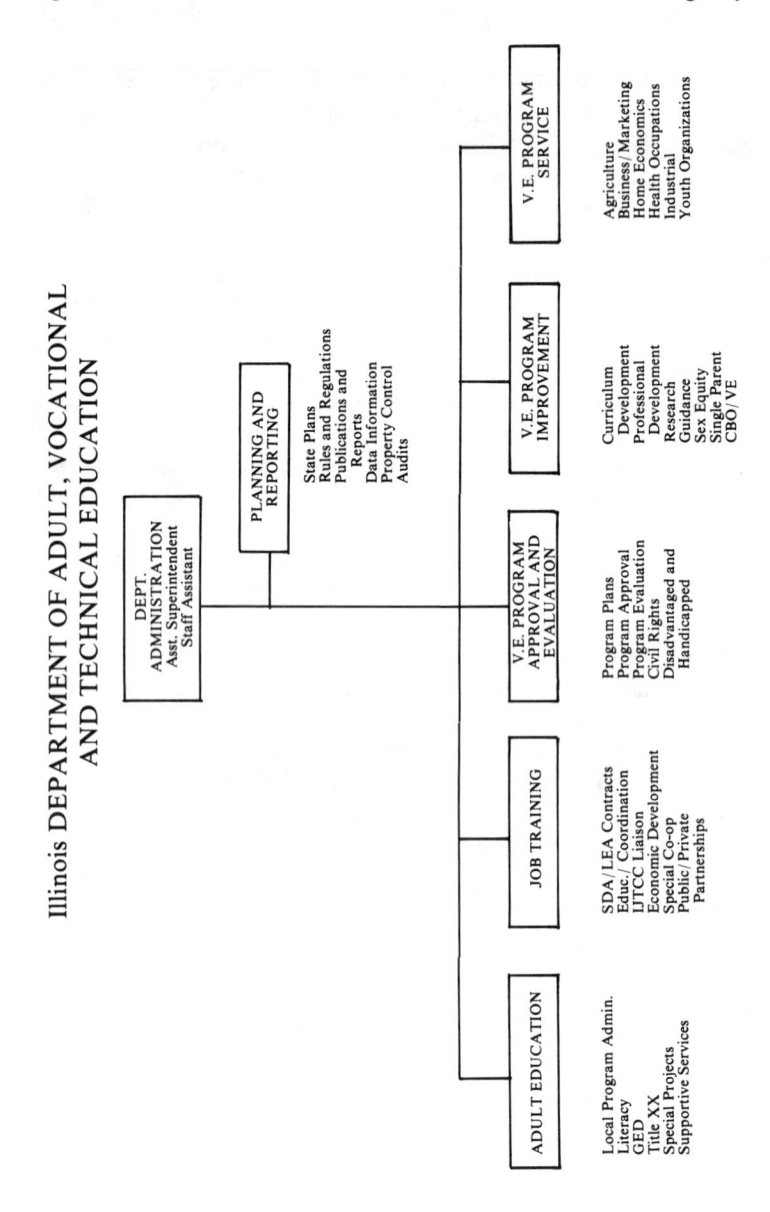

Illinois DEPARTMENT OF ADULT, VOCATIONAL AND TECHNICAL EDUCATION

```
                        DEPT.
                    ADMINISTRATION
                    Asst. Superintendent
                     Staff Assistant
                            │
                            ├──────────── PLANNING AND
                            │              REPORTING
                            │
                            │              State Plans
                            │              Rules and Regulations
                            │              Publications and
                            │                Reports
                            │              Data Information
                            │              Property Control
                            │              Audits
```

ADULT EDUCATION	JOB TRAINING	V.E. PROGRAM APPROVAL AND EVALUATION	V.E. PROGRAM IMPROVEMENT	V.E. PROGRAM SERVICE
Local Program Admin.	SDA/LEA Contracts	Program Plans	Curriculum Development	Agriculture
Literacy	Educ./ Coordination	Program Approval	Professional Development	Business/Marketing
GED	IJTCC Liaison	Program Evaluation	Research	Home Economics
Title XX	Economic Development	Civil Rights	Guidance	Health Occupations
Special Projects	Special Co-op	Disadvantaged and Handicapped	Sex Equity	Industrial
Supportive Services	Public/Private Partnerships		Single Parent	Youth Organizations
			CBO/VE	

in existing elementary school curriculum. School districts could employ itinerant vocational "consultant" teachers to work with elementary teachers in career vocational activities related to what students are studying. School districts could also conduct specific classes in areas such as agriculture or industry. Or schools could offer a general vocational class that integrates a series of learning experiences in all vocational program areas taught by a qualified and certified vocational teacher. To implement these kinds of ideas requires dollars, changes in perceptions with the public and educators at large, and changes in views within vocational education regarding curriculum and professional identification. However, most importantly it will require commitment, first by vocational educators and then by "general" educators, administrators, school board members, and parents.

Vocational programs should also provide opportunities for vocational and career orientation at the junior high/middle school level. Traditionally, this has been the only time in which "vocational" education has been required of students, for example, a six-week experience in indutrial arts and/or home economics. Vocational education should evaluate this very important period in a student's education. During this time students are growing in many ways, and the variety and quality of experiences at this level can have a very profound impact upon their future.

Especially important is curriculum integration, or at least working relationships must occur among vocational teachers and be encouraged by vocational administrators. Agriculture, business, health, home economics, and industrial educators must work more closely. "General" vocational classes, general labs, courses, or infusion of vocational content are alternative options for delivering instruction. Also significant is the articulation and coordination in instructional planning and delivery between elementary and junior high/middle school vocational and general education personnel. Theoretically, and in many cases in practice, this occurs in other educational disciplines, for example, the articulation and coordination of instruction in science and mathematics in elementary and junior high school.

Historically, the secondary or high school level has received the focus of attention by vocational educators. In large part this has occurred because of the traditional economics and politics of the

Figure 5
K-Adult Vocational Education Program Model

PROGRAM PHASES | Placement 13→

	Awareness (K-6)	Orientation (7-6)	Exploration and Preparation (10-12)		World of Work or Continuing Education
	General Education		General Eduction (Comprehensive High School)	Occupational Education (Area Vocational Center/ Comprehensive High School)	Prv./Pub. Sect./ Bus./Indus./ Community Col.
	Elementary	Junior High			
Agriculture	Infusion or Separate Class, Gen. Class	Infusion, Gen. Labs, or Courses, Gen. Class	Exploration ●Horticulture Co-op Education Work-Study Student Organizations	Skill Training ●Agricultural Mechanics Student Organizations	Employment ●Veterinary Technology
Business and Marketing			Exploration ●Typing Co-op Education Work-Study Student Organizations	Skill Training ●Secretarial Student Organizations	Employment ●Data Processing
Health			Exploration ●Human Anatomy Co-op Education Work-Study Student Organizations	Skill Training ●Nurse Aide Student Organizations	Employment ●Dental Hygenist
Home Economics			Exploration ●Nutrition Co-op Education Work-Study Student Organizations	Skill Training ●Food Preparation Student Organizations	Employment ●Child Development
Industrial		●Manu-facturing ●Construc-tion	Exploration ●Electronics Co-op Education Work-Study Student Organizations	Skill Training ●Carpentry Student Organizations	Employment ●Mechanical Technology

●Example program

A version of this figure was published in D.E. Berkell and J.M. Brown, "Transition from School to Work for Persons with Disabilities."

field. However, vocational education at the secondary school level has been and continues to be entirely elective. Programs have been and continue to be available in comprehensive high schools, vocational high schools, and area vocational schools (also known as area vocational centers, joint vocational schools, area vocational technical schools, area vocational technical centers, vocational technical schools, area career centers) in a single district or regional arrangement. Generally, local programs have a considerable amount of independence and autonomy.

Future vocational programming must seek to break down the barriers among and between vocational education in different program areas, as well as the intraprogram barriers (e.g., the rigid distinction between general and occupational education—industrial arts and trade and industrial education). Major differences exist in student career goals rather than in curriculum, instruction, planning, and support services. Future focus must be on programmatic planning and student needs rather than upon political and economic conveniences. Vocational education programs serve students with differing educational goals as do programs in mathematics, music, and physical education. For example, inter- and intraprogram articulation among vocational programs must occur to ensure that students have the opportunity to explore occupations/careers. This is important for deciding whether to prepare for an occupation/career in high school or decide to pursue a more general (explorational) vocational program and delay career preparation until after high school graduation. Vocational programs should not be planned and implemented as an either/or, locking out students early or limiting their access to services. This is an especially important concern for special populations (Greenan, 1989).

Secondary vocational programs should, therefore, offer students the opportunity for exploration, skill training, cooperative education, work study, and involvement in student organizations. The National Commission on Secondary Vocational Education (1984) expressed that the future organizational structure of vocational education should include field-based learning such as supervised cooperative education experiences and that it be available to all students. Pucel, Devogel, and Persico (1988) cited several assumptions that may affect future curriculum and are also likely to affect the future organization of vocational education, including cultural values, information-ideas, demographics, economics, technology, legalistic and political factors, and institutional factors. They also cited institutional factors such as an increase of participation in decision making, better service with fewer resources, organization and job redesign and restructure, development of new managerial approaches and greater flexibility and openness, and cooperation between public and private sectors. In addition, they indicated several local program organization options that will be utilized in the future: (a) programs broken into courses, (b) programs offered with certificates of completion or diplomas, (c) short interview courses to teach limited skills, and (d) programs offering an associate of applied science degree (p. 14). However, nontraditional delivery systems such as computer assisted instruction and traditional methods such as lecture/demonstration will be used.

The vocational education field should not perceive itself or be perceived by the public as only having a job training mission for certain students. To pursue this track would not take advantage of the full array of services and opportunities vocational education can potentially offer to all students. Future vocational programming should continue to focus upon technical outcomes, but should also include relevant cognitive, affective, social, and economic outcomes (Greenan, 1983). To accomplish these goals will require proper articulation and coordination among and between elementary, junior high/middle school, and secondary vocational and general educators and administrators; the public; school board members; and parents. However, most importantly, it will require the commitment of vocational educators to evaluate their programs, seek positive and productive intra- and interprogram relationships, and view their talents and programs as potentially advantageous for *all* students.

The field of vocational education should focus increased programmatic attention upon placement in the world of work and adult and continuing education. The demographic shifts coming in the next 10 to 20 years will reveal more and more adults and older citizens in the population who are in need of basic skills, technical updating, and/or retraining. A focus upon placement will require attention to the transition needs of high school and vocational program completers into the world of work. High school counselors, placement personnel, and transition personnel will need to create even better relationships with private sector employers. In addition, the growing postsecondary or adult population will require a larger amount of instructional services through community colleges offering associate degrees, area vocational technical institutes, universities and colleges offering 2 + 2 programs, and proprietary schools. Effective postsecondary education in the next decade and beyond will require operational partnerships between institutions and the private sector. Further, articulation between secondary and postsecondary programs will be necessary to ensure appropriate employment or higher education placements and the continuation of necessary supplementary services for students and workers. Commitments and collaboration among and between secondary and postsecondary vocational personnel and the private sector in planning, program delivery, resource management, and evaluation will, in large measure determine the extent to which the field of vocational education will be successful in serving the adult and continuing education population in future years.

In addition, access to vocational programs at the elementary, junior high/middle school, secondary, and adult/continuing education levels for all persons is the provision for equity within programs. Provisions for the necessary support services for students who require them to succeed in their programs will assist in ensuring equity. Support services especially for special populations (e.g., handicapped, disadvantaged, limited-English proficient, minorities, displaced homemakers, incarcerated) must be available to help ensure program completion and successful transition into successive program levels, the world of work, or higher education. Support services such as remedial instruction, adpative equipment and materials, transportation, work study, and tutors are required to prevent students, especially "at-risk" students, from "falling between the cracks."

General and Vocational Education: Interdisciplinary Programming

The field of vocational education should strive to become a recognized educational discipline. Vocational educators need to define their mission, goals, program areas, programs, and educational levels in which they deliver instruction and services. The field of vocational education has faced, does face, and will continue in the future to face critical economic as well as educational problems and challenges in serving youth and adults.

Serving special needs (and at-risk) populations, ensuring equity, teaching basic skills, serving adults and older citizens, and providing technical updating will require knowledge and expertise beyond the field of vocational education. Serving the career and vocational needs of youth and adults in the next decade will require formal working relationships with personnel in other educational disciplines. For example, as more special needs students gain access to vocational programs, vocational personnel will need to work collaboratively with special education personnel. Collaboration is essential to ensure equity for special needs learners. Also, as vocational educators are further required to become involved in teaching "basic" skills, they will need to work with mathematics, reading, writing, English, and science teachers in curriculum development/ revision, planning, instructional delivery, and evaluation activities. Guidance counselors and other auxiliary and support staff will also need to become involved in collaborative arrangements.

Removing traditional curriculum, perceptual, and status barriers will the major obstacles to overcome in developing effective interdisciplinary working relationships. The current intuitive knowledge and empirical research has clearly indicated the curriculum similarities among vocational education and other education disciplines (Greenan, 1983). Further, vocational programs and employment settings require these skills. It seems apparent, therefore, that collaboration is of paramount importance.

Summary:
Challenges for the 1990s

The field of vocational education has had a tradition of changing organizational structures primarily affected by social, economic, and political influences. It has been influenced by other public and private institutions as well as other educational content areas or disciplines. In the next decade and beyond, however, the field of vocational education will play a crucial role in preparing youth and adults for employment, productive lives, and an informed citizenry. The field of vocational education will have to face problems and issues relating to serving increasing numbers of special needs populations, teaching employment related (or generalizable) basic skills, ensuring access and equity for all persons, retraining the adult workforce, and meeting the challenges of constantly changing curriculum and occupational skill and knowledge requirements. To meet the challenges and demands in the next decade and beyond, the field of vocational education, and especially its organizational structure, must reflect a well-defined, internally consistent programmatic emphasis. The field should promote its potential, market its offerings, and strengthen its weaknesses. Vocational educators should strive to become and be recognized as members of an educational discipline. The field needs to organize and deliver programs utilizing a continuum of services from K-adult, and recognize that vocational education includes more than job preparation; it also involves awareness, orientation, and exploration. Vocational service areas must more closely interrelate as programs within a discipline rather than be artificially and rigidly distinguished as technical entities. In addition, the field of vocational education must initiate and maintain positive, formal intergency working relationships. The field will have to design partnerships within the private sector to insure that the necessary resources are provided to and the required skills and knowledge are acquired by students and workers. Vocational educators will also have to develop interdisciplinary working relationships with other educational disciplines such as mathematics, science, English, reading, and special education to meet the challenges facing them in the future. Projected limited resources and more expectations will require optimal efficiency in the delivery of vocational programs and services.

The field of vocational education or, more appropriately stated, the educational discipline of vocational education has begun and will continue to respond to the need for effective organizational structure and service delivery at the national, state, and local levels. It must respond to adequately serve all its constituents. As Seckendorf (1981) has stated, "The issues, forces, and factors are real and the consequences will be significant. To overlook them, or to believe they will not occur, can lead to the loss of an educational program that has had a distinguished record of accomplishment, but which has been criticized, primarily for holding on to the past and for viewing the future as no more than the past" (p. 235). The organizational structure and future directions of vocational education, therefore, must respond in relation to the problems, issues, and challenges facing the field in the next decade and beyond. □

References

Boyer, E.L. (1983). *High school: A report on secondary education in America.* New York: Harper and Row.

Copa, G.H.; Plihal, J.; School, S.; Ernst, L.; Rehm, M.; & Copa, P.M. (1985). *An untold story: Purposes of vocational education in secondary schools.* St. Paul, Minnesota: Research and Development Center for Vocational Education, University of Minnesota.

Dunham, D. B. (1980). *Vocational education: Policies, issues, and politics in the 1980's.* Occassional Paper No. 65. Columbus, Ohio: NCRVE.

Florida Council on Vocational Education (December, 1986). *The governance of vocational education: A choice for Florida.* Tallahassee: Florida Council on Vocational Education (ERIC Document Reproduction Service No ED 278848).

Gentry, D.K. (1978). *Selected sections from a national documentary study of the state level governance of vocational education.* Presented at the American Vocational Association Conference in Dallas, Texas, 1978.

Gentry, D.K. (1983). The issue of governance will not go away. *VocEd, 58* (6), 36-37.

Greenan, J.P. (1983). *Identification of generalizable skills in secondary vocational programs: Executive summary.* Springfield: Illinois State Board of Education; Department of Adult, Vocational, and Technical Education.

Greenan, J.P. (1988). Issues in vocational education. *Journal of Studies in Technical Careers, 10* (4), 273-412.

Greenan, J.P. (1989). Identification, assessment, and placement of persons needing transition assistance. In D.E. Berkell, & J.M. Brown, *Transition from school to work for persons with disabilities.* New York: Longman.

Hodes, L. (1979). *A national study of vocational education systems and facilities.* Rockville, Maryland: Westat Research, Inc. (ERIC Document Reproduction Service No. ED 174772).

Illinois Commission on Intergovernmental Cooperation (1987). *The organization and administration of education for employment in*

Illinois (Research Memorandum No. 77). Springfield: Illinois Commission on Intergovernmental Cooperation (ERIC Document Reproduction Service No. ED 284018).

National Commission on Secondary Education (1983). *A nation at Risk*. Washington, D.C.: USDE.

National Commission on Secondary Vocational Education (1984). *The unfinished agenda: The role of vocational education in the high school*. Columbus, Ohio: The National Center for Research in Vocational Education.

Oakes, J. (1986). Beyond tinkering: Reconstructing vocational education. In. G.H. Copa; J. Plihal; & M.A. Johnson, *Re-visioning vocational education in the secondary school*. St. Paul: Minnesota Research and Development Center for Vocational Education, University of Minnesota.

Parnell, D. (1986). *The neglected majority*. Washington D.C: The Community College Press.

Pucel, D.J.; DeVogel, S.H.; & Persico J. (1988). *Visions for change: The context and characteristics of postsecondary vocational education curriculum in the Year 2000: Implications for policy*. St. Paul: Minnesota Research and Development Center for Vocational Education, University of Minnesota.

Ruff, R.D. (1981). *A study of state level administration of vocational education*. Washington, D.C.: NCRVE (ERIC Document Reproduction Service No. ED 198262).

Seckendorf, R.S. (1981). External influence organization. In G. I. Swanson, *The future of vocational education*. Arlington, Virginia: The American Vocational Association.

Wenrich R.C. (1970). *Review and synthesis of research on the administration of vocational and technical education*. Columbus, Ohio: Center for Vocational and Technical Education (ERIC Document Reproduction Service No. ED 037542).

Worthington, R.M. (1979). *A new direction for vocational education in the 1980's*. Washington, D.C.: OVAE/USDE (ERIC Document Reproduction Service No. ED 224936).

CHAPTER 7

Administrative Leadership Issues in Vocational Education

By Merle E. Strong

THIS chapter will address some of the administrative issues facing vocational education and its delivery across the nation. The emphasis will be on current trends as compared with outcomes, since the strong leadership in vocational education may reverse trends as future directions are determined.

Administration, for purposes of this document, is broadly defined, with the issues addressed being those identified in the literature and by professionals in vocational and technical education. They can be grouped under the following questions: What should be the role of vocational and technical education at secondary, postsecondary, and adult levels? What should be the primary influences that should drive the program? What should be the organizational structure or structures to deliver the program? How should vocational and technical education be financed?

I have a strong abiding faith in vocational education as a result of my experience of more than forty years of teaching and leadership experience at local, state, federal, and university levels. It seems important to make this point in order that readers understand my commitment to vocational and technical education improvement.

This improvement cannot take place, however, without realistically discussing the strengths and weaknesses of the system.

Vocational education, for the purpose of this chapter, will be thought of as education designed to prepare persons for employment upgrading or retraining for occupations not requiring a bachelor's degree. Preparation in four year colleges will not be included except for programs that prepare teachers, administrators, or other support personnel for institutions providing vocational education.

It is important when addressing administrative issues to realize that the vocational education program is quite broad in terms of age levels served, purpose for which instruction is given, and types of institutions in or through which it is provided. Some issues may relate to the total spectrum of vocational education; others may relate only to specific levels or types of programs. Care will be taken to help the reader identify the program levels or types being addressed.

Issues in vocational education seem difficult to separate from broader issues of the nation's economy or issues of the welfare of all citizens, since vocational education deals with the preparation of people for work, and almost all—if not all—people will need to work in order to be contributing citizens. Vocational education will touch most people some time during their lifetime in pre-employment education at the secondary or postsecondary levels or in adult upgrading or retraining programs.

Leaders in vocational education must obviously be aware of and be active in responding to the major state and national challenges if they are to exert real leadership. Among these large issues is the question of how we may provide a workforce that can be competitive in a world economy. Technology is increasing dramatically, which dictates not only new jobs but significant changes in the requirements of existing jobs.

Of great concern in the nation is the problem of how to achieve full workforce participation from a larger segment of our population. Too large a percentage of our population has not participated in the workforce or had an adequate quality of life even though our economy has been judged to be relatively prosperous. The nation's welfare in the future will be dependent upon securing more adequate participation of those groups with whom our nation has not been successful. The challenge for leadership in vocational and technical education is as great now as at any time in our history.

The National Association of State Directors of Vocational Education in a position statement described the "big picture" or global influences that will impact upon our nation's future. They stated that:
During the next two decades, technological advances and increasing international competition together with demographic shifts, may change our nation and our way of life more dramatically than in other time in history. Rapid change, disruptions, unexpected challenges are inevitable. How can we prepare ourselves and plan for individual and national success? Through education—expanding our commitment to education:
- as a means of increasing individual productivity,
- as the key to maintaining our world leadership and sustaining our standard of living,
- as the way to create a skilled, capable, versatile, world class workforce able to indeed thrive on change.

(p.1)

In addition to the report of the state directors of vocational education, there are two other reports by official bodies directed at policy, namely, the First Interim Report from the National Assessment of Vocational Education (1988a) and the Second Interim Report from the National Assessment of Vocational Education (1988b). These two reports were prepared for Congress as a response to the requirements of Section 403 of the Carl D. Perkins Vocational Education Act of 1984, and thus have significant implications for reauthorization of federal vocational education legislation.

While all three reports are related broadly to economic development, the state directors appear to approach the issues from the direction of identifying workforce needs and providing appropriate education, while the NAVE (1988a; 1988b) studies interpret the Perkins Act as being designed primarily to focus on social issues and thus target groups of people to be saved.

Rather than depend on the literature alone, I obtained feedback from state directors on what they saw as the key administrative issues. These individuals should be most qualified to provide this information, since they are a major force in the direction of vocational education in each of their states. A survey instrument was sent out to all state directors. Responses were received from 34 states and the District of Columbia. While response rate was not as high as one might have hoped for, there does not among the group that responded appear to be a bias in terms of geographical distribution, size of state, or state's priority for secondary or postsecondary programs. In the following these responses will be organized around issues identified from the literature.

The Role Crisis—Secondary Vocational Education

Although all educators are caught up in the literature of the educational reform movement, for the most part vocational education has been ignored. It is becoming recognized that the reform has been mainly directed at improving education for those who will pursue four year degrees—education upon which to build more education—as opposed to education that has more immediate relevance for the more than 60 percent of youth who will not pursue further education after dropping out of or completing high school. In response to the cry for excellence in education, many states have responded mainly by adding more required academic courses at the high school level, and colleges and universities, for lack of better screening criteria, have required greater numbers of specific academic courses as their main selection criteria—thus increasing the pressure on high schools to require more academic courses. At this time, there is little evidence to show that this increases "excellence in education."

Vocational educators seem to have become uncertain as to their role in the secondary schools. For survival reasons some have changed their philosophies, while others in this new era believe that programs should have a different purpose from that in the past.

Question 1 in the survey instrument asked: What should be the role of secondary vocational education? State directors were asked to rank order seven items taken from the literature related to vocational education's purpose. Rankings are shown in Table 1. Usable returns for this question were limited to 28, since a number of respondents did not rank order the items as requested. The table reflects the fact that leaders in vocational education are not in total agreement about the role of vocational education. Seventeen of the 28 usable responses indicated that the number one ranked goal was to "provide youth with occupational skills for employment in a specific job or cluster of jobs." This response is reflective of what has been the traditional and universally accepted purpose for secondary vocational education. Other responses that state directors ranked as the first goal for vocational education, and the number of state directors making those rankings, included "providing career education for decision making" (3), "support economic development" (2), "enhance basic skills" (1), and "provide exploratory experiences" (1).

Several inferences can be drawn from examining the array of rankings in Table 1. While 24 of the 28 repondents placed "providing of occupational skills" among the first three rankings, two ranked this role as number four, and two ranked it as number six. This suggests that there is lack of belief by several state directors that it is important to prepare students for employment in specific jobs or clusters of jobs at the secondary level.

Current researchers (National Assessment of Vocational Education, 1988a), in an attempt to describe curriculum in "an informative but concise way," developed a secondary school taxonomy, grouping courses by curriculum area, subject, field, and level. The four curriculum areas were academic, vocational, personal and other, and special education.

They described the vocational curricula as including three major

Table 1

Rank Order by Importance of Secondary Vocational Education Goals

Role   Rankings by No. of States n = 28

	1st	2nd	3rd	4th	5th	6th	7th
Support Economic Development	3	4	3	3	5	3	7
Provide youth with occupational skills for employment in a specific job or cluster of jobs	17	5	2	2	0	2	0
Provide career education for decision making	3	3	5	8	6	2	1
Provide exploratory experiences	2	3	7	5	5	5	1
Enhance basic skills	3	3	5	4	5	7	2
Enhance general education	0	4	2	1	5	3	12
Provide preparation for postsecondary education	0	6	4	5	2	5	6

divisions: (1) consumer and homemaking education, which is generally intended to prepare students for roles outside of the paid labor market; (2) general labor market preparation, which they have described as instructional areas that provide skills related to employment but not specific to a particular occupation; and (3) specific labor market preparation.

The first and third categories are compatible with what have been traditionally agreed upon as vocational education. Historically, home economics was defined as preparation for the occupation of homemaking. Since then the context in which homemaking takes place has changed. The influx of many modern conveniences and the large percentage of homemakers who are in the labor market have produced changes in the family structure. Nevertheless, the functions of homemaking are understandable, and training for the work of the family is a necessary and appropriate field of study for both men and women in our society.

Category three, "specific labor market preparation," has been central to the purpose of vocational education in the past. This role has distinguished vocational education from other types of education.

It is that part of the total education curricula identified in the National Assessment of Vocational Education's (1988a) second category, called "general labor market preparation," that is troubling. As defined by the study:

> General labor market preparation consists of a set of courses or instructional areas that provide skills that are related to employment but are not specific to a particular occupation. This division includes Typing I, Introductory Industrial, Work Experience/Career Exploration, and general skills, such as business math. (pp. 1-4)

It is this category that leads to vocational education's identity crisis. Traditionally, the term "practical arts" was used to describe much of the content that is included in this category. Practical arts was designed for all students and thus was defined as a part of general education. In the 1960s U.S. Commissioner of Education Sidney Marland promoted the term "career education"—a term related to content from elementary through the life span, with vocational education being only the "preparation for an occupation" part of it.

Now it would appear that much of education at the junior and senior high school level, other than the so-called academics, is being included by many as part of vocational education. This in itself is not necessarily good or bad, but it does raise certain questions. Is it possible or desirable to have a uniform definition or set of purposes for secondary vocational education, generally agreed upon across the nation, in order that we may communicate effectively with students, parents, the public, and among educators? Can we accurately describe to the Congress and others from which funding is being sought how funds will be used? Should a school or a state claim to have a vocational education program if only "general labor market education courses" are provided?

The lack of clarity of purpose is further highlighted by reports such as *The Forgotten Half: Non-College Youth in America* (The William T. Grant Foundation Commission on Work, Family and Citizenship, 1988a) that stated:

We recommend that the goal of vocational education be directed away from specific job training to the more realistic—and valuable—goal of motivating students to acquire the skills and knowledge they need for both work and active citizenship. (p. 51)

This recommendation requires some reflection. Accepting the fact that motivation for learning is an essential and worthy goal, the recommendation and reflection of the report would dictate that the opportunity for education for an occupation be delayed until the postsecondary level. How does this relate to the fact that for approximately 60 percent of youth, postsecondary education is not a reality at this time?

The identity crisis for vocational education at the secondary level will remain until more clear definitions and purposes are articulated and agreed upon. Communication is highly distorted when personnel in some states speak of vocational education starting in the elementary school and others identify it as preparation for a specific occupation in high school. Also, this lack of agreed upon purpose makes sound evaluation very difficult, if not impossible.

Role of Postsecondary Vocational and Technical Education

Almost all state directors of vocational education agreed in their first order rankings that the role of vocational education at the postsecondary level was to provide youth and adults with occupational skills for employment in specific jobs or clusters of jobs, or to support economic development. Several suggested that the two purposes were the same or similar—a postion with which I would agree. However, states and specific postsecondary institutions are at different levels in their philosophies and priorities for implementation of specific programs and services for the private sector. For example, some institutions have held rather rigidly to the idea that the main and almost exclusive thrust of vocational education should be that of providing the traditional courses and programs in the school setting, as opposed to working directly with employers to help them meet specific needs through customized types of programs or consultive activities. This would suggest that there is much to be done by vocational educators if they are to become a recognized resource for helping industry nationally.

Rankings for "job placement services, counseling and testing, and career education" tended to cluster, following items specific to preparation for occupations. There was little support for "providing exploratory experiences" and "the enahancement of general education" as primary roles for postsecondary vocational and technical education.

In contrast to the responses for secondary education, the comments by state directors regarding the purposes of postsecondary education were much more focused on development of occupational skills, training workers to meet labor market needs, and retraining and upgrading of workers.

Forces for Priority Setting

Historically, there seems to have been general agreement that the driving force for vocational education was to meet the needs of the workforce. Beginning with the Vocational Education Act of 1963, federal legislation took on an increasingly social dimension. More recently other factors, such as economic development and the support of basic education, seem to be influencing programs.

State directors were asked to rank forces for priority setting. Approximately two thirds of the directors ranked "workforce needs" as number one, "economic development needs" as number two, and "social needs" as number three. Workforce and economic needs seemed to be considered generally as a single entity, or as one state director stated, "the needs of the workforce drive vocational education," and "economic development is a result." Another director observed that "vocational education cannot solve social ills." At the same time, several directors pointed out that much of the federal legislation is directed toward trying to solve social ills through vocational education.

While there seems to be some inconsistency between perceptions of vocational education and the primary force in setting priorities, this may be due to state directors' views of the educational needs of students and society. Thinking may have been colored by such reports as *A Nation at Risk* (1983). Some vocational educators at the secondary level were coerced into positions of supporting more academic types of education, even though it may have been at the expense of vocational education, and many vocational programs were eliminated since students were forced to take more academic courses. This trend may be reaching an end. While there may be some quality gain, particularly for the most able students, the problem facing the nation is lack of individuals with the specific skills required to fill available positions. A recent report (The William T. Grant Foundation Commission on Work, Family, and Citizenship, 1988b) had this to say about our secondary programs:

Our schools, moreover, have become distracted from their main mission. Educators have become so preoccupied with those who go to college that they have lost sight of those who do not. And more and more of the non-college bound now fall between the cracks when they are in school, drop out, or graduate inadequately prepared for the requirements of the society and the workplace. (p. 3).

There seems to be a new awareness that while the quality of teaching academic subjects needs to be upgraded, thus improving results for all students, the simple solution of requiring more years and classes may not be adequately serving a large part of our high school age population. An issue is what is the most appropriate content? How can the application and strengthening of basic content be accomplished? How much emphasis should be placed on providing specific occupational skills?

Linkages with Business and Industry

There has been much discussion about the desirability for education to develop stronger and more effective linkages with business and industry. For vocational educators the issues is not whether this is desirable, but how can it be more effectively carried out?

Question 5 of the survey asked state directors about innovations or successes they have had in developing linkages with business and industry. A number of responses were provided, and all state directors indicated pride in their accomplishments. Among the most frequent responses were examples of "quick start" or other types of training developed specifically for a business or industry. The effective use of advisory committees was the next most common response.

These responses would not seem to be particularly innovative, since the use of advisory committees has been recommended throughout vocational education history. And if serving specific needs of business and industry is thought of as an innovation, one should read some of the history of vocational education, particularly related to War Production Training. In defense of the state directors' responses, they did mention a number of existing activities being carried out in their states, including the providing of small business development centers, technical assistance centers, and economic development centers.

There are many examples of innovative approaches in providing services to build linkages with business and industry, but are they universal with all schools at all levels? I would suggest if all schools or school departments at all levels would heed the challenge and take a proactive role in building effective linkages with business and industry, then vocational education's role would not only become more clear, but there would be no question as to the role of vocational education as the workforce provider of the nation.

Vocational Education and Social Issues

As previously mentioned, there is a strong component in federal vocational education and other employment-related legislation designed to solve social problems. In an attempt to assess the impact of identified social problems on vocational education, state directors were asked. "What current or future issues, if any, do you anticipate in coordinating delivery of programs serving dislocated workers, disadvantaged youth, or welfare recipients?" Most directors identified several issues which generally fell under the headings of "governance," "definition of programs and purposes," "needs for additional services," and "needs for funding." Issues related to governance were mentioned by more than half of the respondents, with a major concern being the need to facilitate cooperation between delivery agencies so that services can be comprehensive but not duplicated. A number of responses pointed to the tendency of the federal government to make a variety of agencies responsible for providing services for the same target population. And, even with legislative language requiring agencies to cooperate, most agencies were unwilling to relinquish their "turf" and combine their programs with other agencies, particularly if it required the loss of administrative control over the target population.

A concern that was expressed related to the balance of vocational education academic needs in programs serving target populations. Basic skills are important for all employees. In addition, however, specific occupational skills will be needed for a good portion of our population as a condition of employment. This is particularly true for those who are low on the socioeconomic and educational ladder.

Approximately ten percent of directors expressed the need for additional funds and for liberalization of the matching provisions. Better support services, including child care, were also a concern. Other issues cited included the need to eliminate disincentives for work, development of the work ethic, and the need for greater parental involvement. Any one of these issues provides a substantial challenge for leadership.

Included in the comments about social issues was a suggestion that state directors should indentify innovations or successes in their states for attracting more minorities into vocational education programs. This is certainly a critical issue. On the one hand, there are those who "preach" that to become involved in any specific training at less than baccalaureate level is a form of tracking. Conversely, without specific training, the college preparatory or general academic programs at the high school level have failed to motivate or otherwise serve the needs of many students. Data indicate not only that minorities tend to be underrepresented in technical positions requiring less than a four year degree, but that they are underrepresented in two year associate degree programs also. Vocational leaders need to indentify those factors that will lead to greater success in recruiting and preparing minorities for technical positions.

Organizational Structure

Another reason for divergent opinions among state directors on the role, priorities, and value of vocational education is the wide difference in the organizational structure for delivery of vocational education from state to state. Organizational structures range from a single board of education responsible for all education within a state to independent state vocational boards. Some states place the control of vocational education at the secondary level, while others have the control located at the postsecondary level. The vocational education authority related to the Job Training and Partnership Act and other legislation dealing with training also varies.

Thus, there is a great difference in the span of control and authority among state directors. While some are in strong leadership positions, both in terms of span of control and their location within the structure of education, others find themselves somewhat low in the "pecking" order, and thus in a position where strong leadership at the policy or legislative level is extremely difficult. The complexities and great differences among state organizations would suggest that states have not agreed on the best overall organizational structure, and it is not likely with this current framework that the organization for and delivery of vocational education will become more uniform.

Organizational structure within the states will continue to be a very important issue, however. At issue are a number of questions including: What will be the strength and influence of the program in a state? Will federal legislation drive the program both financially and program-wise, or will the funding and leadership support be used primarily to expand and improve specific program directions? The level of emphasis for the program will also be influenced strongly by structure. If one looks at a state's program in which the predominant emphasis is at the secondary level, it will often be found that the director's primary authority is at that level. The reverse is then true for postsecondary programs. While it can be successfully argued that the positional authority is not a single criterion for effectiveness of the leader, it is certainly important. Regardless of level of positional authority, vocational educators must be the key state persons in bringing about the changes required to make vocational education more effective.

Serving Special Populations

State directors were asked the question: "What current or future issues, if any, do you anticipate in coordinating delivery of programs serving dislocated workers, disadvantaged youth, or welfare recipients?" Responses were categorized under the headings governance, definition of programs and purposes, needs for additional funding. Under the classification of governance, the majority of directors responding were concerned with facilitating cooperation between delivery agencies in order to achieve optimum impact while not duplicating services. The needs of special interest groups are obviously many and diverse, with education being only one very important link. This area, perhaps, is one of the most challenging for leaders in vocational and technical education.

The complexity resulting from a number of agencies working together calls for different dimensions of accountability, modifications in delivery structures, and varied criteria for evaluation. While the advantages of cooperation of a number of agencies with varied expertise to meet complex needs is noteworthy, the involvement of the several agencies may in turn make coordination of services difficult.

Under the heading of "definition of programs and purposes," a number of needs were grouped from the state directors responses. It was indicated by several state directors that improved teaching of basics at the lower grades was critical so that students could benefit from vocational programs. Another important issue related to identifying who should be served in vocational education, particularly at the high school level. Traditionally, the commonly accepted terminology was that vocational education was for those who could "benefit from instruction," and it would seem with few exceptions that it would be difficult to make the case that one who could not read or write could be successful in a skilled or technical occupation. However, vocational education in recent years has been expected to accept everyone, with the expectation that through some magic we are best equipped to teach basic skills after others have failed during the school career of the pupil up to that point. While most would agree that vocational educators should and can strengthen basic skills, primarily through their application, is it not likely that to accept a large or total responsibility for providing basic skills for high school students may be setting vocational education up for failure?

Including basic skills as a central part of vocational education confuses its focus. Also, it provides a kind of a tracking that may not be desirable. If students have not learned to read, write, and cipher through grade school and later academic classes, does it make sense to put them into vocational education to see if they "might catch on"? Would it not make more sense to place such students in intense remedial programs until they have acquired some level of competence, then let them choose vocational programs?

The Delivery System

Vocational education at the secondary and postsecondary levels is delivered through a number of different organizational models. This is inadequate research to assess which of these models are most effective and under what circumstances.

At the high school level in recent years, the "comprehensive high school" has been championed by many as the most acceptable structure, even to the point that it may be at some risk that one would raise a question or promote discussion. It is my position that the comprehensive high school has not necessarily fulfilled expectations. Comprehensive high schools often do not have a student population of a size that can justify or maintain a program in academic areas, let alone vocational education. Vocational programs and leadership either become almost nonexistent, or at least weakened to a level of ineffectiveness.

In "The Unfinished Agenda: The Role of Vocational Education in the High School" (no date), the National Commission on Secondary Vocational Education completely ignored in their discussions and recommendations the fact that a number of patterns of delivery exist. At issue is the question: What institutional and organizational arrangements are most effective for what purposes and for what students? Among the institutions in place are vocational/technical high schools, area schools, and the more recently developed magnet vocational schools.

At the postsecondary level, the community college represents the predominant institution providing technical programs. However, some states have technical institutes as the main type of delivery system, and several states operate technical institutes somewhat parallel to community colleges.

Significant questions relative to postsecondary vocational/technical programs concern what should drive the curriculum and how can or to what degree should articulation with four year degree granting programs take place. A principle articulated historically was that the vocational education programs should be designed to meet the needs of employment in specific occupations or clusters of occupations. It was believed that this principle required that the needs of the workforce should be instrumental in determining the content of the program. The opposite position would suggest that curriculum content be determined by the university or next higher level of education. Since universities usually require that, in order to transfer, a course be the same as or parallel to a course they have in the curriculum, it is easy to visualize what would happen to specialized programs (vocational and technical education) if transfer considerations become primary in curriculum building.

While it is commendable for two year postsecondary institutions to increase their quality and, perhaps, their rigor, it may not be appropriate that they do this by making the content of their courses similar to university courses. If this is carried to the extreme, the institution will loose its uniqueness, and thus its reason to exist.

The open door policy may be at risk if selection of students is based on taking in only those who can do college transfer work. The old adage that "everyone needs training and everyone can be trained" has been reflective of the philosophy at most postsecondary two year institutions. However, examples exist in which new types of institutions were required to be developed to fill the gap of serving the less talented or less well prepared youth and adults.

Funding

The incomplete returns of questionnaries from state directors do not permit me to provide summary data representative of the nation.

In the expenditure of Perkins Act dollars there was great variance among the states in their use of funds for secondary, postsecondary, and adult programs.

Authors with the National Assessment of Vocational Education (1988b) found that "on average, states allocated 42 percent of their program year 1986-87 Title II federal funds to postsecondary education"(pp. 2-5). The variation among states was also found to be quite dramatic, with one state indicating that it allocated all its federal money to postsecondary programs, while another state indicated that only eight percent was provided to this level. This wide variation may reflect the level of emphasis in a state of secondary or postsecondary education but conclusions cannot be drawn without understanding the states' total funding patterns.

There seems to be no question that leadership in vocational and technical education believes that federal funding is extremely important, even though it represents in the case of many states less than ten percent of the funding for vocational and technical education. There seems to be lack of agreement about the changes that should be made in present legislation. This lack of agreement may be tempered by what rate leadership believes is feasible, given the budget constraints and perhaps past priorities of federal officials.

There is belief among some that the proportion of the federal funding allocated to disadvantaged and handicapped may not reflect the broader program needs. However, the plan would likely be to increase funding for other areas, not to lower allocations for special needs groups. ☐

References

American Society for Training and Development (1988). *ASTD means better business for you and your organization.* Alexandria, VA.

Carnevale, A. P.; Gainer, L. J.; & Meltzer, A. S. (1988). *Workplace basics: The skills employers want.* Alexandria, VA: American Society for Training and Development.

Commission on the Future of Community Colleges (1988). *Building communities: A vision for a new century.* Washington, DC: American Association of Community and Junior Colleges.

Goodlad, J.I. (1984). *A place called school.* New York: McGraw-Hill.
National Assessment of Vocational Education (1988a, January). *First interim report.* Washington, DC
National Assessment of Vocational Education (1988b, September). *Second interim report.* Washington, DC
National Association of State Directors of Vocational Education (1988). *Vocational technical education: Meeting growing needs.* Washington, DC
National Commission for Employment Policy (1988, September). *Evaluation of the effects of JTPA performance standards of clients, services, and costs, final report.* Washington, DC
National Commission for Employment Policy (1988, September). *JTPA performance standards: Effects on clients, services and costs, executive summary.* Washington, DC
National Commission on Excellence in Education (1983). *A nation at risk: The imperative for education reform.* Washington, DC: U.S. Government Printing Office.
National Commission on Secondary Vocational Education (1984). *The unfinished agenda: The role of vocational education in the high school.* Columbus, OH: The National Center for Research in Vocational Education.
Teuke, M.R. (1988 Autumn). *The LaFollette policy report,* 1(1). Madison, WI: Board of Regents of the University of Wisconsin System.
Wacker, G.B. (1987). *The future of working Wisconsin: Proceedings from the future of working Wisconsin conference.* Madison, WI: University of Wisconsin-Madison, Vocational Studies Center.
William T. Grant Foundation Commission on Work, Family and Citizenship (1988a, January). *The forgotten half: Non-college youth in America, an interim report on the school-to-work transition.* Washington, DC
William T. Grant Foundation Commission on Work, Family and

Citizenship (1988b, November). *The forgotten half: Pathways to success for America's youth and young families final report.* Washington, DC

CHAPTER 8

The Curriculum

By David J. Pucel

CURRICULUM is at the heart of the educational process. It is what educators design and implement to accomplish instructional goals. Usually it is a set of formal or informal courses constituting an area of specialization. The vocational curriculum is composed of courses pertaining to vocational education.

A curriculum at any point in time is a reflection of society. As variables change in society, so does the nature of curriculum. Therefore, what constitutes an adequate curriculum at one point in time may not be adequate at another. For example, vocational curriculum before the industrial revolution was relatively informal. Vocational skills were primarily taught outside of schools through apprenticeship. Arrangements were made for a person (apprentice) to work alongside a person who was practicing in the occupation (master). The ability to perform the occupation was communicated by an instructor (master) presenting knowledge or performing activities, and the learner listening and watching. The learner then imitated the instructor. If the learner did not adequately master the content, the learner watched the instructor again or reviewed the knowledge. This procedure was repeated until the content was mastered.

During the 19th century apprenticeship as almost the sole form of occupational training began to be questioned. Outside pressures began to be applied to the schools to modify their character so as to become more closely related to the new and changing political, social, and economic life surrounding them. Newell, Superintendent of Public Instruction for the State of Maryland, reflected this well in 1878, when he said the following:

> If our public-school system were perfect, it would develop and direct in youth all the activities which adult life would call into exercise. Every one admits that the best interests of society demand good carpenters, good blacksmiths, good machinists, and good cooks, as well as good penmen, good calculators, and good elocutionists. We live just as truly by the labor of the hand as by the labor of the head, and yet all the machinery of education from the primary school to the higher school is devoted to the cultivation of brain-power exclusively. The hands need training to make them efficient workers in the actual business of life, but our schools think it beneath them to train the hands. (Proceedings of the American Institute of Instruction, 1878, p. 80)

These thoughts about the role of schools occurred during the same time as the industrial revolution, which created a significant increase in the demand for skilled and unskilled workers. Industry found it no longer possible to train all of them through apprenticeship, and it was no longer necessary for all workers to be competent in all aspects of a skilled trade or craft within the factory setting. By 1900, industrial employers were insistent that they needed the secondary schools to prepare skilled mechanics and that general manual training was not meeting the need. They wanted education (which was later to be termed vocational education) focused on the preparation of people for a career in a skill or trade. The implications of this pressure on the public schools and curriculum were reflected in a presentation by Elmer Ellsworth Brown, from the University of California, as follows. "The recognition of the importance and need of purely vocational schools of secondary grade puts a new aspect on the problem of the school curriculum . . ." (Brown, 1900, pp. 41-42).

At this point, educators were faced with a challenge to prepare people in skilled and semi-skilled occupations in relatively large quantities. Little was known about the process of delivering such instruction. Questions such as: Which skills are needed by each worker? What types of procedures and knowledge do they need in order to perform? How should each type of worker be trained? and Who should do the training? began to evolve as important questions. These questions, which were informally addressed by the master in an apprenticeship program, needed to be formally addressed in the teaching of large numbers of people.

Recognizing the need to prepare people with vocational skills and the reluctance on the part of formal public schools to do so, federal legislation was passed to provide incentives to schools to develop such programs. The most noteworthy legislation was Public Law 347 of the 64th Congress which was passed in 1917, and its subsequent supplements. This law became known as the Smith-Hughes Act. Incentives were also provided to universities to prepare people to teach vocational education. At this point a formal curriculum in vocational education began to evolve. It had a clear focus, that of preparing people in the skills of industry, the farm, and the home.

Allen (1919) was one of the first writers who specifically addressed the process of developing curriculum to teach vocational skills in industry and the schools. His techniques were based on teaching people to perform the jobs of the emerging industrial revolution, which were primarily associated with operating machines and manipulating tools and objects. Vocational education as an entity in public schools was born within that context. Originally the focus was on preparing people in skills in trades and industry, agriculture, and home economics. Over the years legislation was expanded to include distributive education (marketing), business education, health occupations, and other areas of occupational training. The definition of what constitutes vocational education began to expand. However, the structure and goals of the curriculum remained quite consistent. The focus was on occupational skill development, and content identification and teaching methodologies were focused on that development.

As the need to prepare more precisely trained people increased, so did the precision of curriculum development tools. In 1942, Fryklund's book, *Trade and Job Analysis*, presented more refined and developed more specific procedures for analyzing jobs to determine the content to be taught. In 1950, Micheels and Karnes published the book *Measuring Educational Achievement*. That book systematically addressed the evaluation of learner progress. It provided detailed procedures for developing tests to measure the information possessed by learners and presented some general procedures for assessing their manipulative performance. The procedures suggested built upon the works of Allen and Fryklund and assumed that the teachable content was the information, topics, and operations to be performed on the job. In 1956, Bloom published a book that dealt with a major step in applying the systems approach to education—that of specifying performance objectives. It presented classifications which could be used to describe human behaviors as performances, in terms of cognitive, affective, and psychomotor objectives.

During the early 1960s a new generation of curriculum procedures began to evolve, known as the *systems approach*. The systems approach had been used in product engineering for some time. A system was defined as a regularly interacting or interdependent group of items forming a unified whole. In engineering it was defined as a process. The process involves the accurate identification of a problem and its requirements, the setting of specific performance objectives, the application of logic and analysis techniques to the problem, and the rigorous measurement of the product designed to solve the problem against the specific performance objectives (Butler, p. xi).

During the same time that the systems approach was being introduced into education, the concept of "mastery learning" was also being introduced. Carroll wrote an article in 1963 entitled "A Model of School Learning." Carroll suggested that if you wanted all people to master a task, you should vary the amount of time that each individual could study the material. You should also vary the instructional approach used with individuals, depending upon how they learned best. People who learned more slowly would take more time, but most people could master most tasks. The notion of mastery learning introduced the concept of individualized instruction into education.

In 1973, The United States Department of the Air Force published the *Handbook for Designers of Instructional Systems*. It presented what became known as the ISD (Instructional Design) model. That model captured the refinements in occupational skill development training to that point and integrated them into a systematic instructional design process. Its comprehensiveness made it appealing to vocational curriculum developers.

In 1975, Pucel and Knaak published the book *Individualizing Vocational and Technical Instruction*. That book brought together the concepts of mastery learning, the systems approach, and criterion evaluation. The result was a systematic approach for designing, delivering, and evaluating individualized vocational instruction, focused on task mastery. It provided detailed information on how to analyze content using task analysis, the logic of mastery learning applied to vocational education, techniques for developing individualized learning materials, and detailed procedures for developing criterion tests (including manipulative performance and product evaluations).

Since 1975, the term competency-based education has evolved as the predominant term to describe that type of education when used in vocational education and training. In most applications it is essentially the same as what Pucel and Knaak defined as individualized instruction. It is self-paced instruction, aimed at the mastery of a task, with criterion measures to verify task mastery.

The process of curriculum development aimed at skill development had been significantly refined since the first writings of Allen in 1919. However, besides these substantial changes in suggested curriculum practice aimed to occupational skill development, the social expectations for vocational education began to change quite dramatically during the 1960s. More inclusive concepts relating to preparation for employment began to emerge, and with them a multiplicity of goals for the vocational curriculum. Vocational development theories proposed by Super (1957) and others suggested that people arrived at and prepared for occupations in stages. Vocational education was called upon to develop programs aimed at these stages, such as job exploration and awareness, as well as occupational preparation. In addition, the place of specific occupational training in high school began to be questioned. The social goals of educating the handicapped and disadvantaged also received increased prominence. Concepts such as preparing people for productive roles which may reflect only partial job competence began to emerge. With each of the new goals the focus of vocational education began to change from a relatively clear role of preparing people to work in an occupation to a multiplicity of roles. Debate raged over whether curriculum designed to develop job skills met the multiple needs of learners. Social and political groups began to exert increasing pressure on Congress to modify federal legislation regarding vocational education to allow for expanded purposes. At first the changes in the legislation were permissive, in that new goals could be funded. With increasing pressures the new goals became mandated and "setasides" were specified within legislation which could only be used for specific purposes (e.g., sex equity, handicapped, disadvantaged).

During the 1980s there has also been an increasing awareness that the nature of society and jobs has changed drastically since the early 1900s. Society had entered the information age, with large components of service. The almost sole focus of vocational education skill training on the psychomotor activities associated with the jobs of the industrial revolution was no longer appropriate. There was a need to expand vocational curriculum to increasingly include instruction in the cognitive and affective aspects of jobs.

The underlying assumptions of what constitutes productivity in industry, which were in place during the industrial age, were being questioned. Those underlying assumptions are well stated by Strassmann (1985) as follows:

> The underlying assumptions about what "productivity" is go back to the industrial-age model of what a person, aided by a machine, does. [They were that] . . . the handling of complexity requires information which is a manager's, not a worker's, prerogative. A person's superior coordination of eye and hand are what wages will purchase—until improved machines buy it for less. A person's brain is not a valuable asset per se under such assumptions, because the engineer designs into the manufacturing sequence everything which needs to be done. The employee's thinking is only useful insofar as is retains simple procedural instructions. (pp. 103-104)

Strassmann's position may be a little harsh, but it represents a perspective of the past regarding preparing people for employment which is obviously not consistent with perceptions of the future. Pucel, DeVogel, and Persico (1987) conducted a study of assumptions about the future that have high probability of impacting the future direction of vocational education.

In general, the assumptions indicated that there will be slow but steady economic growth, increased personal consumption of goods and services, and a decline in the proportion of jobs in the goods producing sector of our economy. There will be an expansion of the service sector of the economy, with a pluralistic, multicultural social mix in the United States. There will be an increase in mass communications and advanced information technologies, with the importance of the individual being expressed in trends towards participative styles in organizations, values of self-fulfillment, and self-actualization at all levels of society. With the increasing automation of repetitive tasks, workers at all levels will need to be increasingly competent in cognitive and affective, as well as psychomotor, skills. Educational institutions will incorporate technology to increase effectiveness and efficiency, and employers and private groups will increasingly deliver educational services.

It is apparent that although we will still need people in society who can operate machines and manipulate objects and tools, and that should still be a major focus of vocational education, that focus is no longer perceived as sufficient. Many of the occupations in society today require cognitive and affective skills in larger quantities than psychomotor skills. Therefore, vocational education is being called upon to incorporate the teaching of those skills into instructional programs with the same level of planning, precision, and commitment as they have devoted to psychomotor skills.

New curriculum development systems, such as The Performance-Based Instructional Design System (PBID) (Pucel, 1987), are being developed to accommodate the necessary changes in curriculum. They are being developed based on the belief that professional students of education tend increasingly to work as scientists (Beck, 1965, p. 95). Educators are assembling knowledge about what works best with which types of learners. They are looking to learning theories as a basis for designing educational practice. They are also examining their goals in terms of the society within which the education is to take place.

Curriculum Change

Historically there has been substantial resistance to curriculum change. Abbott and Eidell (1970) address the issue of educational innovation in the light of social change. Their observation is that the resistance of educational organizations to curriculum change may be viewed positively as stability. However, they claim that educational institutions are, by and large, non-responsive to primary changes in the social or technological environment which warrant curricular change. They claim that this resistance to curriculum innovation has implications for organizational survival.

Burns and Brooks (1970) suggest that school curricula at all levels of education need to be critically reviewed in the light of present cultural needs, global pressures, and technological innovations. They stress the need for both a thorough revision of curricular content and for a re-thinking of learning processes. They indicate that although education has traditionally lagged behind societal change, society can no longer afford this practice.

Many groups in society have been questioning the value of vocational education at the secondary level. They suggest that the secondary vocational curriculum has not kept up with the needs of society. The Education Commission of the States published *A Summary of Major Reports On Education* in November of 1983. Ten major reports on education in the United States were summarized. These reports generally agree that all students should complete a core curriculum, but they did not agree on what a "core curriculum" means. However, the emphasis was obviously on making the secondary schools more academic.

Five of the reports ignored vocational education and its role in the high school. Two reports indicated that vocational education has not fulfilled its promise of training people for work. They recommend using vocational education as a basis for providing hands-on experience and connecting it more closely with career education. One report specifically recommended eliminating vocational education from the high school curriculum. Only two of the reports suggested that vocational education should be continued without suggesting major modification. However, every one of the reports indicated that vocational education should be appraised and improved.

These recommendations clearly indicate that educational policymakers do not have a very high opinion of vocational education and the role it can play and has been playing in the secondary education of American youth. Even if the quality of the current vocational education programs was excellent, it is questionable that they would see it as an essential part of the high school curriculum. There appears to be little question that vocational education is needed at the postsecondary level. However, there are debates over where it should take place and what it should look like. It has most often taken place in public and private postsecondary technical institutes, community colleges, adult extension programs, and through training in business and industry. As the pressure on the high schools to move away from skilled training has increased, more and more skilled training has moved to postsecondary education. Federal legislation has become more prescriptive in terms of ensuring some portion of the funds be used to fund postsecondary programs. However, the technical institutes and community colleges are also receiving pressure to provide a broad-based occupational curriculum which includes more than the development of psychomotor skills associated with occupations. Curriculum is being modified to include larger components of cognitive and affective goals and preparation in the sciences, math, and other fields which support specific occupational preparation.

Adult extension programs are often called upon to provide education in support of apprenticeship programs and instruction aimed at updating and retraining people. They are also being called upon to provide "customized" training for employees of particular companies. As the proportion of people who are already employed who need to make major occupational changes due to changing technology and a global economy increases, there is also increased pressure to articulate the regular postsecondary curriculum with the adult extension curriculum. This is desired to facilitate the flexible preparation of those already employed and to allow learning as part of adult extension programs to be transferred to the postsecondary programs.

As technology has become more complex and jobs more specialized in terms of its use, training in business and industry has also expanded greatly. Public and private vocational programs in schools often cannot train people specifically enough for a particular company. Sometimes the technology of a company represents industrial processes secret to that company. Therefore, companies are finding it effective and efficient to expand their training programs in light of social pressures for productivity.

Issues for the Future

This brief history of the evolution of vocational education and concepts related to change point out the difficulties in trying to describe the vocational education curriculum of the present and the future. It is apparent that there are a number of curricula which meet different purposes of vocational education rather than one vocational curriculum. While all are in some way related to work (both paid and unpaid), curricula within vocational education are almost as different from one another as they are from curricula outside of vocational education. Because of these great differences, it is no longer possible to describe one generalizable curriculum development procedure, one educational level at which vocational education takes place, or one purpose for all programs. The following issues are seen as important to the future of vocational education curriculum. They pertain to issues of curriculum purpose and implementation.

Issue 1. What is vocational education? A major issue facing vocational education and the curriculum of the future is: What is vocational education? At its beginnings it was possible to say that it was designed to prepare people to perform skills associated with occupations. It focused on occupational skill development. It was clearly differentiated from programs which were considered to be the practical arts (e.g., general home economics, general business education, industrial arts). Although those programs pertained to work, they were not thought to be focused on preparing people for jobs. Vocational education was viewed as a separate specialization from math, science, and other programs in the schools. It built upon skills learned in those areas, taught through other fields of education, but did not claim to teach them. It prepared people who could benefit from training in the occupations for which programs were developed. Ability to benefit was based on whether people had reasonable potential for employment in the occupations for which training was provided. It focused on occupations which required training at less than the baccalaureate level.

With the historical evolution referred to earlier, vocational education has come to mean many things to different people. Each has sought and adapted funding and programs to implement their definitions. It is considered by some to mean everything that is taught within a vocational school or in the name of vocational education.

Some consider it to mean all education which prepares people for work. Some consider it to be those programs which prepare people in the skills of an occupation at less than the baccalaureate level. Some consider it to be synonymous with developing work readiness. Some consider it to include the teaching of the basic skills of reading, writing, and arithmetic as an alternative to teaching them through courses taught in those subject matter fields. Some suggest it includes preparing people for family life, including values. Some suggest that it should not provide skill training in the high schools and that skill training should be held off until after high school. Others suggest skill training should be done in high schools, in postsecondary institutions, as well as in business and industry. Some suggest it should be focused on skills that can be used by many companies within an industry. Some say it should also be focused on specific companies and it is all right to offer programs within those companies.

In addition, there are social missions that have been attached to vocational education which affect its curriculum. Work is a key part of a person's life, and discrimination and denial of the opportunity to participate in work must not be tolerated. Concern for making sure all people have an equitable opportunity to prepare for work, along with the view that vocational education is that portion of public education specifically focused on preparing people for work, has brought competing forces to be applied to the vocational education curriculum. Some suggest that people must be prepared to the standards of the businesses and industries that will employ them. Others suggest that people should be given the opportunity to take part in any training, whether or not there is a reasonable expectation for employment. They suggest the goal is not employment but self-exploration. Others suggest that people need opportunities to become aware of alternative forms of work so they can judge their merits. Others suggest that since different jobs pay more, pay equity can be accomplished by changing the mix of people who prepare for those jobs. They suggest that vocational education can be a vehicle for modifying the social mix in occupations as a basis for sex and racial equity. What is vocational education? Which of these often competing goals is it supposed to accomplish?

Issue 2. Where should vocational education take place and what purpose should it have at each place? Some argue that vocational education as skill training should take place at the postsecondary and adult levels after people have developed foundational skills and and secondary educations. At the postsecondary level some argue it should take place in technical institutes, others in community colleges, and others in industry. Others argue that skill training should also be provided at the high school level. Others argue that vocational education should also be provided at the elementary and secondary levels, but its focus should be on providing a context for learning other subjects such as science and math. Others argue that it should be at the elementary and secondary levels, but its focus should be on occupational awareness and exploration. Where should it take place and what purpose should it have at each place.?

Issue 3. Can vocational teachers be expected to meet the variety of expectations for vocational education? It is obvious that with such a mix of expectations for vocational education, defining the curriculum and its goals within one clear set of procedures is impossible. Therefore, another issue is the definition of a set of curriculum procedures which can be used to develop vocational education. Carpenters have techniques for building houses, and doctors have techniques for operating. What techniques should be taught to people who develop vocational curriculum?

If the goal is occupational skill development, the techniques are quite clear. They have evolved, as was pointed out earlier in this chapter. However, those techniques are not appropriate for developing curriculum in family living. They also do not fit well with the goal of developing programs focused on awareness at the middle school level. They also do not necessarily agree with procedures for teaching reading to deaf students who must read to succeed on the job. In preparing people to enter vocational education as a field, what should they be taught about the process for preparing to teach and how to teach? Special education teachers, math teachers, counselors, etc., all receive significant amounts of specialized training to be able to carry on their specialized roles. Is it reasonable to expect vocational teachers to be able to take on all of these roles and to develop and teach curriculum which is capable of meeting all of these types of needs?

Issue 4. Does vocational education have a unique role which justifies its inclusion in education? If vocational education is going to accomplish all of the goals it has claimed for itself, what is the role of other areas of education? If vocational education is going to teach basic skills, focus on the needs of the handicapped and disadvantaged, change the social mix within occupational fields, prepare people for employment and assist with technological change in specific companies, etc., what is left for others? Or, is the answer that vocational education must recognize the roles of other areas of education and perform a unique role in an area of recognized specialization (e.g., job skill development or job exploration). Is this ambitious set of aspirations for vocational education a reason for people currently wondering if it has any value as compared with other areas of education? Is it attempting to be a jack-of-all-trades and a master of none?

Some also argue that the role of vocational education should be that of providing a vehicle for students to apply what they learn in other areas of education. In other words, it should be a place where people can see the practical application of content learned in fields such as math, science, and social studies. This relegates vocational education to the role of an alternative procedure for teaching those areas. What will happen to vocational education if those fields of education include practical work-related exercises in their curricula? Does vocational education have a unique role which justifies its existence in education? Does it have a content of its own? If a curriculum relates to an area of specialization, what is vocational education's specialization?

Sample Scenarios for Vocational Curriculum

At this point it is not possible to describe future vocational curriculum with any assurance, because it is not possible to predict how the issues presented above will be resolved. Therefore, a number of alternative scenarios are presened.

Scenario 1. Vocational education at the primary and secondary school levels has been abolished. In its place all of the other fields of education have modified their curricula to include demonstrating how what is being taught relates to work and life in our society. Home economics programs focused on family living and values have been combined with social studies education.

Skill training designed to prepare people for jobs is provided at the postsecondary level in community colleges and through business and industry.

Scenario 2. Vocational education at the primary level is called upon to provide an activity-based curriculum around simulations of job skills. Those activities draw upon manipulative skills and other areas of education. Vocational education at the high school level is focused on job exploration and the development of work-related attitudes. Occupational skill development is minimal. All students are expected to take part in these programs. Skill training designed to prepare people for jobs is provided at the postsecondary level in community colleges and through business and industry.

Scenario 3. Other fields of education are responsible for teaching areas such as math, science, and social studies. They are also held responsible for showing the relevance of what they teach to jobs and living in society.

Vocational education at the middle school level provides job exploration. The focus is on work sampling and allowing all students to experience performing skills associated with various jobs.

Vocational education at the high school level is primarily focused on job preparation. Just as higher level mathematics and sciences are designed for select groups, vocational education is focused on preparing those people who wish to prepare for skilled employment. This includes adapting vocational courses to accommodate the special needs of learners. However, vocational edcuators work with special educators to meet their needs. Students who do not have sufficient basic skills receive remediation from licensed math, science, English, etc., teachers. Vocational educators are responsible for preparation in occupational skills.

Skill training designed to prepare people for jobs is provided at the postsecondary level in community colleges and through business and industry. It is focused on occupations requiring larger amounts of formal occupational training. Postsecondary vocational education takes place in an environment such as a community college where specialists in other areas of education are available. Special educators, math, science, English, and instructors from the other fields of education work with vocational educators to provide all skills necessary. The vocational educator is the specialist in occupational skill development. □

References

A summary of major reports on education (1983). Denver, CO: Education Commission of the States.

Abbott, M. G., & Eidell, T. L. (1970). Administrative implications of curriculum reform. In R. W. Burns & G. D. Brooks (Eds.), *Curriculum design in a changing society*. Englewood Cliffs, NJ: Educational Technology Publications.

Allen, C. R. (1919). *The instructor the man and the job*. Philadelphia, PA: J. B. Lippincott Company.

Beck, R. H. (1965). *A social history of education*. Englewood Cliffs, NJ: Prentice-Hall.

Bloom, B. S. (1956). *Taxonomy of educational objectives: The classification of educational goals, handbook I: Congitive domain*. New York: David McKay Co.

Brown, E. E. (1900). Secondary education [Monograph]. In N. M. Butler (Ed.), *Monographs on education in the United States, 1*, 44-42. Albany, NY: J. B. Lyon Company.

Burns, R. W., & Brooks, G. D. (1970). *Curriculum design in a changing society*. Englewood Cliffs, NJ: Educational Technology Publications.

Butler, F. C. (1972). *Instructional systems development for vocational and technical training*. Englewood Cliffs, NJ: Educational Technology Publications.

Carroll, J. B. (1963). A model of school learning. *Teachers College Record, 64*, 722-33.

Handbook for designers of instructional systems, vol. IV (1973). Washington, DC: Department of the Air Force.

Fryklund, V. C. (1942). *Trade and job analysis*. Milwaukee WI:The Bruce Publishing Co.

Micheels, W. J., & Karnes, M. R. (1950). *Measuring educational achievement*. New York: McGraw-Hill Book Company, Inc.

Newell, M. A. (1878). *Proceedings of the American Institute of Instruction*.

Pucel, D. J.; DeVogel, S. H.; and Persico, J. (1987). *The context and characteristics of postsecondary vocational education curriculum in the year 2000: Implications for policy*. St. Paul: University of Minnesota, Minnesota Research and Development Center for Vocational and Technical Education.

Pucel, D. J. (1987). The performance-based instructional design system. *Journal of Industrial Teacher Education, 24* (4), 27-35.

Pucel, D. J., & Knaak, W.C. (1975). *Individualizing vocational and technical instruction.* Columbus, OH: Charles E. Merrill Publishing Co.

Strassmann. P. A. (1985). *Information payoff.* New York: Free Press, Macmillan, Inc.

Super, D. E. (1957). *The psychology of careers: An introduction to vocational development.* New York: Harper & Row.

CHAPTER 9

Special Programs for Special Needs Students

By Michelle D. Sarkees and Lynda L. West

THERE will be a number of challenges for educational and industrial planners in the future. Projections indicate that schools will be faced with an increasing number of special needs individuals. There is a high probability that many of these individuals will become enrolled in vocational education programs, in an attempt to create an educational program that is relevant to their needs as future community members and workers. Future programs for special needs students will require more experienced personnel, improved technology, increased options for training, and improved support services.

This chapter will: (1) provide information relative to identifying special populations; (2) discuss implications for necessary changes in the educational system so that special populations will not become dropouts; (3) identify key issues in designing, developing, and implementing special programs for special needs students in vocational education; (4) discuss important considerations in curricular content for special needs learners in vocational education; and (5) identify crucial changes in the methods of delivering vocational education programs to special needs individuals.

Identifying Special Populations

During the past several decades there has been a great emphasis on providing services for special populations in vocational education programs. At the same time there has been much labeling and categorizing of individuals who are considered to have special needs. Whether labels and/or categories will change in the future is anyone's guess. However, the existing special needs populations will continue to require assistance if they are to succeed in developing their vocational potential through participation in vocational education programs.

The Carl D. Perkins Vocational Act of 1984 (Public Law 98-524) identified specific groups within the special needs category as handicapped, academically disadvantaged, economically disadvantaged, limited English-proficient, single parents, and criminal offenders. Phelps (1985) defines a special needs learner as an individual who encounters or is likely to encounter difficulty in educational or employment settings because of a disability or economic or academic disadvantage; who has different linguistic or cultural background or outdated job skills; and who requires individually prescribed and unique teaching strategies, supportive services that vary in type and extent depending on individual need, and additional resources from society for his or her acceptance.

Since the passage of the Smith-Hughes Act in 1917 there has been an increasing focus on special populations in federal vocational legislation. The Vocational Education Act of 1963 (P.L. 88-210) encouraged the use of federal funds to provide access for special populations to vocational training or retraining suited to their needs, interests, and abilities.

The Education Amendments of 1968 (P.L. 90-576) further stressed the need to provide special needs individuals with vocational education skills in mainstreamed situations. This population was divided into two distinct categories with disadvantaged individuals receiving a 15 percent setaside of federal vocational funds in each state to provide them with assistance in vocational program activities. Handicapped individuals received a 10 percent setaside for the same purpose.

The Education Amendments of 1976 (P.L. 94-482) increased the funding formula for special needs programs and services. Sex discrimination in vocational education was targeted for elimination. The Carl D. Perkins Vocational Education Act of 1984 (P.L. 98-524) assured equal access to vocational education programs for special needs individuals. Specific benefits included equal access in recruitment, enrollment, and placement activities; vocational assessment to determine abilities, interests, and special needs; guidance, counseling, and career development activities; and counseling services to facilitate the transition from school to post-school employment.

Other federal legislation has also placed an emphasis on assisting special populations in developing their vocational potential. The Civil Rights Act of 1964 (P.L. 88-352) focused on the rights of every American citizen and provided a framework for handicapped individuals to confront discrimination.

Section 503 of the Rehabilitation Act of 1973 (P.L. 93-112) states that employers who receive federal contracts of $2,500 or more will develop and implement an affirmative action program to recruit, hire, train, and advance in employment handicapped individuals. Employers must also make "reasonable accommodations" in the work environment to meet the needs of these workers.

Section 504 of the Rehabilitation Act of 1973 (P.L. 93-112) prohibits discrimination on the basis of handicapping conditions in all federally funded programs and activities. Vocational education programs would be included in this assurance.

The Education for All Handicapped Children Act of 1975 (P.L. 94-142) provides necessary funding for public schools to ensure that all handicapped students ages three to 21 receive a free appropriate education, including vocational education.

The Job Training Partnership Act of 1982 (P.L. 97-300) provided funding and programs to assist economically disadvantaged individuals to receive training. Local business and industry were encouraged to become involved in employment and training of unemployed individuals. Benefits to special needs populations included job search assistance; remedial education, upgrading, and retraining; expense allowances; and support services such as child care, health care, and transportation.

Projections into the future indicate that schools will be faced with an increasing number of special needs individuals in the next few decades. Feichtner and Sarkees (1987) project that of the 3.6 million children who entered our nation's schools for the first time in 1986 the number that will fall into at-risk categories will be as follows: One out of four will come from poverty homes; 14 percent will be from single parent households; 15 percent will be handicapped; 15 percent will be limited English proficient; 14 percent of their mothers will be unmarried; 40 percent will come from broken homes; 10 percent will have illiterate parents; 25-33 percent will be latchkey children; 25 percent will never finish school.

There is a high probability that many of these learners will become enrolled in vocational education programs in an attempt to create an educational program that is relevant to their needs as future community members and workers. Therefore, the general characteristics frequently exhibited by special needs populations will continue to challenge vocational instructors, support personnel, and administrators. These characteristics include: poor reading skills; poor math skills; poor speech and writing skills; negative self-concept; low motivation; behavior problems; short attention span; low aspiration; poor attitude; frequent absences; resentment of authority; broken home; poor personal hygiene; problems with the law; drug/alcohol abuse; disruptiveness; overage; and potential to dropout.

Implications for Changes in the Educational System

Johnston and Packer (1987) in the publication *Work Force 2000* state that the two most important components to solving the problems facing the labor market for the 21st century will be the educational system and the business community. There will be 23 million new jobs by the year 2000. The work force will be 80 percent comprised of immigrants, women, and minority men; many of these individuals will be from a special needs population. Therefore, as a result of cultural adjustment problems, language barriers, different learning styles, and huge gaps in basic literacy skills, the educational system must change or face failure in meeting the needs of both these individuals and the labor market.

Cetron (1985) completed a study commissioned by the American Association of School Administrators. This study was conducted in an attempt to plan for the future of the American education system through an understanding of the basic issues that affect education in our local districts. The results of this study indicate that the challenge of meeting the needs of special populations in educational programs, far from being behind us, will continue to confront us for some time to come. Cetron states the following projections:

One of the primary objectives of schools in the future will be to prepare individuals to enter a rapidly changing labor market.

Schools will work with both youth and adults in the periodic retraining effort that will take place due to technological displacement and frequent job changes.

Many adults in this country are marginally literate. These individuals will find it difficult to train or retrain for available jobs due to their lack of basic skills.

There will undoubtedly be a greater dropout rate in the future as school standards increase. As a result, programs will have to be developed to help students meet academic standards, and school sponsored work programs will be needed stimulate student interest.

By the year 2000, minorities will compose 29 percent of the population. Schools will be the main providers of literacy programs for minority adults. These individuals will learn the basic skills they need to retain a job while they are holding down a job.

Schools will be forced to focus on the benefits of educating all people in contrast to the huge cost of neglecting special populations.

As minority groups gain educational and political power, tension will grow unless equity issues are dealt with. This tension will clearly be seen in our schools.

Funding incentives from the private sector will be sought to ensure high quality training programs in our schools for the growing minority population.

A wide variety of family services will be necessary as more women enter the labor market and the number of single parent households increases. Crucial among these will be transportation and child care services.

Schools of the future will be community education centers, with private and public agencies renting space to provide a variety of services to individuals of all ages, from infants to golden agers. These services may include vocational programs, medical services, adult education classes, and meals.

Issues

Over the past few decades there have been major topics which have surfaced as the key issues in designing, developing, and implementing special programs for special needs students in vocational education. Each issue has undergone change and vast improvements have taken place.

Future issues are likely to be familiar ones which require still further change as the student population changes nationwide. Future programs for special needs students will require more experienced personnel, improved technology, increased options for training, and improved support services.

Assessment

Special needs students are required by the Carl D. Perkins Vocational Education Act to receive vocational assessment prior to instruction. Among the mandates and assurances for special populations, assessment has been a key issue and the focus of much discussion. Vocational assessment is defined by Dahl, Appleby, and Lipe (1978) as "a comprehensive process conducted over a period of time, involving a multidisciplinary team, with the purpose of identifying individual characteristics, education, training and placement needs, which provide educators the basis for planning an individual's program."

Vocational assessment is a comprehensive, multidisciplinary process that educators can use for a variety of purposes. It is used to identify vocationally relevant interests, abilities, and aptitudes of special needs students in planning the most appropriate program placement, education, training, and resources needed by the student for success in vocational programs. Irvin (1988) wrote, "there are various types of information derived by combining a variety of measures from the medical, educational, personal-social, and occupational domains." Over the years there have been various positions taken on vocational assessment. The implementation of vocational assessment within school settings has created a variety of models and

approaches to the process. Currently there are the following models according to Irvin (1988):
(1) Vocational Evaluation Center Model
—standard battery of assessments is adminsitered to all referred students
—typically functions outside of the ongoing educational program
(2) Curriculum-Based Model
—information is gathered in the settings where they provide educational services, the classroom, school and community settings
—team input and decision making are the cornerstones of this approach.
(3) Comprehensive Model
—a blend of both features of the center and curriculum-based approaches
—interdisciplinary team includes vocational assessment staff
(4) Conceptual Model
—has a three stage approach which includes readiness, assessment, and application
—addresses purposes, sequence of implementation, and contexts of valid, effective, and efficient vocaional assessment. (pp. 115-116)

Regardless of the approach to vocational assessment utilized by educators, Veir (1987) wrote that information collected usually concerns such topics as:

Functional educational levels; prevocational skills and readiness; educational records; general coordination, motor skills, and stamina; prior work experiences; ability to follow directions; relationships with peers; responsiveness to authority, ability to manipulate equipment; classroom management strategies; work attitudes; punctuality and reliability; learning styles; reading levels; specific skills needs; informal work samples; vocational and career interests; vocational program tryouts; health and medical records; work and social habits; and family history. (p. 221)

Veir (1987) stated that information is collected through informal

and formal assessment processes. Informal information is collected through observational data, anecdotal records of student behavior and performance. Records and data are reviewed by educators to insure the information is current, relevant, valid, factual, specific, and dated. Formal assessment involves the use of commercially produced instruments and equipment. Formal assessment includes:
Achievement tests; intelligence tests; standardized tests; personality inventories; social maturity tests; aptitude and dexterity tests. (p.228)

The vocational evaluation process is complex. It requires cooperative efforts among the fields of vocational education, special education, and rehabilitation. In the future, vocational assessment may well require cooperative funding, in addition to cooperative program planning. Hopefully, the future of vocational assessment will bring dramatic changes in the collaborative efforts which will result in the cooperative use of facilities, resources, personnel, funding, and support services, with less red tape in policies and procedures. This type of red tape prevents the primary purpose of all vocational assessment, to improve instruction and vocational training of special needs students which will enhance their vocational opportunities.

Program Planning

The process of planning vocational programs for special needs students requires careful consideration of personnel, facilities, curriculum content, support services, and follow-up. Over the past decade many changes have occurred. Regular vocational programs were not accessible to many special needs students. Over the years, as legislation mandated services and access and as philosophies changed, special needs students were allowed to enroll in vocational programs, first in separate programs, then in regular programs. The Carl D. Perkins Vocational Education Act (P.L. 98-524) mandated equal access in recruitment, enrollment, and placement for special needs students. Program planning has taken on new meaning and renewed significance as a result.

There are various components of program planning which affect the delivery of vocational education to special needs students. West (1987) writes that program development encompasses all ancillary services that support instruction, as well as curriculum content.

Therefore, there are many contributors and participants in program development:
> Educators (administrators, special education teachers, vocational instructors, and counselors); support personnel (resource personnel, facilitators, paraprofessionals, evaluators, and tutors); consultants (specialists, teacher educators, and state education agency personnel); agency personnel (vocational rehabilitation, mental health, and social service personnel, among others); employers; and students and parents. (p. 115)

As a result the components which are critical to program planning are: (1) curriculum content, (2) instructional delivery, (3) support services, (4) administrative policies, (5) intra- and interagency collaboration, (6) labor market projections, (7) skill acquisition and evaluation, and (8) follow-up activities. Each component requires examination, planning, and refinement in order to improve the quality of education and training. In the future, these critical components will dictate the changes in vocational and transition programming for special needs students. As legislation and federal initiatives change, programs and services for special needs students need to reflect the changes which must take place.

Instruction

Gaylord-Ross (1988) wrote that in spite of complex policies and interagency flowcharts, vocational education ultimately boils down to successful teaching of valuable skills and attitudes. The power of instructional procedures is paramount to effective teaching (p. 109). Special needs students have long been a part of public education, but the modification of curriculum and instruction to meet their needs is a relatively recent phenomenon according to White (1987). He said that a sophisticated awareness of the importance of sound curriculum and instruction for handicapped, disadvantaged, and limited English-proficient students is only now beginning to emerge. Goals were often formulated in terms of developmental growth in reading and mathematics, and specially designed instruction became little more than the modification of content to enable students to pass regular classes. Enrollment in vocational education was seen as an end itself, without regard to options upon graduation or providing equal education opportunity for all (p. 137). Much progress has been made. Unfortunately, access to public schools has yet to produce a corresponding access to independent living or employment for special needs learners (p. 138).

One of the major issues in instruction was, and still remains today, the fear of curriculum softening (usually referred to as "watering down the curriculum"). The selection of appropriate and, in some cases, alternative curriculum, is critical to the individual education plan (IEP) for handicapped students as well as any other special needs students, whether they have a written educational plan or not. The selection of curriculum content for special needs students requires deliberation by a team of educators who understand the strengths, interests, and aptitudes of the individual student as well as the vocational program options and curriculum content which most closely match the student's needs.

Administration

Administrative support has been one of the major issues in vocational education for special needs students. The policies and procedures which govern and guide vocational education for special needs students are critical to the learning environment. Leadership is an important factor in the educational climate when planning support services or instructional delivery. Administrators can provide the strong supportive base which enhances a vocational instructor's program or they can negate any effort on behalf of the vocational instructor to provide a positive learning environment for special needs students.

The administrator is the acknowledged educational leader, and consequently has a major responsibility for effective vocational programming for special needs students, as well as for all students enrolled in vocational programs. Kolde (1987) wrote that administrators must demonstrate a positive attitude, keep communication channels open, and establish a team effort to provide effective programming. She believes that administrators can provide active and participatory leadership through various activities which:
- provide quality instruction to meet the needs of all students, both academically and socially;
- ensure that the facility design is barrier free;

- provide appropriate equipment to meet the needs of the handicapping conditions of the students;
- assign an adequate number of staff to meet the needs of the handicapped and disadvantaged students;
- plan for future improvements and expansion of the programs, i.e., numbers, space, equipment, staff;
- monitor and review all program components on an ongoing basis;
- maintain quality programs which meet the needs of both the labor market and the individual student;
- promote the benefits of least restrictive environment and the vocational special needs program through public relations efforts. (p. 356)

Administrators must make a professional commitment toward vocational programs for special needs students. Through their support and encouragement, quality programming will grow. They are a role model for other educators. They keep vocational instructors, resource personel, and support staff informed on federal legislation and state policies as well as compliance and monitoring procedures. Last, but not least, administrators are critical to the public relations efforts within and outside the educational community. Strong, supportive administrators provide additional opportunities for special needs students beyond the boundaries of the classroom.

Support Services

Asselin (1987) wrote that the career-vocational preparation process is comprehensive and must involve coordination of professionals from a variety of disciplines, settings, and programs in order to serve the diverse population of special needs students. Since the field of vocational special needs has been growing and changing, the most effective delivery of career-vocational preparation involves professionals outside vocational education and special education. Professionals from the fields of rehabilitation, counseling, evaluation, social and community services, human services, and labor are becoming interested and active in developing pre-employment and employment skills of special populations (p. 202).

The Carl D. Perkins Act (P.L. 98-524) reinforced the importance of support services for all special needs students by including the assurances and mandates that special needs students receive special services which would enhance instruction and opportunities for success in vocational education. Special educators already had a mandate to do the same task through the Education for All Handicapped Children Act's (P.L. 94-142) Individualized Education Program (IEP). When the IEP is developed by a team and it includes vocational education, there should be input from vocational education, whether it is the vocational instructor or a resource person who is intimately involved in the delivery of support services in vocational programs.

There are many support services which are utilized by special needs students. Sarkees and Scott (1985) have grouped support services into five categories:
1. Coordination of auxiliary services:
    Housing
    Health services
    Child care
    Transportation
2. Outreach services:
    Public relations that inform citizens about what vocational education is doing
    Recruitment services that actively seek students for programs
3. Instructional support services:
    Basic skills assistance
    Job readiness training
    Work experience
    Information about laws and regulations governing specific occupations
4. Guidance service:
    Counseling
    Information
    Provide relevant experiences
5. Placement services:
    Job listings
    Resume preparation
    Interview skills
    Job follow-up (p. 93)

Support services are usually necessary if special needs students are to successfully enter and complete vocational training. However, there is no uniformity among the states or even within states as to what support services can be provided adequately or how to deliver them. Therefore, there is a wide variety of differences within vocational education regarding the delivery of support services.

Intra- and Interagency Collaboration

Sarkees and Scott (1985) wrote that many states have developed cooperative interagency agreements which describe the role and responsibilities of vocational education, special education, vocational rehabilitation, and a number of other agencies to maximize the services provided for handicapped individuals. Such agreements have been developed as the result of the current national drive to expand and improve the services delivery systems used to provide individuals with disabilities with appropriate vocational education opportunties. In addition to collaboration among agencies, it is important that cooperative planning be promoted at the state and local levels, since it has been mandated at the federal level. Coordinated planning is a coordinated effort by various individuals and agencies to provide a comprehensive and realistic instructional plan for a special needs student (p. 185).

Legislative mandates and federal initiatives have urged agencies receiving federal funding to plan, implement, and evaluate collaborative relationships. Without planning and coordination, services are likely to be duplicated or excluded. The Education for All Handicapped Children Act (P.L. 94-142), Section 504 of the Rehabilitation Act (P.L. 93-112), the Carl D. Perkins Vocational Education Act (P.L. 98-524), the Job Training and Partnership Act (P.L. 97-300), and the transition initiative established by the Office of Special Education and Rehabilitation Services (OSERS) are the major causes for increasing interagency collaboration. This interagency collaboration is meant to increase the opportunities and services needed to adequately develop vocational potential and successfully secure meaningful employment and independence. The following is a list of potential opportunities and services which require intra- and interagency collaboration:
  1. access to vocational training programs,
  2. career development activities (awareness, orientation,

exploration, and preparation),
3. vocational guidance and counseling services,
5. curriculum modification,
6. specific skill training,
7. remediation assistance,
8. prevocational skills,
9. employability and work adjustment skills,
10. diagnostic and related services,
11. public school collaboration with other agencies and institutions (e.g., Community Based Organizations—CBO),
12. placement services,
13. transition services. (p. 187)

The future will require stronger as well as expanded intra- and interagency coordination efforts. Educational institutions, rehabilitation agencies, employment service agencies, community organizations, and business/industry will become increasingly involved in the education and services needed by special populations. It is crucial that there be increased awareness and understanding of the various agencies, their services, and the collaboration necessary for the delivery of effective and more cost-efficient services.

Transition

Berkell and Gaylord-Ross (1989) wrote that in the past two decades major changes have taken place in the delivery of education and social services. These changes reflect an increased public recognition of the fact that the service needs of these individuals extend beyond the boundary of the school and include preparation, training, and support for community integration. One of the most crucial and complex components of community integration is the transition from school to work. The successful transition from school to work and to adult life is the ultimate indicator of effective schooling and service provision. Transition encompasses a period that includes high school, graduation, postsecondary education or adult services, and the initial years of employment. It is a process that requires preparation and support through secondary school and follow-up services after employment has begun (p. 3).

Transition has been defined by Madeleine Will (1984), assistant secretary for the Office of Special Education and Rehabilitative Services (OSERS), as a bridge between the security and structure offered by school and the risks of adult life. It is a shared responsibility involving many contributors and participants. Transition literature reflects that there are multiple employment options which are considered as transition takes place: (1) competitive employment, (2) supported employment, and (3) sheltered employment.

Competitive employment is defined as employment where a special needs individual works in an actual work setting with nonhandicapped/non-special needs coworkers. The person is paid at least minimum wage and is considered a regular employee. Supported employment is seen as an alternative that lies between competitive employment and sheltered employment. It has three essential elements according to Lagomarcino and Rusch (1987): (1) wages paid, (2) work performed in an integrated setting, and (3) ongoing support services provided. Sheltered employment is conducted within a work-oriented facility in a controlled environment with individualized goals which utilize work experiences and related services to assist handicapped persons to progress toward their maximum vocational potential.

Berkell and Gaylord-Ross (1989) wrote that the concept of transition has involved moving students from school programs to least restrictive adult programs. One form of transition merely makes appropriate referrals from school to adult services and ensures that individuals are followed-up by an agency and not lost in the service system. A second level of transition formalizes interagency working agreements between schools and adult service agencies. A third level of transition deals with actual program implementation. There are numerous components of transition programs including training, instructional technology, counseling, family involvement, and the administration of support services. While many impressive demonstrations of transition programs have been described, we are still in the developmental stages in designing and implementing comprehensive transition programs and services. The future holds great promise for an increased formalized delivery system of transition services (pp. 17-18).

Evaluation

West (1987) wrote that designing evaluation for vocational special needs programs needs to examine a variety of issues in order to determine the quality and effectiveness of the program. These issues include:

> Administration of the program; adequacy of staffing to meet program design; coordination between vocational education and special education; identification of the one or more target populations the program intends to serve; funding sources available to support the program; purpose of the program; curriculum content and appropriate course offerings; resource and support service to supplement individual needs of the target population; comprehensiveness of support services; assurances that the legislative mandates are met. (p. 133)

Maintaining quality vocational programs that truly encourage and support special needs students requires assistance in several critical areas according to Kolde (1987). She maintains that administrators must ensure that special needs students have the following available to them:

> Diagnostic assessment and career guidance; supplementary and remedial activities, including leadership development; supervised on-the-job learning opportunities; and counseling and assistance during the school-to-employment transition. (p. 361)

The future challenge for vocational education is to improve the quality of instruction, program delivery, support services, interagency collaboration, and transition beyond the extent to which it currently exists. While the philosophy and goals of providing quality programs is in place, only evaluation data can determine if the commitment to quality programs and support services actually exists and is being implemented.

Projections for the Future

There will be a number of challenges for educational and industrial planners in the future. While educators continue to assist industry in educating and preparing new workers for a variety of new kinds of jobs, industry must come to terms with assisting existing workers in accommodating to changes being created by swift and far-reaching employment changes. Industry must also attempt to adjust to a work force that is in a state of flux while coming to terms with the forces of worldwide competition that may require a continued change in automation or other production techniques.

Major factors in the future will dictate that the delivery of vocational education services change to parallel the fast pace of technological changes and different employment opportunities and environments. Edward Cornish, past president of the World Future Society, has stated that "We all have a responsibility toward the future and the only way we can discharge that responsibility is by thinking about the possibilities of the future, selecting those possibilities we want to realize and then working to realize them."

All Day, Year Round Schools

Vocational programs in the future will, by necessity, need to move toward an open-entry/open-exit format which is competency-based in nature. Special needs learners will identify the specific competencies which they need to develop. These will be documented in an individualized program format. Individuals will then enter a program and leave when the competencies have been mastered at a level which is competitive for the industry in which they will apply them. Individualized pacing with a variety of instructional materials will become commonplace. The addition of computer-assisted instruction, interactive video systems, and home computer systems will augment this process (Wircenski, Sullivan, and Weatherford, 1985).

Cetron (1985) predicts that one of the major responsibilities of public schools in the future will be to prepare individuals to enter into and keep pace with a labor market that will constantly be changing. Youth and adults will both be enrolled in public school settings. Youth will be involved in educational programs to develop a foundation of basic skills and critical thinking skills that will generalize across a number of job areas as technology changes the face of job titles and responsibilities. The variety of skills that entry level workers will be expected to bring into the labor market will be increasingly complex. This will be a great challenge for special needs learners who may need additional time or assistance in order to accomplish this.

Cooperative work-study programs will be increased in the future through collaborative planning among educational programs, agencies, and business and industrial sites. Private sector cooperative work sites will require that learners spend certain periods of time at school or at home for instruction in related vocational and academic foundation areas. At other periods of time individuals will spend time involved in specific employment skill training. If a primary objective of the educational systems of the future is to produce productive employees with appropriate skills and attitudes to enter the labor market, students should begin to develop these while they are in school. The most authentic environment in which to learn these necessary competencies is in actual employment settings. Cooperative programs are especially effective in preventing potential dropouts from leaving school before completing the essential base of skills necessary for independence and survival in the work force and community, but will require flexibile programming options for the learners' school schedule. Individuals may be scheduled at work sites during the day and would require instruction in the school program during early or late evening hours. In addition, summer months may prove to be more flexible to cooperative work situations than the regular school months.

Some vocational and technical facilities may be in such demand that several "shifts" may need to be scheduled during each day to meet the demands of people interested in enrolling in programs. Therefore, it is possible that blocks of time may be scheduled almost around the clock.

Adults enrolled in public education programs, secondary programs, "adults in prime time," as well as those involved in postsecondary settings, will be entering programs periodically during their years in the labor force. They will require reeducation and retraining whenever their job title or responsibilities change substantially. Due to the rapid pace of technological advancement, workers will be displaced and shifted to new job areas rapidly.

Programs will have to be scheduled at times that will be convenient for adults in need of upgrading or retraining. Most adult workers must work full time while updating their existing skills. It is essential, therefore, that schools in the future organize and provide flexible scheduling to reflect a variety of availabilities during the day as well as during the year.

Cooperative Work Study Programs

Work-study programs can be effectively utilized with adolescent and adult special needs individuals, merging the resources of the educational programs and the industrial sector and providing participants with true reality-testing situations regarding the world of work. An important characteristic of these programs is the transfer of learning to real life work experiences, thereby combining academics and technical skills.

A cooperative relationship must be developed to include the special needs learner, school-based personnel, agency representatives, adult service providers, parents, and industry personnel. Without this necessary collaboration work study programs may become fragmented and ineffective, characterized by duplication of some services and gaps where essential services are not provided.

Some major barriers to success in work study program development in the past have included:
1. trying to force individuals to be at work study sites where employers or workers are not ready to work with the program;
2. trying to force students to accept jobs that they are not interested in;
3. failing to communicate with special needs individuals and/or parents about work study responsibilities and time commitments. (Kingsbury, p. 181)

Wircenski, Sullivan, and Weatherford (1985) predict that:
Cooperative education programs will increase significantly in the years ahead and reach occupational fields not now usually included, in spite of the problems anticipated with expanding the practice. In fact, cooperative education may be the only alternative for comprehensive high schools that want to extend students' vocational education opportunities beyond the one hour each day that will be possible as academic graduation requirements are increased. (p. 4)

Cooperative work study programs in the future should be designed to provide a number of experiences for special populations. When the components of work study programs are carefully planned and implemented they can provide: (a) an opportunity to develop essential skills, (b) an opportunity for career exploration experiences to be used in the career decision-making process, (c) a base of crucial employability skills, (d) a bank of generalizable vocational skills that will transfer to a number of job settings, (e) a source of initial work experience which can be used for personal resumes or job application references, (f) a foundation of specific entry level skills for an occupational area, and (g) a potential opportunity for full-time employment.

Appropriate supervision must be provided while special needs individuals are involved in cooperative work sites. Follow-up must also occur to assume that learner progress is ongoing in terms of technical and employability skills. Technical update and job upgrading procedures resulting from emerging technology must also be incorporated as an ongoing part of the program. Finally, long range follow-up must be built into the process with a variety of options for schools or support agencies to reenter the situation and provide assistance when needed. The spirit of transition from school to postschool experiences should pervade cooperative work study program planning, implementation, and evaluation at all times. The transition process can be more easily facilitated through a team approach.

Computer-Driven Instruction

New technologies such as computers, job simulation equipment, videodiscs, and interactive video programs will continue to be a prominent part of the learning environment in the future. It will be possible for students to spend several days at home each week completing assignments, receiving instruction, and studying. The traditional "classroom environment" will be much different from the way it is today. Special populations will have to be prepared to use this technology both in their educational programs and in certain aspects of their future career plans. Word processing will become a basic skill that should begin in the early grades.

Sophisticated systems may be in place in classrooms where a high technology station would allow instructors to utilize network systems, to manipulate information and to send individualized material to the desks of learners. This station would also enable instructors to monitor individual progress and provide immediate feedback. The computer networks in the future will allow for interaction among students, larger groups of students, and instructors and students in other locations.

Computers centered in the home environment will be as important as those based in the schools. Prices for computers and accompanying software are becoming affordable to a greater number of people. Educators will need to provide opportunities for basic computer literacy as well as more advanced skills as computer systems are upgraded. Schools will also be in a position to provide guidance and advice on relevant software that parallels the student's educational program. Parent education programs may need to be established to provide the basics necessary to fully utilize home computers.

Self-discipline and time management skills will have to be emphasized, as a great deal of time may be spent on computer driven instruction, drill and practice exercises, reports, or homework either at school or at home. Without a feeling of self-confidence and the ability to manage a block of time while at the computer terminal, special needs individuals will never master the tasks required of this technology.

Special needs individuals comprise a group which will reap the benefits of the new computer technology era. This technology will provide them with opportunities for education and employment which has never been available before. Computers can aid in adapting instruction as well as in providing direct instruction. Applications of computer driven instruction for special needs learners in the future will include: (a) tutorial or remedial software used to assist learners by providing information used to acquire new knowledge and skills; (b) drill and practice software used to reinforce instruction so that it will be comprehended and retained; (c) programs designed to develop critical thinking and problem-solving skills by promoting the discovery learning technique; and (d) simulation software which encourages students to relate what has been learned to the real world of work.

Industry Education Linkages

In order for vocational technical programs to reflect the rapid changes that will continue to be reflected in the industrial environment of the future, stronger industry education linkages must be established. The changing needs of the employment sector must be communicated by industry to educators. Otherwise, programs will not properly prepare special needs individuals for jobs as they emerge and/or change.

Sarkees and Scott (1985) identify a number of services commonly provided by cooperative planning between business and educational sectors in the past. These include:
1. assistance in planning programs that would be appropriate and realistic for special needs learners;
2. advice concerning appropriate program objectives, curriculum content, and occupational competencies to be included in programs;
3. identification of community resources that may help special needs learners succeed in programs;
4. assessing the educational and manpower needs of the community (possibly through a needs survey);
5. identification of entry-level job proficiencies;
6. establishing and promoting positive community public relations;
7. advice concerning equipment, laboratory, and facilities modifications for special needs learners;
8. assistance in locating potential on-the-job training sites for special needs learners who require further reinforcement during or after completion of a specific program; and
9. assistance in identifying job placement situations for special needs learners.

Business and industry can contribute greatly to strengthening programs and services for special populations involved in vocational education programs in educational institutions. Suggested directions for stronger industry education linkages in the future include the following:
1. Business representatives could team teach in vocational programs to share new technology, processes and ideas.
2. Businesses could contract with schools to provide training services for adults in need of retraining. This would be especially pertinent if adults need reinforce-

ment or remedial services while being upgraded and/or retrained, as many educational personnel have an expertise in this area.
3. Specific action plans could be developed between business and industry representatives to outline roles and responsibilities in providing quality programs for special populations. This would help to eliminate both the duplication of services and the absence of necessary services. Community groups could also become involved in this planning and implementation process.
4. Equipment, supplies, and training facilities could be placed on loan to school personnel working with special needs individuals in order to better prepare them for the actual requirements of the jobs which they will someday apply for.
5. Shadowing, tours, and work study opportunities provided by industry could contribute greatly to vocational and career decision-making experiences for special populations.
6. Information could be provided by industry regarding successful special needs employees who could serve as role models and mentors to others who are still involved in preparatory programs.

Collaborative efforts between business and education could result in the development of resource directories. School based personnel working with special populations could be provided with a Local Business and Industry Directory which would include the name of the company, local contact, and types and descriptions of available resources or services. Industrial personnel working with special needs individuals could be provided a Local Education Directory which would include the names of secondary and postsecondary institutions providing vocational programs as well as a list and description of support services which could be helpful to industry.

Parent Education Programs

Parents should be expected to play an increasingly active role in the educational planning and review of their sons and daughters in the future. There is no doubt that the role of the parent is an

important one in the overall success of special needs learners. Vasa, Steckelberg, and Meers (1979) make three assumptions about the involvement of parents in the education of their children:
1. Parents care more about their children than the school does. They have a vested interest in their children, with ultimate moral and legal responsibilities for them. Due to recent judicial and legislative decisions, parents have taken a more active role in the decision-making process for their child's educational programs.
2. Parents have a right to know more about and be involved in their child's education. They must be provided with information which will allow them to make a contribution to their child's education. This includes input in all phases of the educational process, including assessment, programming, and evaluation.
3. Parents can be effective teachers. There is no need for parents to totally delegate responsibility of their child to the school system. They can provide valuable support, reinforcement, and counseling. In addition, they can assist school based personnel by providing valuable data about the child including family background, behavioral history, goals and aspirations, successful and unsuccessful teaching techniques, community experiences, work history, and prevocational experiences.

Research has shown that parents contribute significantly to the career decision-making process of their children. There is little doubt that parents are a principal influence on adolescents' expected occupations. In addition, family structure is one of the most important factors in determining all aspects of a child's life and exerts a powerful influence over career aspirations. (Dillard and Campbell, 1981; Auster and Auster, 1981). Expectations, maturity, and career directions of individuals are heavily influenced by parental association and role modeling. Also, positive career development and decision making are greatly enhanced by early experiences in the family. (Bearg, 1980; Bardwick, 1971).

Recently, educators and business/industry personnel have recognized the need for collaborative efforts in career planning for students. They have also recognized the importance of developing programs for involving parents. The following strategies are suggested

collaboration activities:
1. Conduct meetings to increase parents' understanding of curricula and activities being offered in the school for handicapped and disadvantaged persons (i.e., linkages between subject matter and careers, cooperative programs between schools and local businesses/industries).
2. Conduct joint meetings of parents, educators, community organizations representatives, and business/industry persons to address the need for basic skills, employability skills, and specific job skills for handicapped and disadvantaged persons.
3. Publish informational materials that will provide parents with suggestions and activities for providing (home based) career experiences that will complement those offered in school.
4. Provide parents with opportunities to serve as career resource persons in their children's classrooms.
5. Provide parents with opportunities to assist school personnel in obtaining, cataloging and updating career education resource materials.
6. Open up business and industry settings on weekends for field trips for special needs youth and their parents who are interested in learning more about competitive employment options. (Sarkees and Scott, 1985, p. 206)

Essential components for future parent education programs should include information relative to:
1. basic theory of the career development process;
2. goals and stages of career development programs;
3. components of effective career development programs for special needs learners (occupational information, decision-making skills, employability skills, daily living skills);
4. rights and responsibilities of parents in the vocational development of the child (legal and moral);
5. role of the parent in the development, implementation, and evaluation of vocational goals for the child;
6. basic understanding of vocational education, program offerings, operation of programs, offerings, and employment opportunities;

7. available support services provided by the school to assist special needs individuals in successfully participating in vocational programs;
8. available services from service organizations, advocacy groups, community agencies, and adult service providers;
9. transition options for special needs individuals for post high school success.

Summary

Projections for the future indicate that schools will be faced with an increasing number of special needs individuals. There is a high probability that many of these learners will become enrolled in vocational education programs in an attempt to create an educational program that is relevant to their needs as future community members and workers.

Several basic issues will undoubtedly face educational institutions and vocational programs as they retool to meet the needs of these populations. Future programs for special needs students will require more experienced personnel, improved technology, increased options for training, and improved support services. The crucial issues will include a focus on vocational assessment, program planning, instruction, administration, intra- and interagency collaboration, transitional services to post school opportunities, and evaluation.

Major factors in the future will dictate that the delivery of vocational education services change to parallel the fast pace of technological changes and different employment opportunities and environments. Some important considerations for planning programs for special needs learners include basic skills, time management skills, leisure time skills, career decision-making skills, information about continuing educational and training opportunities, generalizable skills, critical thinking skills, and employability skills. In addition, the impact of the future will cause a restructuring of the delivery of vocational programs. This will include all day, year round schools, more cooperative work study programs, computer-driven instruction, more industry education linkages, and parent education programs. ☐

References

Asselin, S. (1987). Identification and utilization of support services in serving vocational special needs students. In *Handbook of Vocational Special Needs Education* (Second Edition). Meers, G. (Ed.). Rockville, MD: Aspen Publishers.

Auster, C. and Auster, D. (1981). Factors influencing women's choices of nontraditional careers: The role of family, peers and counselors. *The Vocational Guidance Quarterly*, March, 253-63.

Bardwick, J. (1971). *Psychology of Women: A Study of Bio-Cultural Conflicts*. New York: Harper and Row.

Bearg, E. (1980). Parental role modeling as a career awareness tool. *Elementary School Guidance and Counseling*, 14 (4), 266-68.

Berkell, D. and Brown, J. (1989). *Transition from School to Work for Persons with Disabilities*. New York: Longman Publishers, Inc.

Berkell, D. and Gaylord-Ross, R. (1989). The concept of transition: Historical and current developments. In *Transition from School to Work for Persons with Disabilities*. Berkell, D. and Brown, J. (Eds.). New York: Longman Publishers, Inc.

Cain, E. and Taber, F. (1987). *Educating Disabled People for the 21st Century*. Boston, MA: Little, Brown and Company.

The Carl D. Perkins Vocational Education Act (1984), Public Law 98-524. Washington, D.C.

Cetron, M. (1985). *Schools of the Future*. New York: McGraw-Hill Book Company.

Cunningham, D., Putzstuck, C., and Barbieri, M. (1988). *Working Together to Support At-Risk Youth*. Denton, TX: University of North Texas, Department of Occupational and Vocational Education.

Dahl, T.; Appleby, J; and Lipe, D. (1978). *Mainstreaming Guidebook for Vocational Educators Teaching the Handicapped*. Salt Lake City, UT: Olympus Publishing Co.

Dillard, J. and Campbell, N. (1981). Influences of Puerto Rican, black, and anglo parents' career behavior on their adolescent children's career development. *Vocational Guidance Quarterly*, 30 (2), 139-48.

Gaylord-Ross, R. (1988). *Vocational Education for Persons with Handicaps*. Mountain View, CA: Mayfield Publishing Company.

Greenan, J. (1987). Generalizable skills instruction. In *Handbook of*

Vocational Special Needs Education. Meers, G. (Ed.). Rockville, MD: Aspen Publishers, Inc.

Irvin, L. (1989). Vocational assessment in school and rehabilitation programs. In *Transition from School to Work for Persons with Disabilities.* Berknell, D. and Brown, J. (Eds.). New York: Longman Publishers, Inc.

Johnston, W. and Packer, H. (1987). *Work Force 2000: Work and Workers for the Twenty-First Century.* Indianapolis, IN: The Hudson Institute.

Kingsbury, D. (1987). Cooperative work experience programs for students with vocational special needs. In *Handbook of Vocational Special Needs Education.* Meers, G. (Ed.). Rockville, MD: Aspen Publishers.

Kolde, R. (1987). The administrator's special needs programs. In *Handbook of Vocational Special Needs Education* (Second Edition). Meers, G. (Ed.). Rockville, MD: Aspen Publishers.

Lagomarcino, T. and Rusch, F. (1988). Supported employment: Transition from school to work. *Interchange,* 8 (1), 1-5.

Meers, G. (Ed.) (1987). *Handbook of Vocational Special Needs Education* (Second Edition). Rockville, MD: Aspen Publishers.

Phelps, L. A. (1985). Special needs students: Redefining the challenge. *Voc Ed,* 60 (3), 24-26.

The President's Committee on Employment of People With Disabilities (1988). Special report: an examination of the impact of the Carl D. Perkins vocational education act of 1984 on our nation's citizens with disabilities. Washington, DC.

Sarkees, M. and Feichtner, S. (1987). Working together: The special needs team. *Voc Ed,* 62 (2), 22-4.

Sarkees, M. and Scott, J. (1985). *Vocational Special Needs,* Homewood, IL: American Technical Press.

Sarkees, M., West, L., and Wircenski, J. (1988). *Vocational Education Programs for the Disadvantaged.* Columbus, OH: Center for Research in Vocational Education.

Vasa, S. and Steckelberg, A. (1980). Parent programs in career education for the handicapped. *Career Development for Exceptional Individuals,* Fall, 74-82.

Vasa, S., Steckelberg, A., and Meers, G. (1979). *Career Education for the Handicapped Child: A Guide to Parent Education Programming.* Columbus, OH: The National Center for Research in Vocational

Education.

West, L. (1987). Designing vocational programs. In *Handbook of Vocational Special Needs Education* (Second Edition). Meers, G. (Ed.). Rockville, MD: Aspen Publishers.

White, S. (1987). The modification of curriculum and instruction: Catalysts for equity. In *Handbook of Vocational Special Needs Education* (Second Edition). Meers, G. (Ed.). Rockville, MD: Aspen Publishers.

Wircenski, J.; Sullivan, R.; and Weatherford, J. (1985). Vocational education: A look ahead. *Curriculum Report* 15 (2), 1-6.

CHAPTER 10

The Relationship of History to the Future of Vocational Education

By Angelo C. Gilli, Sr.

BY keeping a record of the past through the writing of its history, with accuracy and comprehensiveness, a tool becomes available through which we can illustrate what society is capable of accomplishing. Through examining past events on a selective and analytic basis, the following become determinable: (a) the nature of our predecessors in the world in which they were living; and (b) what their accomplishments were—both for themselves and others who were affected by their endeavors. The historian who succeeds in steering this course can help us to understand all aspects of civilization—its limitations, from the past to the present—and provide some valuable insights into possibilities for pushing back our limitations in the future (Berlin, 1988).

A good writer of history strives to satisfy the readers' curiosity with regard to happenings of earlier times. Also, if done with honesty and candor, it can instill in the reader of that history a feeling of healthy skepticism about our contemporary society being a permanent fixture here. A thorough historical treatment of culture and society will show that the mores which people embraced and the practices that evolved out of them have been changing all along and will continue to do so until the end of time. Another virtue of well-written history is that it renders available a knowledge of what previous generations ran up against, possessed, and accomplished. Profit can be reaped from this, by learning about the possibilities, along with the uncertainties, limitations, and contradictions. That is what good history is-all about.

The questions raised by historians, as well as their reasons for what they select and reject, is a reflection of what is deemed important "today." These are "prejudices" embraced by historians that are mirrors of our experience in our living in the here and now—our contemporaneousness. But this is what it is to be human and we need to address this reality and deal with it in the best way we know how. In that way, we can minimize misinterpretation of the actions of earlier peoples and events that transpired in a previous time and another milieu.

What History of Education Brings to Future Education

Much of the history of education that has been written has consisted of "house histories" and has dealt with ideas of education reformers. Such treatments are considered lopsided and offer little in the way of helping to find our way into education of the future (Talbott, 1972). A high quality "history" of education is the variety that provides insight into the elaborate and intricate involvements of education with the rest of society. As logical as that sounds, it is a tall order, and the difficulty in writing history in that manner is the major reason why we have to look long and intensively to find such works in the literature.

During the past half century or so, teaching has entered the ranks of the professions, alongside of the others—law, medicine, science, and theology. This development has provided the basis for historical scholarship in education to become a separate discipline. Such an approach is opposed by traditional historians. Reasons for their opposition are several: First, the danger of a specialized history becoming a separate discipline is that it could become isolated from the mainstream of historical study and of society as a whole. Secondly, although not as openly expressed by the "professional" historians, is their reluctance to share the business of writing history with specialists in the various professions—a turf problem. The historians' sense of proprietorship with regard to writing history runs strong, just as individuals in other professions tend to resent intrusions by outsiders. On the other hand, can we rely on professional historians to have a complete understanding of education (especially vocational education)? And so the debate goes on.

Interactions Between Education and Society

While the earlier approaches to educational history focused upon particular institutions, it has become clearer that useful efforts in this field should be directed toward the interplay between society at large and the role of education within it. This is easier said than done. An initial difficulty in such an endeavor is to determine which factors in society should be examined in relation to education (especially since it would be impossible to deal with all of them), and to decide the weight to assign those that are chosen. The dynamics of the interactions between the structure of society and education require careful analytic explanation based upon factual information, not weakly based and idiosyncratic assumptions. Implicit to understanding such connections is to clearly determine *who* got educated—that speaks to the issue of the interplay of education within the societal structure and to many of the pronouncements regarding needs, goals, objectives, and the like (declarations that we are so prone to fall back upon in education). And from that, other critical concerns appear that need responses: What does the answer to that question have to do with the social and economic mobility of people in that society? What has been the role of education in this process? Furthermore, and perhaps even more important, what have been the results of mobility brought about through the acquisition of more or certain kinds of education? What has it meant to the persons who benefited and to those who have not gained from it, and what has been its effect upon flexibility of social stratification? What has been the impact upon the political arena? In what ways have the economy and economic development been affected?

Even more difficult to assess, because relatively fewer records are extant, are the effects of education upon the lower classes (Keen, 1987). It is comparatively easy to make judgments on the matter regarding the elite members of our society, because of the prevalence of journals and other literary evidence produced by the upper classes. But what about the commoners who did not maintain written records of their personal and work lives? We need to take measures to avoid stressing the wrong thing: The *intentions* of the educational reformers are relatively unimportant when compared to *consequences* of their efforts (Burnham, 1984).

In our desire to ferret out education's role in the historical process, we must guard against the possibility of distorting our perceptions of the role of education. We would like to know both sides of the question: How does society affect education and in what ways does education in turn affect society, and when does this exchange of influence fail to take place (O'Brien, 1988)?

The writing of educational history has undergone considerable changes in recent years. Many authors have taken second looks at earlier approaches because contemporary education is seen as being in a troubled condition. Present day dilemmas urge new questions upon us that in turn demand new approaches to the study of happenings of the past, in the interest of achieving a more correct understanding of them. Let us hope that some of the endeavors of today will help lead us to some workable solutions for some of the problems that seem so intractable at the moment.

Evolution of Vocational Education Practices and Future Education

One is tempted to believe that vocational education glacially evolved from some primitive beginning, gradually emerging into its present forms. But that would be a mistake. The major permanent feature of vocational education is that it always has been a component deeply imbedded in and reactive to the prevailing cuture. Each society had its own version of where preparing persons for work belonged in the everyday world and just how such preparation was to be provided. Therefore, the institution of vocational education, although known by other terms up to rather recent times, has been a changing phenomenon—on occasion by slow evolution and other times by abrupt variations that were imposed by cultural demands that suddenly came upon the scene. Furthermore, sometimes societal changes, especially those brought in a relatively sudden manner (such as the abolition of slavery, or the inauguration of child labor and minimum wage laws), caused interfaces with society that were incompatible. Such incongruities have been "forced" in some cases and "strongly enticed" in others into the interstices of society through legislation. For example, the inclusion of vocational education in the public school systems of the various states may have never reached its contemporary status if it were not for a number of public laws that have emerged since 1862, and especially since 1917. But such statutes did not suddenly appear out of nowhere. More often than not, they were the outcomes of citizen concerns that gradually resulted in a build up of pressures to which lawmakers responded. Although many of the public laws may have found the light of day because of various kinds of compromises and "deals" made between prominent lawmakers of the time, they were clearly on the national agenda before then, often for many years (Gilli, 1973, 1976). Other chapters in this work more accurately address the varieties of legislation that have had effect upon vocational education over the years.

The purposes of vocational education have varied in ways that are imcompatible: Long ago, it was among the devices employed to distance the "masses" from the upper strata of society and to keep them under the control of the upper class; in more recent times, it has been advertised as a way to individual economic independence and self-autonomy. In all cases, the dominant culture of the prevailing society dictated the purposes of vocational education. This aspect of vocational education has not changed over the centuries: Its place is dictated by the greater society. In our early years as colonies and later as a young nation, a major concern was the availability of a complacent, manageable, and cheap labor force. Coupled with it was the concern over avoiding the overloading of the pauper rolls. Later, vocational education was viewed in a more humanistic vein, as one of the possible career development avenues for some youngsters and adults (Enright, 1987). But elements of the earlier concerns (economic) still exist deeply within the fabric of society, although in a less obvious fashion. A good historical treatment of vocational education since early times could provide an understandable connection between these disparate institutions, and increased comprehension of their legitimacy during their period of existence (Gilli, 1980). Such knowledge would be an invaluable bridge to better preparation of youngsters for the future.

We are doomed to making choices. Consider the concepts of liberty and equality: Can we have both? They share opposite ends of a balancing system. Increasing one must be accompanied by a reduction in the other. When are these two elements truly in balance? The zero point on such a bipolar scale is contingent upon cultural perceptions at the moment the weighing-in is made.

An example is the distribution of income: Those with the most money have the greatest chance of acquiring even more. This has been tempered (some would say tampered with) in varying degrees over the years by instituting various taxation rates. While this places a restraint on those earning greater incomes, it does nothing for those on the lower end unless the money so derived is passed over to the other side of the scale. So, from time to time, special interventions are instituted to provide additional money to the lower income group. And with each choice, while we open some doors, we also irreparably close others. We will always have to deal with value collisions: with each winner there must be one or more losers. Such is the very essence of society—the continual opening and closing of options.

Moving from the Known to the Unknown

And so it is with regard to the provision of vocational education in past times, the present, and the years ahead. The clearest solutions that we have, and can understand the best, are derived from observations of and experiences obtained from past events. Even then, we run the risk of interpreting past events in terms of contemporary values, which can really put us off track considerably. Nevertheless, we think our best solutions are learned from events that have transpired and have been examined ex post facto. But how much do we really know of how the recipients of vocational education felt about it in previous times? We have some inklings, based on census and other demographic data, and a limited number of oral histories that people wise enough to collect them managed to acquire in years past. But, as mentioned before, human products of vocational education, particularly during the times when virtually all of them could be classified as illiterates, left little in the way of diaries, journals, family stories, and the like, that would provide an answer to that query (Gilli, 1988). We have a limited amount of superficial and paternalistic commentary (journals, biographies, autobiographies) from upper class individuals who refer to "their" workers. Most of the literature of this nature is notably lacking in true insight of how the poor folks really felt about their labor and society as a whole. In spite of missing out in learning about that important part of our heritage, we have been quick to pass judgments about the merits and effects of vocational training and education of days past.

These earlier training modes included within-the-family training, apprenticeships, indentureships, forced training within the institution of slavery, and some varieties of compensated on-the-job preparation. The legitimacy of early vocational education had much to do with control of the masses. The compromise sought by the rulers was people control in the interest of community tranquility, enablement of common folk to be sufficiently productive so as to "carry their own weight" and not be a burden on the public coffers, and to have a cheap source of labor on hand (Gilli, 1976, 1980, 1988). It worked to some extent, of course, but the price exacted from the masses is not clearly ascertainable.

Much of what goes on in contemporary vocational education is responsive to pressures exerted by those who have the "ear" of the governing elements in our society. Like all public education and other tax supported institutions, vocational education has a political center of gravity. Is this desirable or undesirable? Actually, it is a double-edged sword, being responsive to both selfish and altruistic demands. Cynics may say that the first takes precedence over the second, but that view can be challenged. There is a consensus today that it is better to run the risk of "unwise" politics than idiosyncratic and authoritarian decisions imposed by a single person or ruling junta regarding the funding of such endeavors as vocational education.

We don't know as much for certain about the present state of vocational education as we do about its past, but we aren't completely in the dark either. Among the certainties is that occupation preparation needs to go on in a variety of ways if we are to adequately address a variety of personal and occupational needs. The major preparatory modes are on-the-job training, other forms of training by business and industry (the largest of all in this list), private training institutions, formal education in the public high schools and colleges, the sundry curricula provided by the several branches of the military, special federal/state intervention type programs, and self-planned learning totally controlled by individuals (and that we know very little about because of its private nature). There is an optimum (and second best) way for each person to acquire the knowledge and skills one requires for the work world. What is best for one is not necessarily the most desirable or efficient for another individual. Society is charged with the responsibility of helping all persons to find and pursue their best vehicle in their quest. Having no pat formulae, we aren't quite certain of the best approaches to helping each citizen in the processes of job decision making, preparation, job seeking, job retention, upgrading and updating, and job changing (Gilli, 1981). It is tempting to use the rear-mirror approach: look back to see what worked best in an earlier time and do it again. In such cases, we need to be careful to see that the people involved have the same characteristics as the earlier ones—the critical ingredient in the entire effort. But careful utilization of previous experiences can be an effective platform from which to launch out to serve present day people in the various approaches to vocational education preparation.

The future is most ambiguous of the trilogy, more so than the present and very much more than the past. It is analogous to an equation in which we have yet to uncover the value or limits of every variable. Each of these elements is sure to have an effect upon vocational education of the future. Several components in this equation are known, to some degree. First among these is that the kind and amount of vocational education made available will be in response to cultural demands—some of which will be contradictory. Secondly, but of equal long-term importance, the need to provide a virtual kaleidoscope of education formats for employment preparation within the various stages (beginning with exploratory activities on to job changing) on a lifetime basis, although strategies and implementations will likely undergo major alterations continually, even including its very name. Beyond these two broad suppositions, it is indeed risky to predict what lies ahead.

The use of regression analysis techniques, as sophisticated as they may be, are applicable only if variables employed in the analysis are those that will indeed influence the future. And that, we simply do not know. But this isn't cause for despair; a touch of uncertainty adds a little bit of spice to life and the way our universe operates. Life has always been such that we move from a region of clear definition (the past-present) toward chaos (the uncertain and unclear future). Some consolation may be found in the realization that this is the way it has always been, and, in retrospect, we have managed to muddle through with provision of at least somewhat relevant and appropriate vocational education up to now. Those of us who possess some degree of self confidence and faith in what is coming up in the future feel we will do at least as well in the years to come. But we can do even better than that, if we can learn to better utilize lessons from the past.

Every solution arrived at in vocational education has unfailingly generated new situations that gave birth to additional needs, and another family of challenges. There is no way for us to perfectly prepare for the unknown consequences that are forced by previous decisions ad infinitum. In the final analysis, our anticipation of the next set of demands will be more subjective than rational—we can only "guesstimate" and conjecture about what is ahead and bank on making the right decisions. There are such things as "good" guesses; they are the mental ventures that emerge from a wisely concocted amalgam of intuitions and comparisons of what we are responding to with a selected group of similar past sets of circumstances. Expressing this in another manner, we need to learn how to more wisely use our empirical information.

Utilizing Past Trends in Vocational Education to Interpret Present Developments

The statement above leads to a very powerful conclusion: The more knowledge about previous related circumstances and their attendant factors we have at our command, the greater the intelligence we can employ on our futuristic ventures. We have to be smart enough to recognize upcoming situations that fit past vocational education treatments and incorporate our experiences into them, and factor out all the other past events that are irrelevant. The fact that a given response was satisfactory in an earlier situation should not be the unconditional basis for applying it again. This contention is a major basis for the claim that historical information is critical for the formation of future plans in vocational education.

Present developments are only temporarily contemporary; tomorrow will find them among the ever growing cluster of past events, and they will be filed with their predecessors in our historical archives.

We need to record these events in forms that can be useful to future generations.

Some of us may believe that the ideal present situation would be one that has evolved in a gradual manner over a space of years, based on the implementation of decisions which led to clearcut outcomes. For example, it would be "nice" to be able to predict the following:

1. Spending more money per student increases the quality of vocational education;
2. Business and industry can always predict the major changes in required training prior to the time it is needed;
3. Work place surveys can accurately determine the number of workers needed in each of the occupational fields;
4. Vocational educators with the greatest amount of out-of-school work experience become the best teachers.

Although some people treat the above as truisms, they are not. There is sufficient evidence to prove their validity in some situations and not so in other circumstances. If they only were, our lives in laying the groundwork for tomorrow's vocational education delivery system would be simplified. But, on the contrary, each of the statements embrace some truth, the amount being dependent upon each situation. The accuracy of any of these statements is determined by the net influence of a myriad of elements in any given vocational education setting. The factors involved (some fixed and others changing over time) intermingle in complex interrelationships that can be different from one place to another, and even from one time to another in the same location. Our best response may be to draw judgments on the basis of known facts for a particular place and point in time, from which cautious predictions are proffered.

For example, "throwing money at vocational education" can only guarantee that more money will be spent. If it is to improve the quality of the process and student outcomes, then a number of measures need to be taken to see that the process is indeed changed for the better, and the increased funds could be the mechanism through which such alterations can be made. The past has shown us, for example, that a "caring" teacher can overcome many other obstacles, such as limited facilities. On the other hand, a teacher with such a viewpoint, while lacking in ability to help students to acquire the skills and knowledge deemed needed, will graduate students with skills that fall short of those cited in the instructional objectives. Furthermore, a good teacher must also be a good classroom manager. Add to these other elements too numerous to mention here. All of this requires us to continue to seek ways to help instructors to acquire the many desirable attributes needed for the particular set of circumstances. This also requires funding—and on and on. We can go through the other statements above (and many others not made) in a similar manner, but our single example suffices to show that using the past trends and experiences to make accommodations for the future is indeed a complicated but necessary endeavor.

Today's Groundwork for Tomorrow's Vocational Education History

Our present status in the sciences and culture as a whole have come about because we have come to a better understanding of the world around us. That in turn is fed back into the acquisition of more knowledge, leading to continued progress. An important component in this development has been the creation of instruments that better enable us to see, feel, and interpret people, places, things, and relationships. For example, Newton came up with the calculus, which opened a wide vista for him and later scientists to understand a rich variety of mechanical relationships. Presently, we are busy trying to invent instruments to further study the opposite ends of our reality—macrocosmos and microcosmos. We have some sense of the territory in between those limits—we know the "lay of the land," so to speak. Many of the future instruments will be cognitive in nature, the most obvious being new mathematical techniques that are made possible by great advances in computer processes.

Vocational education lies well within the center of those limits of the macro and micro explorations. But that doesn't mean our search for new methods and knowledge can be put to rest. Indeed, there are many important actions that can be taken in the interest of making vocational education more "successful." We, too, like scientists and philosophers, need to develop new cognitive instruments and to hone those we already possess, in the interest of continual improvement in the service we provide.

We would be better able to profit from past experiences in vocational education (that is, to base some of our present actions upon such knowledge) if we knew more about what really went on in the process. But, for the most part, we don't really know what students thought about and how they responded to their training and vocational courses during the time they were engaged in the process. The time has come to take steps to obtain such knowledge of today's students. Knowing answers to certain deep questions relating to the actual ongoings during the teaching-learning experiences would improve the chances of finding what needs to be done to improve the process at the classroom-shop level. Being aware of what we would like to have known about the past in vocational education provides us with knowledge of what we should begin to gather now, so that future vocational educators can utilize today's recordings in their planning.

Perhaps from the very day the first person was placed in a teaching-learning situation (likely a "me show—you copy" technique), the participants from both sides of the teacher-student axis knew (or at least intuited) that the attitudes of the people involved in the process were the catalytic elements. Some time later, formal descriptions for the concern were formulated—largely around such concepts as teacher motivation and student motivation.

A critical cognitive instrument for education as a whole, and vocational education specifically, is the probing into how all persons involved perceive the sundry components in their school environment. We have learned over the years that such things do indeed matter. It is one of the reasons longitudinal and cross-section studies of vocational program graduates and dropouts, of their teachers, parents, and employers, have been conducted.

There are risks in such "remembering." From the students' point of view, liking and respecting instructors, subjects, and classroom and school environments are important cluster variables in the learning equation. Although a number of well designed studies have been conducted that ask graduates about these elements, we haven't done nearly enough to probe into what and how learners feel about all these elements while they are in school. Among the dangers found in asking graduates about their views "back then" is that some degree of mental "filtering out," the product of memory fragility and adjustments made due to maturation, is certain to have taken place. Requests that old experiences be reexamined means they will be reviewed through the "new" eyes of a more mature and older person, whose rear-view mirror type vistas of the matter are invariably colored and even changed by virtue of experiences acquired through additional schooling and employment after the time in question. There is even a likelihood that, in reflecting about previous school experiences, the responders "forgot" some of their less mature reactions that may have had major effects on their schooling at the time. Waiting until years after going through a vocational program before asking the receivers to comment on selected aspects of the experience may introduce a screening effect (intentional to some extent, but also unconscious) that masks those seemingly little ingredients in the students' lives that were helping and hindering the process of their vocational education.

Anecdotal Records

Can we do something about the shortcoming of inaccurate determination of such components in their teaching-learning situation before it's all over? The answer is yes. It calls for the utilization of a cognitive instrument, one that has been in existence for a long time, but not often used beyond the early elementary school grades (and in many cases, not used very effectively in those situations either). It is the keeping of anecdotal records. The data and information obtained and stored in such efforts could become the base data for in-depth analyses of learning by vocational education students.

Anecdotal record keeping, to be a most effective information gathering and storage technique for tomorrow's historical data of the kind that can be analyzed and thereby interpreted for projecting techniques to be used in vocational education, should be based on addressing carefully selected concerns. These ought to revolve around a number of items. Primary among these are the ones that deal with each student's initial achievement level, social-economic characteristics, week by week interest in schooling, the sustained level of regard and respect for schooling and the teachers, interest in the vocational subjects being taken, quality of interactions with peers and others in the school setting, treatment of facilities and equipment, attitude toward control, and acceptance of responsibility for his actions.

Even after such delimitation, there will be bad and good anecdotal record management unless specific measures are taken. Those kept in a perfunctory way, simply to meet requirements imposed by administrators, will be useless, or at best of only limited applicability for future utilization. How can assurances of keeping good records of this type be obtained? There are several approaches that may help.

First, prior to imposing the requirement upon the faculty, it is imperative that their work schedules be modified so that the task is integrated into their duties, and not seen as an "add on" (which would be a sure death knell for the effort). Admittedly, this may indeed be the major drawback to its implementation, but the matter needs to be addressed up front. Anecdotal record keeping needs to be treated as part of teacher "planning time." Set-aside time should be arrived at through negotiations. Fifteen minutes per week for maintaining anecdotal records for each student is a realistic allocation for the activity. In other words, with twenty students, a weekly total of five hours should be provided—time that should be spread over the entire week, preferably not at one sitting.

Second, "how to do it" instructor training is a must. The inservice should be imbued with the belief that using the acecdotal record approach would heighten instructor awareness of the melange of classroom transactions that transpire, from which teaching improvements can evolve. Teachers need to be shown what items and thoughts should be included and excluded in the observational part of this venture. But merely telling them what to watch for, and how to observe, doesn't go nearly far enough. In the beginning, the anecdotal record keeping should be coached and critiqued by competent professionals who are masters of the process. Worthy of consideration in this regard is the possibility of teachers providing weekly oral anecdotal information to counselor-type individuals who would, through careful questioning, screen out the debris from what is really at the heart of the matter and insert the germane information into the student's anecdotal record. Such a technique, on a school-wide basis, is presently uncommon or non-existent. In spite of that, it can be an effective strategy that can: (a) set the stage for picking up the important soundings of the classroom happenings, and (b) provide a thorough recording of the findings before they are lost or forgotten.

Third, stress needs to be laid on the need to record those observations that shed light on the day-to-day actions that directly relate to student learning progress; and this includes the negative as well as positive ones. Teacher views of student attitudes, a mixture of subjective and objective reporting, are important to record as they surely color all teaching-learning exchanges. Striving for strict objectivity from the teacher could negate much of the usefulness of anecdotal record keeping, as some of what goes on with students is not of an overt nature, but "sensed" or intuited by observant instructors. These are among the thoughts that need to be preserved, as they lend the most insight into the heart of what education is about. An analogy will help to illuminate our next point. It is commonly believed by the uninitiated that honey bees are among the hardest workers in the world. That conclusion has been drawn by countless observers because bees are seen as constantly flying and buzzing around. Lately, however, intense observation of them by apiarians has discovered that, while the bees are supposedly procuring pollen, they are actually spending more than half of the efforts in just "killing time" by flying about in a random manner (Hubbell, 1988). The same can be said about students in classroom and shop settings: The differentiation of mere student activity from those actions that are truly integral to achieving school goals needs to be made. Therefore, a third prerequisite to good anecdotal record keeping is astute observations by faculty of their charges. Inservice for teachers in this area of expertise is sorely needed. Much of the encoding of the data by programmers can be done within carefully pre-established categories, so as to enable the information to be analyzed later.

Fourth, anecdotal record keeping should be monitored and supervised on a weekly basis by a qualified person. In this way, teachers who are straying from the desired obervational mode can be guided back on course. The utilization of a counselor-type person to work with each teacher would be an effective way to install a continual quality-control facet in the activity.

Fifth, the weekly records should be translated into a pre-planned computer file with a minimum of delay. Each student's identification should be coded to assure privacy. Such transfers should take place shortly after the records for the week have been reviewed and found to be in order. Early in the planning of this important activity, with involvement of persons knowledgeable of computer programming and statistics, the major components being recorded should be translated into numbers and/or letters so their storage in the computer file will be in a suitable form for future statistical analysis. This means that the type of statistics to be incorporated (such as multiple regression and other methods) must be decided upon *in advance*. It is critical that this matter be attended to prior to any attempt to acquire and store information in computer files. The first purpose of the entire activity being described here is to be able to store data relating to student behaviors and attitudes relative to their vocational schooling in ways that are easily retrievable, from which the information can be examined and utilized in predetermined statistical techniques. That leads to the ultimate objective of the whole activity: to provide a means to incorporate this anecdotal-derived knowledge into retrievable and forms that can be used in planning future vocational education efforts. Thus, we come to the best way, in my judgment, in which historical information can be used in improving vocational education up ahead.

The contention here is that the attitudes and other mental postures of learners while they are in the school environment, which is the time they are carrying all the actual mental and emotional baggage associated with their learning, is more predictive of future outcomes than what they say about these experiences later on in their lives.

Teacher Diaries

The daily thoughts of teachers are of great value as well. A review of instructors' views regarding their day-to-day classroom experiences is another way for uncovering factors that affect the processes of vocational education (both good and bad). The notion of asking teachers to maintain daily diaries of their thoughts about their classroom life is not as far fetched as it may at first seem. Chances are that a number of vocational educators keep diaries of some sort or another anyway. It obviously wouldn't work to demand such an activity from every teacher, but offering inducements to some of them to do so would be worth checking out. Again, the purpose is to pick up the soundings of the teachers with regard to certain pre-identified factors. In that respect, it could be considered a "directed diary keeping" activity. The programming concerns expressed earlier would be of great importance here, as such data would be analyzed, particularly in conjunction with that derived from anecdotal records, to identify both causal and casual relationships between selected elements in the teaching-learning equation.

Another important inclusion in the teacher journal would be a place where the faculty person could record free-flowing thoughts about the school situation that come to mind but fall outside the rubric of prescribed items. Such a provision enables the instructors to record other concerns that enter the schooling scene that, while they fall beyond the parameters of the present outline, are considered by the instructor as having significant impact on the teaching situation at the time.

Helping Teachers Deal with Change

History has revealed to us that many persons are loath to make changes in their work style and activities. Studies on the adoption of innovations show that teachers fall among the distribution of the normal curve when it comes to taking on something new in the classroom. Vocational educators are no exception to this phenomenon. Instructors can quietly make a proposed change "fail" when they decide to do so—which is likely to occur when they perceive the change as being of no value to them or their educational objectives (Gilli, 1976). Educators' range of rate of adoption of new practices fall along the normal curve distribution—one extreme is comprised of teachers who are quick to learn about a new development and incorporate it in their work (innovators), to the opposite end of the curve where lie those faculty who are likely never to incorporate the change (laggards is the kindest word that can be applied to them). The majority of vocational educators fall between the two extremes, which translates to there being elements of acceptance and rejection simultaneously present in the attitudes of most vocational teachers when it comes to integrating new ideas or practices into their school practices.

There are relatively good ways to deal with this reality. An important strategy to put into effect is to establish the means for well-respected innovative instructors to master the new developments, followed by making provisions for them to gradually teach and coax their cohorts into adopting the innovation. Most successful adoptions are made from the "inside," and not by introducing outsiders to push for it. Even under the best of circumstances, a sizable number of the faculty will not incorporate the innovation into their professional practices, but it's the best way we know of at the moment.

What We Can Learn from Parents while Students Are in School

Parents are a source of information about the educational situation of their offspring. Carefully designed and conducted interviews with and surveys of parents, perhaps randomly selected if obtaining access to all of them is not feasible, is a valuable source of information for present evaluation and future planning. Certain factors related to parents, including their attitudes toward selected components in their child's vocational education situation, could serve as important elements for statistical analysis. The outcome of this effort when controlled for reliability and validity, in conjuction with other knowledge, would be uncovering certain facets that could be factored into planning for future programs.

As an obvious example, parents displaying a negative attitude toward their offspring's enrollment in a particular vocational program, coupled with items picked up by other information gathering approaches, can be made to reveal critical relationships that affect the student's educational outcomes. Again, such relationships must be hypothesized beforehand, so that the elements to be searched for in parental contacts are known and understood at the onset.

What We Can Learn from Employers Immediately after Graduates Begin Work

A critical moment in the career development of graduates occurs when they begin their first full-time job. Within a few months of that important event, an interview with the work supervisor, again with carefully pre-identified questions in mind, can provide valuable information that would hark back to strengths and shortcomings of the graduate's vocational programs. Observations of the job supervisor's attitudes toward the new worker are important inclusions in the verbal scans, as they can be incorporated in the analysis leading to predetermined relationships between school preparation and transition to the work environment.

Using Historical Data to Improve Future Vocational Education

A master scheme for utilizing the acquired information for planning future vocational programs can be based on the statistical treatment of the data acquired through the historical approach discussed here (e.g., use of anecdotal records, teacher diaries, interviews and surveys of parents and employers, and longitudinal cross sectional surveys of graduates).

The wise use of historical information, which in effect is empirical in nature, is an excellent method to keep vocational education viable, and to make it even more pertinent to the world at hand for our students in the future.

Hazards and Limitations

Several caveats are in order. Predictions, based on solid statistical analysis of the historical information, are usually sufficiently modest (the chances of mispredicting can be easily provided within the parameters of the chosen statistical techniques employed). The user must always add the precaution that the answers obtained are based on the information drawn upon, which is limited in accuracy for a host of reasons.

On the other hand, overly modest use of statistical and other knowledge obtained from the historical method can mute the usefulness of hard earned findings. The user needs to step out and apply the findings within the acceptable limits—no more and no less.

Conclusions

The present contains countless elements of the past, some of which stand out on their own, and others that form at least part of the foundation for other components in our vocational settings. The future will be the result of these same factors of yesteryears, joined in various combinations with a host of contemporary elements in vocational education. We cannot escape the result of actions taken before our time, and this will continue to be true in the future.

Since so much of vocational education is an outcome of what was done to it, and with it, by others before now, it behooves us to establish careful records of the present vocational education process, through use of the devices mentioned above. This would set the stage for our successors to plan for the continuation of vocational education in the most effective ways. The wise utilization of this historical method depends, first of all, on the smart recording of contemporary facts while they are extant, so our successors can subject them to analyses from which they may incorporate them into their planning. This is how history can be used to improve vocational education of the future. The time to start has already begun. ☐

References

Berlin, I. (1988). On the pursuit of the ideal. *The New York Review of Books* 35(4), 11-18.

Burnham, W. (1984). Bridges & boundaries. *The New York Review of Books* 33(21 & 22), 40-41.

Gilli, A. C., Sr. (1976). *Modern organizations of vocational education*. University Park, PA.: Penn State.

─── (1980). *Education for work*. Elmsford, NY: Collegium.

─── (1981). *At the crossroads: where do I go from here?* Elmsford, NY: Collegium.

─── (1988). *Public education in Queen Anne's County, MD.: 1723-1980*. Unpublished manuscript.

─── *(1973). Principles of post-secondary vocational education.* Columbus, OH.: Merrill.

Hubbell, S. (1988). *A book of bees*. New York: Random House.

Keen, N. (1987). Neediest cases. *The New York Review of Books* 33 (21 & 22), 42-43.

O'Brien, M. (1988). On transcending the mollusk: Cosmpolitanism and historical discourse. *The Gettysburg Review* 1(3), 457-72.

Sprinthall, N. A. & Thies-Sprinthall, L. (1983). The teacher as an adult learner: A cognitive-developmental view. *Staff Development* 82(2), 13-35.

Talbott, J. E. (1972). Education in intellectual and social history. *Historical Studies Today*, 193-210. New York: Norton.

CHAPTER 11

Issues in Vocational Education Research

By Curtis R. Finch and John H. Hillison

MANY persons, particularly education practitioners, view research as a necessary or even unnecessary evil. They perceive the research process as something conducted with little thought to program improvement. In fact, research is alive and well and contributing to the improvement of vocational education. Although there has not been as much relevant research conducted as would be hoped, studies completed over the years have made significant contributions to the betterment of vocational education. (See, for example, Finch & O'Reilly, 1988; Asselin & Finch, 1988).

This chapter focuses on the past, present, and continuing role of vocational education research.

Spirit of Research Past

Consideration is first given to the heritage of vocational education research, including a relatively recent history of the research movement. This is followed by a glimpse at the current status and alternate futures for vocational education research. And last, a set of issues associated with future research are presented and discussed. Each issue provides food for thought in terms of future research activities.

Many sources of influence have flavored the world of vocational education research. Among these are legislative influence, methodological influence, and various uses of scholarship and inquiry in the field.

Legislative Influence

Legislative influence has evolved primarily from federal involvement in vocational education. Much research-related legislation was established as a part of various vocational acts; however, the earliest influence emanated from the Federal Department of Education. Established in 1867, 50 years before passage of the Smith-Hughes Act, this department was charged with responsibility for data collection and dissemination of statistics (Evans, 1967). The purpose of this data collection and dissemination was to indicate the progress and condition of education in the states and territories (Evans, 1967). Such responsibilities were later assumed by the Office of Education and more recently by the current Department of Education.

The Smith-Hughes Act of 1917 did not provide funding specifically for research efforts in vocational education. However, extensive statistical reports were required by the Act. An example of such reports was the annual report prepared by the Federal Board for Vocational Education. This report included statistical information about each vocational service area, publications, progress by states, and other related information (*Second Annual Report*, 1918). The Barden Act of 1946 also permitted support of studies and reports concerning administration and management of vocational education (Evans, 1967). The Act specified ". . . for securing necessary educational information and data as a basis for the proper development of programs of vocational education and vocational guidance" (Vocational Education Act, 1946, p. 1).

The Cooperative Research Act of 1954 had as its purpose ". . . to make grants to, and contracts with, public and private institutions, agencies, and organizations for the dissemination of information, for surveys, for exemplary projects in the field of education . . ." (*Cooperative Research Act*, 1954). This Act called for the Commissioner of Education to establish a 15-member advisory council on research and development, including members with expertise in the field of educational research and development or related fields. The Act was renewed by Congress several times and functioned through the 1970s. This Act was most significant because when funded in 1956 it represented the federal government's first commitment to educational research beyond data collection and dissemination (Evans, 1967). The Vocational Education Act (VEA) of 1963 set a major precedent for funding research and development in vocational education. The 10 percent set aside for research activities provided a stimulus for conducting research in vocational education (Miller, 1985). Part C of the 1968 VEA amendments supported research, demonstration, and curriculum development. A 50-50 split was made of part C funds that permitted the Commissioner of Education to make grants to state agencies while the second 50 percent was controlled by each state board in accordance with the state plan. The Commissioner's 50 percent could be used for : (a) research in vocational education, (b) training programs to familiarize people in vocational education with research findings and pilot and demonstration projects, (c) experimental, developmental, and pilot programs, (d) demonstration and dissemination projects, (e) development of new vocational education curricula, and (f) projects in the development of new careers (*Vocational Education Amendments*, 1968).

Methodological Influence

The influence of research methodology on vocational education research is as varied as its legislative counterpart. Today's vocational education research comes from a heritage rooted primarily in the fields of educational psychology, general education, and agriculture. A typical early educational psychology study involving humans used twins as subjects, matching as a basis for equating subjects and using correlation coefficients for analysis. Wingfield and Sandiford (1928) noted that a study conducted by Galton as early as 1883 used both identical and fraternal twins, which produced data lacking in objectivity, but ". . . nevertheless his main conclusions have stood the test of time" (p. 276). Wingfield and Sandiford (1928) also noted that E. L. Thorndike conducted extensive research with twins. In one 1905 study they noted that Thorndike ran correlations between twins, and between twins and siblings on certain mental skills such as addition, multiplication, and spelling. He reported r scores ranging from .29 to

.90 with twins having the higher relationship.

By 1926 Burks was warning educational psychologists about the use of correlations. Her major concern was with researchers who used correlational statistics to explain causation. She reported, "Logical considerations lead to the conclusion that the techniques of partial and multiple correlation are fraught with dangers that seriously restrict their applicability" (p. 532).

During the 1920s, educational researchers began to be influenced by educational psychologists. At this time, educational researchers also used descriptive research methodology quite extensively.

Schwegler and Winn (1920) conducted a descriptive study in which they matched children by chronological age and attempted "to study the relative intelligence of white and colored children by the use of scientifically reliable devices." (pp. 838-39) Their bibliography contained citations for eight references (out of a total of 17) for either psychology or educational psychology.

A relatively early example of experimental research in an educational setting was a matching study conducted by Leonard (1930) in which he attempted to determine the value of special practice sessions. He determined differences between groups by examining mean scores.

Barr (1931) reported several examples of the use of correlation coefficients in educational research. He noted "the literature of education contains numerous correlation studies of the factors constituting or conditioning different products and abilities, such as the studies of arithmetical ability, etc." (p. 57). He further noted that "it is difficult to know which factor is the cause, and which the effect or that the obtained correction is not due to a common factor, or to coincidence" (p. 57).

As would be expected, vocational education researchers have been influenced by researchers in educational psychology and general education. The heritage of matching, correlation, and early attempts at experimental methodology all appeared in vocational education research until more sophisticated experimental design and statistics were drawn from the field of agriculture.

Because the Hatch Act of 1887 provided federal funds for the land-grant agricultural experiment stations, agricultural research grew in popularity and became quite sophisticated. Educational research had to evolve past the use of matching and heavy use of correlation coefficients before it could fully appreciate the more sophisticated agricultural research and put it to use. By the late 1930s and early 1940s this step was being taken. As part of his work at the Rothampsted Experimental Station, R. A. Fisher identified the need for a better means of equating agricultural experimental plots and the need for a more sophisticated way to analyze the data obtained from experiments. Fisher (1937) described using a deck of cards numbered 1-100 and a table of random numbers. As early as 1926 he used randomization in a field study examining the influence of nitrogen on oat yields (Eden & Fisher, 1927). Campbell and Stanley (1963) described the importance of randomization to the field of educational research. They indicated that "Perhaps Fisher's most fundamental contribution has been the concept of achieving pre-experimental equation of groups through randomization" (p. 2).

The agricultural research field also helped to develop and popularize several important experimental research designs now commonly used by vocational education researchers. One such design is the post-test-only design. It was generally impractical to collect pretest data on either crop plots or livestock. Many prominent agricultural researchers such as Fisher, Snedecor, and Yates used post-test-only designs extensively. The Latin square design was used at an early time by Thorndike, McCall, and Chapman (Campbell & Stanley, 1963). However, Fisher popularized its use in agricultural experimentation. Researchers in agriculture had a common problem with varying soil types that the Latin square design helped eliminate. Other designs used by vocational education researchers that can be credited to pioneering work in agriculture include the factorial design and the missing plot design (initially used in agronomy experiments with plots of land). The randomized block design was named ". . . because of its parallel to agricultural experimentation, in which randomization is performed within blocks of land" (Lev, 1948, p. 414).

With randomization and sophisticated design being commonly used, agricultural researchers could employ sophisticated statistics to analyze their data. Fisher published information about analysis of variance as early as 1916. In fact, the F ratio was named in Fisher's honor. By the 1930s, researchers funded by Hatch Act experiment station funds were frequently using analysis of variance. Lindquist

(1940) called for educational researchers to pay more attention to agricultural research and statistics. He noted "... a thorough training in the use of the methods of analysis of variance should be considered an absolute essential in the general preparation of research students in education (p. v)."

Educational researchers, including those in vocational education paid attention to such suggestions. Today, researchers utilize research designs and statistics that are as sophisticated as colleagues' in other fields. Vocational education research, as a part of educational research, has a rich history. It is the product of legislative encouragement and methodological influence from research conducted in the fields of educational psychology, general education, and agriculture.

Spirit of Research Present

Present day research continues to draw upon funding available at the federal level as part of the Carl D. Perkins Act, which includes funding for the National Center for Research in Vocational Education. Research conducted in the field continues to show its heritage of descriptive influence with some experimental design being employed and a new interest being shown in qualitative procedures.

Recognizing that vocational education research does little good if it is not shared with consumers, avenues for dissemination such as the Educational Resources Information Center presently exist. Several service area specific organizations meet at different times throughout the year and devote a portion of the their agendas to research reports. However, a number of organizations and journals play a prominent role in encouraging the conduct and dissemination of vocational education research.

Organizations

The American Vocational Education Research Association (AVERA) held its first annual meeting on December 16, 1966. V. E. Burgener, chair pro-tem of the steering committee, presided over the meeting, which was held in Denver, Colorado. The Association has grown since that time to over 300 members from research centers, universities, and state departments of education across the United

States. Its purposes are to stimulate vocational research and development activities, stimulate the development of vocational research training programs, encourage cooperative efforts in vocational research, and facilitate the dissemination of vocational education research findings (*Operating Policies*, 1986). AVERA holds its annual meetings as the research section of the New and Related Services Division of the American Vocational Association.

A Special Interest Group sponsored by AVERA was established on February 7, 1968. At that time the AVERA executive committee decided to petition the American Educational Research Association to form the Vocational and Technical Education Special Interest Group. The present Vocational Education Special Interest Group meets annually at the American Educational Research Association annual meeting.

Journals

Several scholarly journals have helped stimulate the conduct and dissemination of vocational education research. Both general across-the-board journals and journals specific to traditional vocational service areas encourage research in the field.

The Delta Pi Epsilon Journal was established on a trial basis in 1957. It was made a permanent publication at the 1959 Delta Pi Epsilon National Council meeting. The *Journal* is now recognized as the leading refereed research journal in business education.

The *Journal of Agricultural Education* was initiated in 1961 as *The Journal of The American Association of Teacher Educators in Agriculture*. In 1975 the *Journal* became a refereed publication. It is considered the primary source of refereed articles for teacher educators in agricultural education.

The *Journal of Vocational and Technical Education* was established by the National Council of Omicron Tau Theta in 1984. It is a refereed journal that publishes articles emphasizing vocational education philosophy, theory, research, and practice. Its purpose is to serve as a vehicle for communication within the entire profession of vocational education.

The *Marketing Educators' Journal* was started in 1975 as the *Distributive Educators' Digest* and is sponsored by the Marketing Education Association. The purpose of the *Marketing Educators' Jour-*

nal is to provide a means to communicate research findings and research-related information about marketing education. The *Journal* is a refereed publication and the major research journal for marketing educators at the pre-baccalaureate and marketing teacher education levels.

The *Journal of Vocational Home Economics Education* was established in 1983. This refereed journal has as its major purpose disseminating research findings to home economics education teacher educators and others in the field such as state and local supervisors. The *Journal* was created to facilitate communication among members of the home economics education profession and the vocational education community at large. It is published by the National Association of Teacher Educators for Vocational Home Economics.

The *Journal of Studies in Technical Careers* was started in 1978. It is a refereed journal emphasizing research, theory, and concerns for postsecondary vocational-technical education. The *Journal* is published by the College of Technical Careers, Southern Illinois University at Carbondale.

The Occupational Education Forum has been published biannually since 1973 under the sponsorship of Alpha Chapter, Iota Lambda Sigma. It is currently published at Virginia Polytechnic Institute and State University. The *Forum* is a refereed journal devoted to professional reports in practical arts, vocational, and technical education.

The Journal of Vocational Education Research was founded in 1976 with the purpose of serving as a communication link with the vocational education research community. It is sponsored by the American Vocational Education Research Association (AVERA). The *Journal* contains refereed articles reporting vocational education research and theoretical issues in the field.

The Journal of Industrial Teacher Education was established in 1963. It is published by the National Association of Industrial and Technical Educators. This refereed journal reports scholarly inquiry and commentary broadly related to industrial and technical teacher education, military training, and industrial training.

As may be noted, most journals have been established since 1960, with many emerging in the 1970s and 1980s. Research-based articles are thus a rather recent addition to the vocational education field.

Vocational education researchers are fortunate to have numerous outlets for the dissemination of research findings. This information sharing keeps the field abreast of the latest information and also encourages continued research.

Spirit of Research Future

Predicting what the future will hold is at best a difficult task. We do not have the confidence of ancient oracles who were respected for their comments about the future even though such statements were often far from accurate. We also lack the data necessary to make completely accurate predictions about what will be in our future. Since futuring is an inexact science, it is sometimes helpful to use methodologies that help us make better predictions. One such approach is the scenario. Scenarios present alternate outlines or synopses of the future. Interested parties may review various alternatives and decide for themselves which one seems most plausible under certain conditions (Finch, 1985).

Presented in the next several paragraphs are best case, middle of the road, and worst case scenarios for vocational education research during the next decade. They vary primarily in terms of dollars and human resources available to conduct research. In all three scenarios, general support for vocational education continues to grow at a moderate rate. Vocational education courses and programs continue to be offered in a variety of secondary and postsecondary education settings. Additionally, the economy continues to hold steady with a moderate inflation rate and a six to eight percent unemployment rate.

Best Case Scenario

The federal government had been extremely generous to vocational education research during the 1990 to 2000 time period. Support seems to have emerged from a variety of sources, each of which has contributed to the overall welfare of the field. Recognizing the value of the programmatic inquiry, federal legislation was passed in support of a national vocational education research network. In addition to continued and expanded support for the National Center for Research in Vocational Education, legislation provided for "research centers of excellence" at various comprehensive universities around the country. These centers were established so that interdisciplinary teams of researchers could seek answers to pervasive problems in the field. Each university is, in turn, linked to the National Center through a collaborative network so that duplication of effort is held to a minimum.

Research support has been provided for five year periods with renewal funding based on progress made toward problem resolution. The federal government has also provided financial support for vocational education researcher preparation. Opportunities are made available for qualified students to pursue up to three years of graduate study if they agree to work in vocational education research positions for periods equal to that of their graduate fellowships. Numerous benefits have accrued for the vocational education community. In addition to increasing graduate enrollments and establishing a cadre of vocational education researchers, there has been an opportunity to focus on some of the more significant research problems facing the field. Payoff to the field may already be seen. It has been noted that instruction provided to vocational students has improved and that the needs of special learners are better met. Likewise, universities and state departments of education have welcomed the opportunity to employ vocational educators with extensive research skills.

Middle of the Road Scenario

It might be said that vocational education research is business as usual. Although many other education areas have received increased support from the federal government, vocational education research has remained on a flat funding base. With inflation taken into account, this has, in effect, meant a five to six percent annual decrease in funding. Support for the National Center remains at a level which is barely enough to conduct meaningful programmatic research efforts. Interest in research activities remains positive but reserved.

At a few universities, long range research activities have been mounted but this is more the exception than the rule. Even less programmatic activity occurs at most state departments of education. In sum, vocational education research continues to be respected but not widely supported as a means of helping to improve the field.

Worst Case Scenario

The last several years have been extremely difficult for vocational education research. It all seemed to start when funding was reduced at the federal level. Significant cuts were not made to vocational education program funding; in fact, the vocational program budget increased. However, in terms of vocational education research, funding was cut to the bone. The situation began to snowball when various states reduced their own research and development funding with a result being that vocational education research began to be treated like a sinking ship. As research positions were dropped from universities and state departments of education, graduate students began to recognize that research-related job opportunities would be scarce. Most students eventually shifted their graduate program emphasis to more employable areas such as local level administration and community college teaching.

The net result was that interest in conducting research waned, skilled researchers ceased to be prepared, and significant research was shelved in favor of other activities. Even the editors of refereed journals became concerned. With a loss of research production, fewer manuscripts were prepared for consideration by journals. Several editors even modified various journal issues from refereed to invited articles. As would be expected, research program emphasis was reduced at national conferences and research-oriented professional organizations shifted away from research and toward more "acceptable" areas.

An Analysis

Obviously, each of the preceding scenarios presents only a brief glimpse of what the future might bring. Factors such as changes in the economy and allocation of federal funds might paint an entirely different picture. What seems to be most important, however, is the fragile nature of vocational education research. To some degree, the quality and quantity of research has been driven by federal dollars. This situation reflects a lack of significant local support available to vocational education researchers but, since federal funding does flow on a regular basis, little effort is made to build local support for research.

This delicate state of affairs extends to the type of vocational education research conducted. Periodically, a "hot" topic surfaces and monies are made available to study it. After a relatively short period of time during which little in-depth inquiry has been conducted, another topic is introduced which may supercede the current topic. Then the cycle repeats itself. Thus federal funding for research may be both a blessing and a problem, particularly if researchers desire to conduct programmatic research in a significant area.

Issues Related to Future Research

Numerous issues may be raised about the future direction of vocational education research. Most important among these seems to be the potential for investment in research activities and the ways and means by which research may be conducted.

Can research be an investment in the future? This question is most difficult to answer. Perhaps the best way to approach such a question is by saying "it depends." One must first look at the benefits derived from vocational education research. It may be easily noted that greatest benefits to the field have resulted from programmatic research efforts. Few examples of programmatic inquiry in vocational education exist, but those which come to mind include the typewriting research conducted by Leonard West, the meaning and value of work research completed by H. C. Kazanas and others, and the vocational teacher education research and development conducted by Calvin Cotrell and others. Research *can* be an investment in the future but only if researchers choose to pursue critical problems and do so in a systematic, long-term fashion.

Is programmatic research feasible? The potential does exist for conducting programmatic research. However, several difficulties must be overcome before this approach to research becomes widespread. First, many vocational education researchers are unwilling to band together and focus on finding solutions to critical problem areas. Most people, particularly those in universities, tend to conduct research associated with a relatively minor problem and then submit the results for possible publication. This is a fairly successful approach from a promotion and/or tenure standpoint, but lacks in terms of contribution to our knowledge about a significant area. Second, programmatic research lacks the immediate payoff of research focusing on short-term problems. Many do not want to toil for three to five years conducting a series of studies. They instead want to see immediate results, even though those results may have little long-term impact on the field. And finally, programmatic research must often be orchestrated by some agency or center. It is extremely difficult to conduct long-term research efforts outside of a center framework. A few research universities have been successful at such orchestration but the number is indeed small.

Can meaningful multidisciplinary research efforts be conducted? It is becoming clear that researching vocational education is a very complex task. Individuals and even groups from one field may, in fact, not have the expertise to conduct meaningful research. Enter the multidisciplinary research team. Composed of researchers from a wide variety of fields, these people may represent areas such as psychology, sociology, and anthropology in addition to vocational education. Their purpose is to plan a broadly based attack on a pervasive problem area. Of course, one may ask if such a team can be assembled and used effectively. Multidisciplinary teams have been formed at various research centers and universities and their success has been mixed. This situation stems from the fact that many vocational education researchers have behavioral science backgrounds and may not be able to communicate properly with persons from other disciplines. Some vocational education professionals are beginning to become quite proficient in the use of qualitative research methods but it may be some time before general expertise levels reach a point where multidisciplinary research is conducted on a large scale.

Who is in the best position to conduct future research? In a general sense, every vocational education professional has an opportunity to conduct research. However, when focusing on specifics, it is difficult to imagine that everyone in the field will participate in research activities. Most likely, programmatic research will be conducted by universities and research centers. Persons at these locations, with input from people at state departments of education, local education agencies, and postsecondary institutions are in the best position to do long-term research. Action research, which seeks solutions to immediate problems, will continue to be conducted at the local level. This research will tend to focus on improving curriculum and instruction in a particular educational setting.

Conclusion

This discussion has centered on issues related to vocational education research. It has been noted that vocational education research has a rich heritage drawn from the general field of educational research as well as the fields of agriculture and psychology. Recent developments in vocational education have seemed to stimulate growth in research both in terms of quantity and quality.

Today there is a great deal of research being conducted but only a small subset of this research will have significant impact on the field. The future may follow a similar path. If we accept a worst case scenario, little research will be conducted. However, a best case scenario paints a very bright picture for the field. If an optimistic picture is the most realistic one, we should reap numerous benefits in terms of improved instruction and learning. Although we cannot predict what will actually happen, it is hoped that the future will provide an environment that is more conducive to the conduct of high quality, programmatic research efforts. Such a vision is not too much to ask. ☐

References

Asselin, S. B. & Finch, C. R. (1988). Preparation and roles of vocational special needs teachers: A research review. *Journal of Vocational Education Research, 13* (4).

Barr, A. S. (1931). The coefficient of correlation. *Journal of Educational Research, 23* (1), 55-60.

Burks, B. S. (1926). On the inadequacy of the partial and multiple correlation technique. *The Journal of Educational Psychology, 17* (8), 532-90.

Campbell, D. T. & Stanley, J. C. (1963). *Experimental and quasi-experimental designs for research.* Chicago: Rand McNally College Publishing Co.

Cooperative Research Act (1954). Public Law 531, 83rd Congress. Washington, DC: U. S. Government Printing Office.

Eden, T. & Fisher, R. A. (1927). The experimental determination of the value of top dressings with cereals. *Journal of Agricultural Science, 17,* 548-62.

Evans, R. N. (ed.) (1967). *Assessing vocational education research and development*. Washington, DC: National Academy of Sciences.

Finch, C. R. (1985). Future oriented methodologies: Implications for applied research. *Journal of Vocational and Technical Education, 1* (2), 3-10.

Finch, C. R. & O'Reilly, P. A. (1988). Trade and industrial teacher education research: Status and prospects. *Journal of Industrial Teacher Education, 26* (1), 19-37.

Fisher, R. A. (1937). *The design of experiments*. Edinburgh: Oliver and Boyd.

Leonard, J. P. (1930). The use of practice exercises in teaching capitalization and punctuation. *Journal of Educational Research, 21* (3), 186-90.

Lev, J. (1948). Research methods and designs. *Review of Educational Research, 18* (5), 410-23.

Lindquist, E. F. (1940). *Statistical analysis in educational research*. Boston: Houghton Mifflin Company.

Miller, M. D. (1985). *Principles and a philosophy for vocational education*. Columbus, OH: The National Center for Research in Vocational Education.

Operating policies and procedures. American Vocational Education Research Association (1986).

Second Annual Report of the Federal Board for Vocational Education (1918). Washington, DC: U. S. Government Printing Office.

Schwegler, R. A., & Winn, E. (1920). A comparative study of the intelligence of white and colored children. *Journal of Educational Research, 2* (5), 838-48.

Vocational education act of 1946. 20 USC 11-15 (1946). Washington, DC: U. S. Government Printing Office.

Vocational education amendments of 1968 (1968). P.L. 90-576. Washington, DC: U. S. Government Printing Office.

Wingfield, A. H. & Sandiford, P. (1928). Twins and orphans. *The Journal of Educational Psychology, 19* (6), 410-23.

CHAPTER 12

The Image of the Profession of Vocational Education

By Lynne Gilli

EDUCATORS are regularly reminded of the cliches surrounding the public's perception of vocational education—its "second class" status, its "image problem," and its reputation for leading to dead-end, low paying jobs. These opinions have resulted from long-standing myths regarding the value and status of certain work roles, imparting a negative stigma and prejudice toward vocational education and perpetuating occupational stereotypes. The low priority given to vocational education has been reflected in the emphasis placed on the basics, while vocational programs remain largely elective rather than essential components of the high school curriculum (Copa, 1984). The "image problem" has been widely documented, but vocational educators have been ill-equipped to present a strong unified effort to promote a more constructive image.

With the failure and ultimate elimination of the Vocational Education Data System (VEDS) survey, the field lacks a national data center that supplies information needed to demonstrate the quality of vocational education programs in terms of their performance. The findings of the VEDS surveys indicated that vocational education programs fulfilled the purpose for which they were intended: to prepare people for jobs. Moreover, students graduating from vocational programs seemed to experience less unemployment than the general population of their peers (National Center for Education Statistics, 1982). But the VEDS provided no solid basis to urge people to enroll in vocational education programs. Another shortcoming of the system was its failure to produce believable enrollment data. Some sources claim that this lack of confidence was due to the fact that a majority of the states did not use automated student record systems (Hoachlander, 1988). For the most part, data in vocational education have been inaccurate and misleading (Sewall, 1987).

Authorized in 1984, the Carl D. Perkins Vocational Education Act (Public Law 98-524) drastically reduced the requirements for collecting and reporting data. The legislation requires the Center for Statistics, formerly the National Center for Education Statistics (NCES), to use sampling methods more frequently and collect information less often. Presently, there is no current information on participation in secondary vocational education programs beyond the senior class of 1982. Thus, lacking up-to-date information on contemporary students and graduates, there is no nation-wide system from which to extract reliable data that demonstrates the worth of vocational education. From follow-up data such as placement and earnings of graduates, employers' satisfaction with vocational completers, and post-high school education, a national perspective of vocational education could be developed that would help to determine its effectiveness. Accurate data collection and reporting on the outcomes of vocational education are critically important to marketing the enterprise.

The Impact of the School Reform Movement

During the 1980s, a number of studies and reports were published on the condition of education, one of the major ones titled *A Nation at Risk*. This report of the National Commission on Excellence in Education spurred unprecedented effort to improve the academic preparation of students in the public schools (Bell, 1984). Another report urging educational reform in the United States, *Investing in Our Children: Business and the Public Schools*, urged that all students be required to obtain a core of basic academic competencies before being allowed to enter a vocational course of study (Committee for Economic Development, 1985). In response to the recommendations offered in these reports, many states mandated increased academic requirements for graduation and/or minimum competency examinations, placing a major emphasis on the basics—English, mathematics, science, and social studies (Bell, 1984).

When national commissions pointed to the need for educational reform, few people recognized the value of vocational education and the contributions that it makes by developing work ethics and providing skilled workers. Instead, vocational education either was not given fair representation or was taken to task for failing to adequately prepare students for future success, both academically and in the world of work. The Panel on Secondary School Education for the Changing Workplace, in its report, said that while vocational-technical education provides specific job skills that can enhance a student's employablility, it does not replace education in the core competencies (National Academy of Sciences, 1984). Thus, the school reform movement, with its emphasis on raising basic skills and increasing graduation requirements, has in many states significantly reduced the amount of time students have for occupational education (Hoachlander, 1988).

Aside from those directly involved with the profession, few people seem concerned about the tenuous position vocational education has been placed in as a result of school reform efforts. During the movement, vocational education could not be defended in a believable manner due to lack of adequate documentation that could not be made available without the establishment of a reliable data system. Up to now, much of vocational education's claim to success has been anecodotal and testimonial in nature, not a convincing approach to use when attempting to obtain the support of hard-nosed legislators and educational decision makers.

A key factor in improving vocational education is to provide programs that strengthen students' basic skills in a measurable way. It seems apparent that vocational and academic offerings must become, and are becoming, integrated and complementary. Increasingly, vocational educators will be required to reinforce, through application, information taught in English, math, and science classes. The teaching of thinking skills, helping students to understand, process, and apply information at higher levels, will have to become a component of vocational education if it is to survive in American schools. Though many teachers may deny these responsibilities—some even claiming that they were not hired to teach basic skills—they will enhance their value and image if they are able to emphasize the basics while teaching job and employability skills. This will call for considerable retraining of present vocational teachers and a major overhaul of vocational teacher education curricula.

Professionalism in Vocational Education

The critics of the profession, many of whom are respected and influential, remain vocal and their charges include the predictable stereotypes. These stereotypes are a substitute for true analysis of what really goes on in vocational classrooms. They have managed to keep vocational programs at a low status on the educational ladder because, when there is an ounce of truth in what they are saying, it is used to cast doubt and despair on the entire profession. While this is not an attempt to list and defend all of the charges levied against vocational education, it is meant to serve notice to vocational educators of their need to become outspoken advocates of the profession. This can only be done when facts are at the disposal of educators to use in order to highlight strengths and identify weaknesses, thus leading to improvements in vocational education that will enhance its image.

To a great extent, individuals in the general public form their opinions about the quality of education in their community based upon informal discussions with educators, administrators, members of the board of education, and other school employees. Vocational educators frequently interact with representatives of the business community, often through craft committee or advisory council activities. It is unfortunate that, many times, it is through information provided by school employees that the public forms its negative opinions about schools. Efforts must be made to ensure that school personnel, including secretaries, bus drivers, and custodians, are involved in promoting an accurate and positive image of the school.

Schools offering vocational education can be very visible in a community. In fact, they may even seem indispensable by providing adult education, meeting room space, day care, and other services that people come to depend on and expect. The key to keeping vocational schools viable, now and in the future, is to remain responsible to the needs of the community by offering programs, services, and graduates that appeal to students, adults, and employers. The following statements address some of the items that must be in place to assure that vocational programs are relevant to local and statewide needs:

1. Teachers are evaluated regularly and encouraged to remain up-to-date in their area of occupational expertise. They hold credentials, such as teacher certification, and are offered opportunities for personnel development. Through effective teaching, vocational educators will enhance their image and that of their profession.

2. Secondary and postsecondary administrators strive to develop articulation agreements in similar areas of occupational instruction. Students are offered options that allow them to earn college credit while in high school, obtain advanced placement, or receive credit by examination. By being offered articulated programs, students and their parents will recognize the importance of vocational education as a path to further education. The advantages of articulated occupational programs may also lead to increased enrollments.

3. Vocational and academic teachers collaborate to develop balanced curricula—where the basics are integrated—leading students to a better understanding of the workplace (The National Commission on Secondary Vocational Education, 1984). The contents of vocational courses are analyzed to determine whether they meet requirements for credit in math or science. Vocational programs that qualify for academic credit are marketed to students, making them aware that they can earn credits in the basics toward high school graduation while enrolled in a vocational program. Whenever possible, vocational courses should be modified to provide credit toward high school graduation. For example, electronics programs can be modified to ensure that the mathematics taught is equivalent to that required for credit in high school algebra. Health occupations curricula can be written to include academic credit for biology, anatomy, physiology, or other areas depending on the level of difficulty and content of the course. By being offered vocational courses that develop basic skills, students will have more time to enroll in programs that serve the dual purpose of preparing them for work while fulfilling high school graduation requirements.

4. Vocational facilities, classrooms, and equipment are modern

and up-to-date. The environment of the school and its climate are reflective of the quality of the learning that is taking place. The building and grounds appear to be clean, students are motivated and enthusiastic, and administrators and staff members are proud of their profession. Since vocational programs often lead to employment, the ethics and habits learned in the classroom are often practiced in the workplace. By perceiving a positive and inviting climate within the school, students and community members will develop a respect for vocational education. Since teachers unconsciously transmit their beliefs to students, the faculty of occupational programs must themselves believe in vocational education as a legitimate and extremely important aspect of American education (Gillie, 1973).

5. Vocational programs are responsive to the carefully assessed needs of businesses and industries, curriculum is relevant to the existing and future labor market, and quality vocational programs are accessible to students. By being offered programs that are relevant to the labor market and to the needs of employers, graduates will be in demand and will have opportunities to obtain entry into satisfying careers.

Vocational teachers have a special problem in that changes in the occupations that they teach occur continuously—at a rate much faster than in academic fields. Despite the required commitment of time and money, ongoing efforts must be made to keep vocational teachers up-to-date in their occupational specialities and refine their teaching skills (The National Commission on Secondary Vocational Education, 1984).

Strategies to Enhance the Image of Vocational Education

Vocational educators cannot afford to let criticisms continue to go unchecked. They must abandon the "woe-is-me" attitude that has eroded the profession and become actively involved in finding ways to enhance the image of vocational education by utilizing a variety of promotional efforts. The time has come to market vocational programs in an attractive and organized manner to the public at large, especially potential students and their parents. It is not enough to tell the public that vocational education is "good"; rather it must be demonstrated in the professionalism of the teachers, the relevance of the programs, and the quality of the graduates. Along with adequate financing, these are the main factors that will help vocational education gain the public's support and recognition.

Educators and parents alike have long held beliefs regarding the relationship between education and jobs. It is generally believed that a good paying, prestigious, and satisfying job can only be attained by going to college (Silberman, 1986). Parents are usually more interested in the long-term wage earning potential of the vocation their children select to pursue, relying on schools to prepare them for the world of work. Often, that thinking includes the beliefs that the more years of education, the better the job opportunities (Woodring, 1979). While there is nothing wrong with this notion, it is important to note that many graduates of vocational programs enroll in some type of postsecondary programs (Silberman, 1987).

The challenge to vocational educators will be in convincing parents and their children that vocational education, either at the secondary or postsecondary level, can be the first step on the ladder to further education and/or a rewarding and lucrative career. One of the best ways to attract students and their parents is to demonstrate the benefits derived from enrolling in a vocational education program. For secondary students, access to quality vocational programs helps them to learn and appreciate the fundamentals of work, often by obtaining their first job. For adults and postsecondary students, vocational education either has immediate application to a job, improves or upgrades job skills, or leads to new employment opportunities (Sewall, 1987).

Published in 1989, the data reflected in the report from the Congressionally mandated National Assessment of Vocational Education (NAVE) may help to dispel some of the public myths surrounding vocational education. Since there are no national data sets pertaining to students who were in school between 1983 and 1988, the report was based on the class of 1982, the most recent class for which complete data exist. Preliminary findings indicate that about 97 percent of those students enrolled in some kind of vocational education course between the ninth and twelfth grades. However, further data from the assessment indicate rapidly declining enrollments in secondary vocational education. Even though secondary enrollments have been decreasing overall, many people claim that the increases in graduation requirements in some states have made it difficult for students to fit vocational courses in their schedules (Lewis, 1988).

Perhaps the results of the National Assessment of Vocational Education will pinpoint the actual causes of the enrollment decline and offer realistic solutions to the problem, such as integrating academic and vocational education. They may also provide justification for improving data collection and evaluation systems for vocational education. If the Congress is to chart a course for future legislation pertaining to vocational education, it is important to have information about the past and present status of the profession.

Marketing Vocational Education

Efforts to market vocational education begin with well developed internal and external communication plans. The internal plan will be targeted to the information needs of people within the school including staff and faculty members, students, board members, and members of parent/teacher associations.

The external plan will be developed around the communication needs of the target audiences indentified as important to reach by the school. They include other agencies, the news media, the general public, employers, clergy, civic leaders, parents, and non-parents, to name a few. The following suggestions are provided for developing and implementing strategies to promote a positive image of vocational education.

Developing a Marketing Plan

Marketing has been defined as delivering the right message to the right audience at the right time, resulting in positive action. On the other hand, public relations efforts build the public's confidence in the schools—thus, they are an essential building block to marketing vocational education courses. Public relations activities are conducted to demonstrate the quality of a program or build respect for a vocational school. They are part of a broad, ongoing management function aimed at earning the public support the schools need to exist. Marketing programs are more sharply focused and are designed to stimulate specific action by specific publics. Marketing efforts are conducted to move people to enroll in specific courses or programs. Both public relations and marketing programs are essential to improving the image of vocational education (National School Public Relations Association, 1987).

In order to effectively market vocational programs, a plan must be developed that outlines the specific actions that will be taken, when and where they will occur, who will carry them out, and how much money will be budgeted for the activities. Key to the success of the plan is that it contains an accurate and consistent description of the vocational program offerings. It is far worse to market a bad program than not to market it at all. One way to ensure that vocational programs are accurately portrayed is to convene a public relations or program promotion committee. The members of the committee should be charged with reviewing the mission statement, philosophy, goals, and objectives of the school system. Perhaps these documents will need to be revised in order to ensure that vocational education is part of the overall education delivery system.

Before any events are conducted to promote vocational education, a definition of marketing should be agreed upon. Next, the committee should assess the strengths and weaknesses of the vocational programs offered at the institution (quality of instruction, student enrollment, success of graduates, condition of facilities and equipment). A needs assessment, or attitude survey, can be conducted of significant people in the school and community to obtain their feedback for use in the development of a marketing plan.

It is also important to obtain demographic data that accurately reflect information about the geographic location, population spread, average levels of income and education, economic climate, types of businesses, known community leaders, and institutions of higher education. Try to establish a profile of the people living in the school district: In what age groups are residents? Do they have children in school? What is the racial composition of the community? Are residents employed in professional or paraprofessional positions? This information can often be obtained from census data. It will provide valuable information about the audiences in the market and help target those likely to be interested in educational concerns.

Demographic data can be useful in creating a match between the needs of the community and the services provided through vocational programs. The school's message must communicate the benefits of vocational education to the audience it serves. People pay attention to messages in which they recognize value to themselves (Petro & Durocher, 1988). They are less likely to be impressed with publicity pieces that appear to be self-serving puffery. The public prefers to have the quality of vocational programs and services demonstrated to them. Successful public relations programs in vocational education are those that regularly demonstrate excellence by providing services and products useful to their markets or target audiences.

This can be accomplished by compiling demographic data with other information about current enrollees in vocational programs and follow-up studies indicating the level of employers' satisfaction with graduates. This will aid in preparing a report that portrays the positive role that vocational education can play in promoting the economic development of the community and preparing graduates for employment. Since parents play such a significant role in the career choice that their children make, they should be an audience targeted to receive copies of school publications.

The findings of reports that reflect the positive contributions that vocational education can make should be available, in a published format as well as in an oral presentation, to representatives of businesses. Vocational administrators and advisory council members can develop a brief, fifteen to twenty minute presentation that can be delivered through a speakers' bureau, at club meetings, or in corporate offices.

In the future, there must be more business and industry involvement in vocational education in order to encourage and implement important elements of program improvement (Radcliffe, 1987). Partnerships between businesses and education should be mutually beneficial. Thus, communication can begin by showing corporate executives that vocational education can offer them access to qualified entry-level employees or perhaps even provide customized training programs through adult education.

Obtain Consensus and Support

It is virtually impossible to carry out a public relations plan that is not supported by the members of the staff, student body, and school leaders. They should be involved in meetings to brainstorm and indentify strategies that will communicate a positive image of vocational education in the school and community. Provide them with a background of facts and data at the onset. Inform the local board of education or board of trustees of plans to promote vocational education and involve the members of the local advisory council in the process. Interested advisors and members of vocational student organizations, or other student groups, can also provide valuable assistance in planning and conducting many public relations events. Efforts to promote vocational education should include representatives from every level in the school's hierarchy, as well as people not directly involved with the vocational school. Accept community volunteers or appoint willing business representatives to serve on a core committee for public relations or to become members of a speakers' bureau. These advocates keep vocational educators from the danger of appearing self-serving or "talking only to themselves." They can also help dispel negative stereotypes of vocational education by spreading positive messages to other social settings, both in and out of school.

Personnel Development—Improving Internal Communication

Creating a positive image of vocational education in the school and community will involve more than planning public relations activities and creating pens, mugs, notepads, calendars, and other promotional items. In order to assure that the community is aware of the quality and effectiveness of the vocational programs, students, faculty, and support staff members must be involved in the communications process. Enlist the core members of the public relations committee in efforts to plan and conduct personnel development workshops for everyone who is employed by the school including secretaries, bus drivers, maintenance workers, counselors, faculty members, and administrators.

The purposes of the workshops would be to enhance the effectiveness of both internal and external communications, reinforce the mission and purpose of the school, and encourage participants to know and be able to communicate these accurately. They also provide excellent opportunities to familiarize personnel with the public relations plan and solicit their support and recommendations. People tend to take ownership of ideas or activities for which they believe they are responsible. Promote a team attitude and take a proactive, not reactive, approach to marketing programs.

Ask faculty members to take the plan one step further by introducing it to students, obtaining their input, and identifying ways for them to become involved. Develop lesson plans that provide structure to the implementation of activities outlined in the marketing plan. Focus groups can be formed to provide input regarding attitudes and interests of targeted audiences toward vocational education. The results of these focus group meetings can be useful in planning promotional activities. Contact successful graduates to enlist their help in promoting vocational education by providing testimonials. They can help preserve or pass on the traditions and history of the vocational school, giving it a stable image within the community.

Develop an Annual and Three-Year Plan

The plan to market vocational education should include all of the promotional activities that the group considers feasible and desirable to conduct. Flesh out the plan by writing a program of work for the first year, then project a tentative one for a period of three years.

Be sure to identify the following for each activity: date and time, activity or event, goals and objectives, message and intended audience, procedure or steps involved, responsible person(s), necessary resources, and a realistic timeline and budget. Enlist volunteers and establish subcommittees to assume responsibility for carrying out selected activities that are part of the overall plan.

Calendar of Events

Prepare a calendar of events for both internal staff members and external audiences. The internal one should serve as a master calendar for all events—both internal and external. It should include the pre- and post-activity responsibilities such as scheduling facilities, borrowing equipment, ordering refreshments, inviting guests, informing the media, developing promotional materials, thanking participants, and evaluating the effectiveness of the event. Update the calendar on a monthly basis and use it to generate new ideas and continued enthusiasm.

The external calendar will serve to make the public aware of events that may be of interest to them. Publish it in the local newspaper and mail it to parents, members of the board of education, school administrators and personnel, advisory council members, politicians, and community business leaders.

Public relations must be ongoing in order to be effective. In addition to celebrating vocational education week and holding an annual open house, activities must be planned and conducted that bring people to the schools or the schools to the people (via television or radio advertisements or programs, mail displays, newspapers, magazines, newsletters, billboards, to name a few mediums).

Feedback and Evaluation

In writing the internal and external public relations plans, be sure to include methods for evaluating each activity or product that is developed. Make certain realistic outcomes are expected from the promotional efforts. Do not be too ambitious in setting goals for the first year. Patience will be required in order to assess the long-term effects of efforts to promote vocational education.

It will take several years before identifying the tangible results that might emerge from attempts to promote a positive image of vocational education (increased enrollments, enhanced cooperation with businesses and industries, advanced placement, and articulated programs with other agencies or institutions). After evaluating each activity, use the feedback to update, modify, and improve the three-year plan. Continue to involve members of the staff and student body in planning, conducting, evaluating, and refining public relations activities.

Summary

In order to communicate a positive image of vocational education, encourage anyone associated with vocational programs to dwell on the positive aspects of the school. Satisfied faculty members, students, graduates, and other personnel can be the school's best form of advertisement. Every effort should be made to maintain a positive school climate and publicize the accomplishments of the administrators, faculty members, support staff, and—most important—students and graduates. Other individuals whose support is needed in promoting vocational education are politicians and representatives of businesses and industries. Legislation and funding for vocational education at federal and state levels must be maintained to keep programs relevant to the nation's labor market needs.

In the future, the field can expect to experience sweeping changes because traditional vocational programs have been too skill-specific to prepare students for the variety of job changes likely to occur in their career. Occupational programs must be broadened in order to prepare students to adapt to the rapidly changing world of work. Vocational education will play an important role in preparing the work force of the future because it provides students with useful skills, particularly those that employers view as essential to job success.

Vocational educators have long been doing a good job of supplying skilled workers while addressing the needs of the most difficult-to-serve populations. They are aware of the challenges of the future. Demographic trends indicate that there will be an increasing demand for skilled employees in the future. The workforce will change greatly as more women and minorities seek entry than ever before. The profession is equipped with the knowledge and skills needed to prepare people for the world of work, to keep America productive and prosperous. But there are many misconceptions surrounding vocational education that simply will not go away overnight. Vocational educators must assume the responsibility of projecting and promoting a positive image of the profession on a continuous, ongoing basis. Collectively, they can make a difference. □

References

Bell, T.H. (1984, October). Vocational education and the education reform movement. *VocEd*, 33-34.

Copa, G.H. (1984, October). Insights from the past. *VocEd*, 30-32.

Committee for Economic Development (1985). *Investing in our children: Business and the public schools*. Washington, DC: Committee for Economic Development.

Gillie, A.C. (1973). *Principles of post secondary vocational education.*

Columbus, OH: Charles E. Merrill.

Hoachlander, E.G. (1987, February). The federal role in vocational education. *Design Papers for the National Assessment of Vocational Education.* Washington, DC: National Assessment of Vocational Education, U.S. Department of Education.

Korb, R.A. (1982, April). Students with job training more likely to land jobs. *National Center for Education Statistics Bulletin.* Washington, DC: U.S. Department of Education.

Lewis, A.C. (1988, August). From Washington. *School Shop,* 36-40.

National Academy of Sciences (1984). *High schools and the changing workplace: The employers' view.* Washington, DC: National Academy Press.

National Center for Education Statistics (1982, April). *National center for education statistics bulletin.* Washington, DC: U.S. Department of Education.

National Commission on Secondary Vocational Education (1984). *The unfinished agenda: The role of vocational education in the high school.* Columbus, OH: The National Center for Research in Vocational Education, The Ohio State University (ERIC Document Reproduction Service No. ED 251 622).

National School Public Relations Association (1987). *Marketing Your Schools Kit.* Arlington, VA: NSPRA.

Petro, T. & Durocher, D.P. (1988, June). PR that works. *Training,* 48-58.

Radcliffe, C.W. (1987, February). Comments on the federal role in vocational education and implementation of the Perkins Act. *Design Papers for the National Assessment of Vocational Education.* Washington, DC: National Assessment of Vocational Education, U.S. Department of Education.

Sewall, G.T. (1987, February). The national assessment of vocational education: An introduction. *Design Papers for the National Assessment of Vocational Education.* Washington, DC: National Assessment of Vocational Education, U.S. Department of Education.

Silberman, H. F. (1986, Fall). Improving the status of high school vocational education. *Educational Horizons,* 5-9.

Silberman, H. F. (1987, April) Stereotypes of vocational education are not true. *Education Week,* Volume VI, Number 28.

Taylor, R. E. (1987, February). Vocational education—opportunity and challenge: Perspectives on the national assessment of vocational education. *Design Papers for the National Assessment of Vocational Education,* Washington, DC: National Assessment of Vocational Education, U.S. Department of Education.

Woodring, P. (1979, May). Vocational education: How much, what kind, and when? *Phi Delta Kappan,* 644-646.

CHAPTER 13

A Vision of the Next Ten Years

By Jane Ruff

OVER the past several years many changes have emerged in the field of occupational education. The number of students entering various fields has greatly diminished, to the point where some occupations are no longer represented in the district where I am currently teaching. Others are "hanging by a thread"; yet at the same time employers are actively seeking entry-level people in these same trades. It appears this may be a many-faceted problem which must be actively addressed over the next few years.

In 1948, the state of New York first initiated what has come to be the largest group of occupational training centers for high school students in the state: the Board of Cooperative Educational Services, commonly known as "BOCES." These schools appeared as an answer to the problems districts were encountering in providing vocational training for their students. In particular, rural districts with smaller populations found it very difficult to offer the numerous programs students were requesting and which were at that time needed by the economic community.

Students who attend the BOCES occupational centers are mainly eleventh- and twelfth-grade students enrolled in a two-year program. A handful of tenth-grade students are enrolled in what is termed "multi-occupations"—a series of mini courses, five weeks in length, designed to offer these young people the opportunity to partake of a smattering of a variety of courses before committing themselves to the full two-year program. These students are integrated into the regular classroom, exposed to the lessons, texts, and practical applications, and at the end of a full semester of such exposures are better acquainted with the course content and potential work situations they would face before they decide to enter a particular field. The expectation for all the BOCES students is that they will enter a program which interests them and which provides them with either an entry-level skill or enough expertise about the skill to enable them to continue their studies in a graduate institution. These occupationally oriented courses have proven to be extremely effective in holding students in school who might otherwise find their way into the drop-out column.

Over the years the number of students attending the BOCES centers statewide has gradually diminished. Many factors have been involved in this process: Raw numbers of students attending high school have been on the decline since the baby boom years of the 1970s; our industrialized society has, in many instances, given way to technology with fewer available job openings in traditional occupations such as machine shop, welding, etc.; and the State Education Department of New York recently enacted a program calling for intensified academic training of high school students, thus leaving them with insufficient scheduling time to include the occupational courses they may have wanted to take. As a teacher in an occupational course over the last twelve years, I have seen our center decrease in enrollment from nearly 800 students about eight or nine years ago to a little over half that many in 1988-89.

The future of the BOCES schools (and undoubtedly that of other occupational centers throughout New York and across the United States) will depend upon enrollment generated by other segments of our population. Adults need re-training; high-tech will replace and/or update current course offerings; schools will be open longer hours and throughout the entire year; and these changes will revitalize the concept of occupational education as a whole. It is in these areas that I will address the remainder of this chapter.

The Student Population

The next decade promises a considerable change in the so-called "regular student popualtion" which has been the mainstay of education throughout the major part of this century. Traditionally, children entered school at age four or five, continued until completion of high school or until the prescribed age of minority was reached, and thereafter entered the world of work. As we move closer to the 21st century, more and more of these young people enter some sort of postsecondary education in order to obtain the perceived "good life" that is possible only through attainment of various certifications or degrees.

A proliferation of well-educated adults has begun to emerge through this system. However, an even greater number of the current population is inadequately educated for today's changing work environment. While public and private education of school-aged students must continue and improve in its offerings, other segments of our society must also be recognized as being in need of education—an education which will provide opportunities for employment, socioeconomic growth, and ultimately, benefits for the country as a whole. Stadt and Gooch (1980) discussed a variety of approaches to training which could be used to the mutual advantage of both learners and presenters in their textbook.

Who, then, are these "special populations"? The New York State Board of Regents, in a working paper prepared in 1987, identified many segments of the population which can be considered "at risk" and which must be included in the visions discussed in this chapter. It is recognized that minority groups are among the largest percentage which must be addressed, as the dropout and unemployment rates of these people, despite gains during recent years, continue to be extremely high in comparison to the rates of the remainder of the population. A second and almost as large contingent needing new and/or additional training is dislocated workers—people who have lost their prior positions as a result of advances in technology, closings due to economic conditions, or relocations which for various reasons they could not accept.

Laws initiated some time in the past to protect the handicapped are now being more strictly enforced. While it previously may have been taken for granted that the less fortunate would be better off if they were taken care of by family or the state, it has now been proven that many are not only capable of assisting in their own care but that they can also be productive, useful citizens who take pride in being a part of the mainstream of life. Not only must we educate the handicapped children of this country, we must see that adults who may have previously been denied an opportunity to receive training, or who suddenly have become handicapped through accident or military involvement, now are included in national educational policies.

Sex equity issues have brought forth numerous incidents wherein both men and women have been discriminated against insofar as employment opportunities are concerned. New and increased educational programs must be developed to include both genders on an equality basis; those who wish to make mid-life career changes must be met with open-door policies, while others just beginning to assess their future goals are made aware of the diversity of available possibilities.

There was a time in the history of this country when one retired only when the end was in sight. Retirement meant the finish of work, a final statement that productive life has reached its end and all that was left was to sit on the porch until the grim reaper arrived. Consider, now, the changes which have taken place in this scenario: Retirement is looked upon by many as the beginning of a new era in their lives, a time for a fresh beginning, a time to launch a long-treasured business venture, a time to turn their attention to new people and new horizons. Retirement age has been lowered for many as a result of pension plans; advances in the health field have made it possible for those who are older to be in excellent physical and mental shape. Many of these people will need retraining which suits their areas of interest, while others will seek assistance to further ideas for businesses, projects, etc. As the population greys, so does the need for assisting these seniors expand to the point where adult education will, in many cases, take on an entirely new meaning.

Several articles in the November 1988 issue of *Phi Delta Kappan* dealt with the inevitable changes which will certainly occur in the student population of American schools as more and more legal immigrants arrive at U.S. shores. America continues to be a "melting pot" of nationalities, and immigrants still daily arrive at her doors seeking the Great American Dream. The influx may surpass that of the previous century as great numbers of people from Asia, Latin

America, the Caribbean, and Mexico seek asylum and refuge within our shores. While, previously, immigrants settled mainly in the northern industrial centers, a majority now are concentrated in the South and western portions of this country. Many of these people come replete with skills that can be assimilated into our culture. Many arrive with high school and even college degrees, while others may possess skills which need refinement or changing in order to be put to use here. Language can sometimes be a barrier; thus, education must be provided to insure that none suffer discrimination due to that circumstance.

A final segment of the population needing training is one often ignored because of its obvious existence—those who might be considered "normal" citizens. Today's educational system has succeeded in "turning off" a large segment of society, or has been remiss in providing an environment of learning that stimulates thought and imagination and thus a craving for further knowledge. New methods of instruction must be found that will enhance the image of schools at all levels. If the majority of persons who comprise our citizenry are to possess the degree of ability they should have as a result of having attended our high schools, colleges, and universities, traditional means of education may have to be abandoned or updated to address the needed changes.

Time Elements

For many years instructional time allocation has been looked upon as that which best suits the presenters. In the case of traditional high schools, days have begun around 7:30 in the morning and finished somewhere around 3:00 in the afternoon. So-called extra curricular activities were held later or in the evenings, as well as on Saturdays. Everyone of school age was expected to adhere to this schedule, with perhaps minor changes.

But what now happens to the "non-traditional" students? How can they be educated at a time that suits *their* needs and still allows for the flexibility necessary to fill the classroom teaching assignment? Obviously, an inventive spirit and the willingness to compromise must be the hallmark of all future successful programs. Several suggestions along these lines have been made, some of which are already being instituted while others may come into prominence as time passes.

Certain areas of the United States already are experiencing year around schooling, mostly applicable to vocational classes. This concept allows for more economic utilization of our present schools. Instead of schools sitting semi-idle throughout ten weeks or so in the summer, classes continue to be held. Instructors and students are assigned on a rotating basis, with no long-term vacation but an interim period between semesters. Thus, greater numbers of students can be accommodated in a given year.

Adult training is now being integrated into the regular school curriculum in many occupational centers. Persons who have completed their regular high school curriculum, whether they have graduated or left school for other reasons, are working and learning side-by-side with the traditional students. Benefits of this program are numerous: Younger students observe the consequences of leaving school under-educated and are more prone to learn while in class; older students have a calming effect on the classroom in general—there is less boisterousness on the part of young students—and more attention is paid to the educational process; older students enjoy the opportunities to work with the youngsters, sometimes finding new self-respect through their ability to communicate with and/or counsel their classmates on a peer level.

Not only will schools be open throughout the year, they may well be open at least six days per week on a regular basis. Many schools presently hold adult education or other training classes, especially on new technologies such as computers, etc., on Saturdays. Evenings are also popular times for training for persons employed during the normal work hours. It may be difficult for persons transferring into new fields to avail themselves of traditional schedules. The proprietary schools, as well as community and junior colleges, must begin a rearrangement of their programs if they are to offer training to persons employed on a daily basis. Even four-year colleges may find it necessary to provide a majority of their courses, seminars, and workshops on Saturdays and throughout the summer months in order to satisfy the demands made on them.

Short-term training will be an important part of the educational system over the next ten years. While extended courses may be necessary to completely retrain students, it is obvious not all coursework will need to be thus scheduled. "Crash courses" of intensified training may take the place of traditional courses in order to provide the public with an educational system that allows for the greatest flexibility. Extended hours are another possibility for training in the future; schools may find it necessary to "double up" their schedules in order to accommodate students.

Training done in businesses and industrial settings is already following most of the above guidelines, offering their personnel opportunities to learn new skills or to enhance old ones both during normal working hours and after work. Often these employers resorted to providing their employees training within the confines of their buildings because such training was not offered elsewhere at a time which was advantageous to the workers. Some will continue to do so, while others will increase tuition reimbursement programs, etc., at area establishments that agree to incorporate programs and schedules into a convenient unit which meets the employer/employee schedules.

The Instructional Staff

The question of *who* will provide instruction in the years to come poses several interesting possibilities. With the recent reports on teaching effectiveness as seen in our present schools, there is increased emphasis on the professionalization of teaching in general. In New York State, the Commissioner's Task Force on the Teaching Profession researched this area in depth. Specifically, who will be qualified to understand the task of presenting information to all who need any type of instruction? Is it necessary to have licensed teachers in every classroom situation? Are people who have experienced the world of work actually better prepared to share their knowledge with learners? Can certain skills be better learned on the job? Is experience under supervision at times a bona fide method of learning?

The public is demanding visibly better results of traditional schooling. Teachers have made it clear that if they are to be held accountable for the degree of learning that occurs, they will expect a greater voice in the preparation of curriculum, methods of presentation, and other aspects of school management, as well as what they feel are justifiably higher salaries. While that debate rages onward, instruction will still need to take place in many and varied settings.

More and more businesses and industries are turning to noncertified but work-qualified persons to provide training on new job applications, technologies, etc. Often an expert in the field will be called in to conduct orientation classes for future trainers; the future trainers are company employees who possess the qualifications identified as needed to assist others in learning. These non-academically certified teachers can be highly effective when their charge is simply to increase the abilities workers already possess. They may, however, encounter problems if they are expected to completely re-educate fellow employees in an original procedure, change, etc. It is in such instances that the benefits of formal teacher training become obvious.

If one looks entirely at academic schooling, there are other possibilities that emerge. For some time occupationally certified teachers' regulations have differed from those for people who would teach academics. One such difference is in the subject area training, wherein occupational teachers need a specific amount of "trade experience" in order to qualify for provisional or permanent certification after they have completed a prescribed amount of schooling, and academic teachers are required to obtain both a bachelor's and, eventually, a master's degree to retain their positions. There is a movement afoot now in many states to require a period of internship prior to licensure in any area of education.

Concepts on educational reform in the two decades prior to the year 2000 were discussed in a Carnegie Council report entitled *Three Thousand Futures*. Many of the premises envisioned in that report are beginning to become realities. One such possibility is that of differentiated staffing, in part created by the idea of an internship. No one would receive permanent certification until a series of steps had been followed during which prospective teachers would be mentored by experienced teachers, coached by peers, and thoroughly evaluated throughout the process with an eye to assisting them to become true professionals. New teachers thus would not be left to work through their own problems; they would be given help when it was most vitally needed and while they were still vulnerable to suggestions and methodological changes.

New York state has also instituted a program of funding for what are known as Teacher Resource and Computer Training Centers. Through these centers still another form of teaching is emerging, that of peers teaching each other, experts giving presentations, universities offering courses, and businesses supplying technology personnel all in an effort to re-educate teachers and while under the goverance of the teachers themselves! These highly successful centers have begun to branch out across the state, even offering training to non-teaching personnel such as support staff members and persons in supervision. In other parts of the U.S. similar programs have begun under different titles but with similarly anticipated outcomes. If these programs are to continue and grow, huge state funds must yearly be allocated, and the federal government will assuredly be called upon to contribute its financial support. □

References

Board of Regents, University of the State of New York (July 1987). *Increasing high school completion rates: A framework for state and local action.* Albany, NY: State Department of Education.

Carnegie Council on Policy Studies in Higher Education (1980). *Three thousand futures.* San Francisco, CA: Jossey-Bass.

Commissioner's Task Force on the Teaching Profession (March 1988). *A blueprint for learning and teaching.* Albany, NY: New York State Department of Education.

Divorsky, Diane (November 1988). The model minority goes to school. *Phi Delta Kappan,* 20, 3.

First, Joan M. (November 1988). Immigrant students in U.S. public schools: Challenges with solutions. *Phi Delta Kappan,* 20, 3.

Kellogg, John B. (November 1988). Forces of change. *Phi Delta Kappan,* 20, 3.

Stadt, Ronald W. and Bill G. Gooch. (1980). *Cooperative education: Vocational—occupation—career.* Indianapolis, IN: Bobbs-Merrill Educational Publishing.

CHAPTER 14

The Role of Vocational Education in Preparing Students for the Future

By Albert J. Pautler, Jr.

"THOSE planning school programs for the world of the future must consider the place of vocational education in the curriculum." With this intent, the Smith-Hughes Act of 1917 created and funded federal legislation to support vocational education as a part of the education system. This Act set the direction for the separate funding of vocational education and, in a sense, the framers of the Act must be blamed for causing vocational education to be considered that "other type" of education. The framers intent was that if vocational education was not provided separate funding to get it started, it would not become part of the school curriculum. Unfortunately, a control group to test this hypothesis against was not created in 1917.

Things vocational in those days were considered "manual arts" and were the "high tech" of 1917. You might say that the manual arts movement of those days touched off the start of the debate that still is with us today over the proper role of vocational education in the curriculum of the secondary school. The current lack of mention in some of the "reform reports" of vocational education may logically lead to the conclusion that vocational education does not have a place in the secondary school curriculum.

Federal legislation in the years since 1917 has continued to support the separate funding nature of vocational education. The original idea was to use this federal money as "seed money," with matching funds provided by the various states and local educational agencies. This idea did work and has expanded the delivery system of vocational education that is presently in operation.

Existing federal policy for vocational education can be found in the Carl D. Perkins Vocational Education Act of 1984, which seeks to make for a contemporary program of vocational education. Federal policy in the form of legislation to support vocational education is of continuing concern to educators who consider themselves vocational. Federal policy influences state level policies and local delivery systems of vocational education. A national evaluation or assessment of vocational education seems to take place about every five years, to evaluate the effectiveness of previous federal policies and set the direction for future policies.

Several years ago legislation was created that made it possible for special education students to take vocational education programs. At the present time writers are recommending that "at-risk" students can profit from vocational education at the secondary level. What has happened to the place of vocational education for the "average" or "above average" student? At times it appears that vocational education is becoming a "dumping ground" for special education and at-risk students. When the academic side of the system has problems dealing with social conditions within the public schools, they recommend vocational education as the program of last resort.

What Is Vocational Education?

In 1917 it was rather easy to define the meaning of the words "vocational education." That is no longer the case. Federal policymakers have continued to expand the meaning of vocational education as well as their expectations for those operating vocational programs at the secondary level. Try telling someone that you are a vocational educator and see what you get as a response. You best tell them that you teach electronics, nursing, business education, or agricultural education. It is like an English teacher telling someone that he teaches academic education.

In *Investing in Our Children* the Committee on Economic Development recommended that the term "vocational education" be much more narrowly defined. They recommended consideration of at least five functions. These areas are as follows: an education program designed for very specific entry level positions in the work force; programs that make use of employment counseling; joint ventures with business and industry making use of cooperative education (on-the-job training of a part-time nature); and general employability and job seeking skills including preparing a resume, interviewing, and getting to work on time.

These suggestions must be given serious consideration by all educators as we think about the future place of vocational education at the secondary level. If it is determined that one role or purpose of vocational education is to prepare children for specific entry level positions immediately after high school, a change in terminology is certainly in order. That objective differs from exploratory programs designed to assist in career choice and decision making.

The American Vocational Association *Fact Sheet* defines vocational education as "the segment of education charged with preparing people for work. It is the backbone of the nation's employment related education and training programs. . . . It responds to this charge through a variety of programs that offer instruction in related basic education, career development, general vocational knowledge, improved family living skills, and occupationally specific preparation." This statement is very general and attempts to address vocational education programs at the secondary, postsecondary, and adult program levels. The best advice seems to be to consult with your individual state department of education for a definition for vocational education at the secondary level.

Where Is It Offered?

The American Vocational Association reports that some 26,000 institutions across the country offer vocational programs. This figure includes vocational programs at all levels, not just the secondary level.

At the secondary level vocational education programs can be found in general high schools, comprehensive high schools, vocational high schools, and secondary area vocational centers. A general high school is defined as a school that offers fewer than six vocational programs, while a comprehensive high school is one that offers at least six different vocational programs. A vocational high school is a specialized secondary school that offers full-time programs of study in both academic and vocational subjects. A secondary area vocational center is a shared time facility that provides instruction in vocational education for students in a certain region. Students spend part of the day in their "home" school and part in the area vocational center.

A "program" as used in the previous paragraph would refer to instruction in certain technical areas. These might be in programs such as agriculture, business, trade, and technical subjects. Courses might be in automotive mechanics, electronics, practical nursing, robotics, machine shop, drafting, secretarial subjects, graphic design, etc.

A wide variation in organizational structure exists among the states in how vocational education progams are provided for students. Within large cities vocational high schools are available for students who desire a vocational education. *Education Week* reported that State Comptroller Edward Regan has recommended an expansion in the number of vocational high school and programs for New York City. This recommendation is based upon a three-year audit that showed that vocational high schools had a much lower dropout rate than other schools. The demands for vocational education is four times greater than the present spaces available. The student demand could be met by the opening of 17 new vocational high schools. Should student demand for a vocational education determine the type of educational programs offered? How much of this current demand for vocational education is as a result of the "reform movement" and the Regents Action Plan in New York state? Are New York City students seeking a vocational education as a result of increased academic requirements? What are the stated goals and objectives for vocational education programs? How well do vocational education graduates do in finding employment after graduation? These are key questions that need to be asked.

A Select Form of Education.

Students choosing a vocational education program of studies in high school are entering a select form of education. Such students are making a career decision, one hopes, based upon good guidance and realistic expectations for their future.

In Buffalo, New York, students entering high school may apply for admission to several "magnet schools" or vocational schools. If they do not care to apply for these schools, they would attend the district academic high school for their area. It is a selection process. Those students not selected for admission to either a "magnet school" or vocational school would then attend the district academic high school serving their area. Therefore, vocational education may be considered a select form of education for Buffalo school children who choose to take a vocational program. But, what about those children who applied for admission to a vocational high school and were not selected? Do they loose interest in school and drop out?

This type of situation in Buffalo and New York work against the old image of vocational education being a "dumping ground" for problem children. This does not imply that there are areas in the country where vocational education programs are not used as so-called "dumping grounds" for some children. Recent literature is suggesting that children labeled "at risk" might profit from some forms of vocational education. Vocational educators in attempting to help "at-risk" students may still be considered by academic educators as providing a "dumping ground" for the students. This double standard of education which divides academic and vocational education students into two groups must stop. This attitude which has been displayed over the years must somehow change.

To change the image will perhaps require attempting to change the attitudes of parents, students, teachers, and school administrators. The curriculum structure used to deliver vocational education at the secondary level will also have to change. Several of the "reform" reports call for a change in the delivery system of vocational education, but seldom are details suggested for curricular changes.

The Vocational Image

Various states have been developing public relations programs in order to improve the image of vocational education. Promotional programs for several regional vocational centers in New York state have been developed and implemented as a means to deal with the image held by many regarding vocational education. New York state several years ago dropped the term vocational and replaced it with occupational education. But still what goes on in occupational centers is referred to as vocational education.

Largo High School in Prince George's County has announced plans for a "professional center." This center will be used to teach marketable skills when it opens in 1989. This change of title, no doubt, is a means to avoid the use of the words vocational education, occupational education, or career education.

Educators concerned with programs of a vocational nature need to deal with the image issue of the past and engage in activities that will change the attitudes of people toward things vocational. Those preparing for a career in medicine, law, or religion are preparing for a vocation. Why is there such an image or stigma associated with the term vocational education at the secondary level? Perhaps this image is based upon the attitude that preparation for a career should not take place at the secondary level. Those who support this proposition must also believe that all students must continue their education beyond high school graduation.

But what about those children who drop out before completing high school and those who graduate but have little interest or desire to go on to further formal education? This has been the argument of vocational educators for years as they support the role of vocational education at the secondary level. The recent reform reports have said very little concerning the role of vocational education at the secondary level.

It does not appear that the image of vocational education will be improved if the scope of vocational programs is enlarged to service more special education students and those students considered to be at risk. This does not imply that certain vocational education programs should not be made available to special populations of students. If vocational instruction can be of help to these students, it most certainly should be provided for them. However, average and above average students should also be able to take vocational programs if that is their choice.

The Forgotten Half

The 1988 report of the William T. Grant Foundation Commission on Work, Family, and Citizenship entitled *The Forgotten Half:*

Non-College Youth in America is of interest to those associated with secondary vocational education. This report is concerned about non-college youth who did graduate from high school and are making the transition from school to work. The report calls attention to those 20 million high school graduates who are not likely to go on to some form of postsecondary education.

These youth may have been in the college preparatory, vocational, or general program while in high school. For some reason they did not go on to some form of postsecondary education. Perhaps some wanted to continue their formal education but were either not accepted into colleges or did not have the financial means to go on to school. Others perhaps decided they had enough schooling and wanted to go to work.

When one completes schooling there are three choices: (1) go on to more schooling; (2) enter the world of work; (3) flow into the pool of the unemployed. This transition may occur after high school, community college, college, university, or completion of postgraduate work.

If firm decisions on future educational plans could be made by students upon entering high school, better use of the four-year curriculum in high school would be possible. But we know that this is not possible for all students. Their career plans and personal goals and aspirations change during high school.

The report makes some suggestions for attempting to improve the school-to-work transition for all high school students. Some of these suggestions are as follows:

Monitored Work Experience: cooperative education; internships; apprenticeship; pre-employment training; youth-operated enterprises.

Community and Neighborhood Service: individual voluntary service; youth-guided services.

Redirected Vocational Education Incentives: guaranteed postsecondary and continuing education; guaranteed jobs; guaranteed training.

Career Information and Counseling: career information centers; parents as career educators; improved counseling and career orientation; community mentors and community based organizations.

School Volunteers

The report recommends that communities experiment with multiple elements to construct an improved school-to-work system. "Students should learn in schools and in the workplace and in other community settings." What are the implications for the curriculum of the schools? What are the implications for what we now call vocational education at the secondary level?

New York State Education Commissioner Thomas Sobol, in addressing the 1988 New York State School Boards Association convention, suggested a two-diploma system for high school students. He spoke of one track being academic and the other vocational. This idea is certainly not new. Franklin Keller in his 1953 book, *The Double-Purpose High School*, was advocating this same suggestion that Sobol is again making in 1988. So what is really new at the present time? Not very much is new. Policymakers are still not sure what, if any, role vocational education should have at the secondary level. The idea of the comprehensive high school was that it be able to serve the needs of the entire school population including those who are not planning on going on to further formal education immediately after high school.

Redirected Vocational Education

John Goodlad in *A Place Called School* writes that "vocational education, including guided work experiences, is an essential, not merely an elective, part of general education." The implication is that vocational education is for all students.

Vocational education is the only part of the secondary school curriculum that has been separately supported by United States federal funds for 70 years. Congress must be aware of its unique contribution to the economic well being of the nation. This does not mean that some redirection of the existing system is not in order. This redirection occurs every time new federal legislation is approved for vocational education.

Changing the name of vocational education to occupational education, career education, or technology education will not solve the image problem that many associate with preparing high school students for employment immediately after high school graduation. The image problem will not go away with a change of title. If a change is going to occur, it needs to be a change in attitude among those concerned with the role of the high school in preparing students for employment after graduation. *The Forgotten Half: Non-College Youth in America* is a start in focusing the attention of the nation on the approximately 20 million 16- to 24-year-olds who are not likely to enter undergraduate education. High school may very well be their transition point into the world of work. They may attempt to enter the world of work with or without a diploma. These young people have a desire to find a place in the world of work and contribute to society in general. They also need to find personal satisfaction in what they are able to contribute to society.

Some children still are "forced" to select a vocational high school major or program after grade eight, nine, or ten. This refers to young people who may choose to attend a vocational high school program that will take two, three, or four years to complete. Early career or vocational choice after eighth or ninth grade seems to be too soon to make such a serious decision that may very well have long-term effects. If such decisions could be delayed until at least after grade ten, it would seem to be much more realistic. This would have implications for vocational curriculum as well as scheduling in the high school. It might be that some students would spend half their time in a vocational program during their last two years of high school. Others may spend their entire senior year in a vocational program that will assist them in their transition to the world of work. Such program flexibility may even reduce dropping out during the last two years of high school. Flexibility of programming of vocational education seems essential in the future of vocational education is going to survive at the high school level.

The content of what to offer in vocational education programs must be carefully examined and designed to serve as a transition to the world of work. Since high school graduates are less mobile than college graduates, the vocational programs offered must be geared to the local employment opportunities available to high school graduates. School-to-work transition has always been a goal of secondary vocational education programs. Most state education departments require follow-up placement data on high school vocational graduates. So this should not be new to vocational educators.

Schools operating vocational programs must more narrowly

define what they mean by vocational education. The *Investing in Our Children* report of the Committee for Economic Development made this recommendation. As it now is, the meaning of vocational education is much too vague to mean very much to anyone. It is very important that attention is given to this recommendation at the local school district level. If secondary vocational education programs are designed to prepare students for entry level employment; help students make career decisions; provide employment counseling; provide cooperative education; and provide general employability and job-seeking skills, program sponsors must clearly state these goals. This should help clarify what it is that vocational education is working to achieve at the secondary level.

Lastly, it seems essential that schools establish linkages in the form of partnerships with local business, industry, human service, and governement agencies in order to keep in tune with expectations of employers for entry level employees. Along with this, the entire issue of part-time paid or voluntary work experience for high school children should be discussed. For some students part-time work experience provides the transition from school to work. The positive as well as negative aspects of working part time while in high school should be considered. □

References

American Vocational Association (no date). *Fact sheet: Vocational education today.* Arlington, VA: American Vocational Association.

Commission on Work, Family and Citizenship (1988). *The forgotten half: Non-college youth in America.* Washington DC: The William T. Grant Foundation.

Committee for Economic Development (1989). *Investing in our children.* Washington, DC: Research and Policy Committee, Committee for Economic Development.

Education Week (May 25, 1988). Reversing vocational image: Officials are turning to P. R.

Goodlad, John (1984). *A place called school.* New York: McGraw-Hill.

Keller, Franklin (1953). *The double-purpose high school.* New York: Harper & Bros.

Regan, Edward (April 27, 1988). 13 states agree to test of ambitious cational program. *Education Week.*

Regents action plan. The popular name given the New York State Regents plan for the reform of education in New York state.

Sobol, Thomas (1988). Presentation made to the New York State School Boards Association Convention, Buffalo.

SPECIAL SECTION

Bibliography of Review and Synthesis Literature Concerning Vocational and Technical Education

By Charles R. Doty

SINCE the mid-1960s there has been a tremendous effort to review and synthesize any literature concerning vocational and technical education. Review and synthesis papers were written in order to discover new knowledge with which to solve the increasingly complex problems of providing vocational and technical education in public and private institutions in the United States.

This bibliography was developed to give the reader a perspective of the number of areas of potential problems of any educational endeavor and to give those review and synthesis papers generated since the mid-1960s up to August 1988. Most of the review and synthesis papers are available via the data base called ERIC. ERIC is a nationwide information computer system supported by the National Institute of Education. ERIC's purpose is to collect and disseminate research results, practitioner related materials, etc., that can be used to improve education.

A national network of specialized centers called clearinghouses, each focusing on one special field, acquires information; evaluates, indexes, abstracts that information; and announces this in the ERIC abstract journals. The clearinghouse associated with vocational and

tional and teachnical education is the ERIC Clearinghouse on Adult, Career, and Vocational Education, The Ohio State University, 1960 Kenny Road, Columbus, Ohio 43210.

Those review and synthesis papers in the ERIC system are available on microfiche, a transparent, plastic card (4×6″) which must be read using a microfiche reader. The criterion for the selection of each source was that a thorough review of the literature exists within the publication. Thirty-plus areas are given in this listing:

accreditation	futures
agriculture	guidance and counseling
basics	health occupations
behavioral objectives	home economics
business education	individualizing education
career education	industrial technology
change process	placement
computer	selected areas
cooperative education	special needs
correctional education	systems
cost	teacher education
distributive education	technical education
employer sponsored education	trade education
	transferability
evaluation	women
forecasting	

Accreditation

Stoodley, R. V., Jr. (1983). *Accrediting occupational training programs.* Columbus, Ohio: National Center for Research in Vocational Education. (ERIC Document Reproduction Service No. ED 233132)

Agriculture Education

Carpenter, E.T. & Rogers, J. H. (1970). *Review and synthesis of research in agricultural education* (2nd ed.). Columbus, Ohio: National Center for Research in Vocational Education. (ERIC Document Reproduction Service No. ED 040275)

Lee, J. S. (1985). *Agriculture education: Review and synthesis of the research* (4th ed.). Columbus, Ohio: National Center for Research in Vocational Education. (ERIC Document Reproduction Services No. ED 260300)

Leske, G. & Persico, J., Jr. (1984). *Indicators of quality in cooperative vocational education: A review and synthesis of research in vocational education.* St. Paul, Minnesota: Minnesota Research and Development Center for Vocational Education. (ERIC Document Reproduction Services No. ED 242874)

McClelland, J. B. (1965). *A summary of studies in achievement of vocational agriculture students in college.* Ames, Iowa: Iowa State University. (ERIC Document Reproduction Services No. ED 016822)

Newcomb, L. H. (1978). *Agricultural education: Review and synthesis of the research.* Columbus, Ohio: National Center for Research in Vocational Education. (ERIC Document Reproduction Services No. ED 164979)

Warmbrod, J. R. and Phipps, L. J. (1966). *Review and synthesis of research in agricultural education.* Columbus, Ohio: National Center for Research in Vocational Education. (ERIC Document Reproduction Services No. ED 011562)

Basics

Sechler, J. A. & Crowe, M. R. (1987). *Roadsigns from research. Basics: Bridging vocational education and academic skills.* Columbus, Ohio: National Center for Research in Vocational Education. (ERIC Document Reproduction Services No. ED 288957)

Behavioral Objectives

Melton, R. F. (1978). Resolution of conflicting claims concerning the effect of behavioral objectives on student learning. *Review of Educational Research, 48* (2), 291-302.

Business Education

Lambrecht, J. J. et al. (1981). *Business and office education: Review and synthesis of research* (3rd ed.). Columbus, Ohio: National Center for Research in Vocational Education. (ERIC Document Reproduction Services No. ED 205780).

Lanham, F. W. & Trytten, J. M. (1966). *Review and synthesis of research in business and office occupation education.* Columbus, Ohio: National Center for Research in Vocational Education. (ERIC Document Reproduction Services No. ED 011566)

Mayer, K. R. & Clinkscale, B. G. (1980). *Synthesis of work organization research and application for business communication curricula.* Cleveland, Ohio: Cleveland State University. (ERIC Document Reproduction Services No. ED 198319)

Price, R. G. & Hopkins, C. R. (1970). *Review and synthesis of research in business and office education.* (2nd ed.). Columbus, Ohio: National Center for Research in Vocational Education. (ERIC Document Reproduction Services No. ED 038520)

Career Education

Budke, W. E. (1971). *Review and synthesis of information on occupational exploration.* Columbus, Ohio: National Center for Research in Vocational Education. (ERIC Document Reproduction Services No. ED 056165)

Doty, C.R. (Project Director) (1982). *Career education and the affective domain: Choices, success, concepts, survival skills, testing.* New Brunswick, N. J.: Rutgers-State University of New Jersey. (ERIC Document Reproduction Services No. ED 222667)

Dudley, G. A. & Tiedeman, D. V. (1977) *Career development: exploration and commitment.* Muncie, Indiana: Accelerated Development, Inc. (ERIC Document Reproduction Services No. ED 135946)

Herr, E. L. (1977). *Research in career education: The state of the art.* Columbus, Ohio: National Center for Research in Vocational Education. (ERIC Document Reproduction Services No. ED 149177)

Herr, E. L. (1972). *Review and synthesis of foundations for career education.* Columbus, Ohio: National Center for Research in Vocational Education. (ERIC Document Reproduction Services No. ED 059402)

Hotchkiss, L. et al. (1979). *Theories of occupational choice: A critical assessment of selected viewpoints.* Columbus, Ohio: National Center for Research in Vocational Education. (ERIC Document Reproduction Services No. ED 197111, also see ED 204530)

Hoyt, K. B. & Shylo, K. R. (1987). *Career education in transition: Trends and implications for the future.* Columbus, Ohio: National Center for Research in Vocational Education. (ERIC Document Reproduction Services No. ED 290933)

Lancaster, A. S. & Berne, R. R. (1981). *Employer-sponsored career development programs.* Columbus, Ohio: National Center for Research in Vocational Education. (ERIC Document Reproduction Services No. ED 205779)

Lufting, J. T. (1974). *Review and synthesis of the theory of occupational choice literature with special application to public school teaching.* Minnesota: University of Minnesota. (ERIC Document Reproduction Services No. ED 095409)

Mitchell, A.M. (Ed.) (1975). *A social learning theory of career decision making.* Palo Alto, California: American Institutes for Reseach in the Behavioral Sciences. (ERIC Document Reproduction Services No. ED 122199)

Rever, P. R. (1975). *Scientific and technical careers: Factors influencing development during the educational years.* Iowa City, Iowa: American College Testing Program. (ERIC Document Reproduction Services No. ED 094208)

Tuttle, T. C. & Hazel, J. T. (1974). *Research and implications of job satisfaction and work motivation theories for Air Force specialties.* Lackland AFB, Texas: Air Force-Human Resource Lab. (ERIC Document Reproduction Services No. ED 099551)

Warren, M. A. et al. (1967). *Generalizations related to concepts important for youth orientation to the world of work.* Norman, Oklahoma: Oklahoma University. (ERIC Document Reproduction Services No. ED 029998)

Wenig, R. E. & Wolansky, W. D. (1972). *Review and synthesis of literature on job training in industry.* Columbus, Ohio: National Center for Research in Vocational Education. (ERIC Document Reproduction Services No. ED 062514)

Change Process

Hull, W. L. & Kester, R. J. (1975). *The perceived effectiveness of innovation diffusion tactics.* Columbus, Ohio: National Center for Research in Vocational Education. (ERIC Document Reproduction Services No. ED 110754)

Skelton, G. J. & Hensel, J. W. (1970). *A selected and annotated bibliography. The change process in education.* Columbus, Ohio National Center for Research in Vocational Education. (ERIC Document Reproduction Services No. ED 041108, see also ED 023025)

Wall, J. E. (1972). *Review and synthesis of strategies for effecting change in vocational and technical education.* Columbus, Ohio: National Center for Research in Vocational Education. (ERIC Document Reproduction Services No. ED 062512)

Computer Applications

Roblyer, N. C. & King, F. (1988). *The effectiveness of computer applications for instruction: A review and synthesis of research findings.* New York: The Haworth Press.

Cooperative Education

Humbert, J. T. & Woloszyk, C. A. (1983). *Cooperative education.* Columbus, Ohio National Center for Research in Vocational Education. (ERIC Document Reproduction Services No. ED 229578)

Owens, T. et al. (1979). *Experiential learning programs: Synthesis of findings and proposed framework for future evaluations.* Washington, D.C.: U.S. Department of Labor. (ERIC Reproduction Services No. ED 023025)

Wallace, H. R. (1970). *Review and synthesis of research on cooperative vocational education.* Columbus, Ohio: National Center for Research in Vocational Education . (ERIC Document Reproduction Services No. ED 040274)

Welch, F. G. (1977). *Cooperative education: A review.* Columbus, Ohio: ERIC Clearinghouse on Adult, Career, and Vocational Education. (ERIC Document Reproduction Services No. ED 149185

Correctional Education

Wolford, B. I. (1986). *Correctional education: Perspectives on programs for adult offenders.* Columbus, Ohio: National Center for Research in Vocational Education. (ERIC Document Reproduction Services No. ED 272770)

Cost

Hu, Teh-wei (1980). *Studies of the cost-efficiency and cost-effectiveness of vocational education.* Columbus, Ohio: National Center for Research in Vocational Education. (ERIC Document Reproduction Services No. ED 186609)

Sparks, D. (1977). *A synthesis of research findings which described selected benefits and outcomes for participants in vocational education.* Washington, D.C.: U.S. Office of Education, Bureau of Occupational and Adult Education. (ERIC Document Reproduction Services No. ED 147576)

Stormsdorfer, E. W. (1972). *Review and synthesis of cost-effectiveness studies of vocational and technical education.* Columbus, Ohio: National Center for Research in Vocational Education. (ERIC Document Reproduction Services No. ED 066554)

Warmbrod, J. R. (1968). *Review and synthesis of research on the economics of vocational education.* Columbus, Ohio: Center for Vocational and Technical Education. (ERIC Document Reproduction Services No. ED 023937)

Distributive Education

Ashmun, R. D. & Larson, R. A. (1970). *Review and synthesis of research on distributive education 1966-68* (2nd ed.). Columbus, Ohio: Center for Research in Vocational Education. (ERIC Document Reproduction Services No. ED 038498)

Berns, R. G. et al. (1980). *Marketing and distributive education: Review and synthesis of the research.* Columbus, Ohio: National Center for Research in Vocational Education. (ERIC Document Reproduction Services No. ED 193533)

Meyer, W. C. & Logan, W. B. (1966). *Review and synthesis of research in distributive education.* Columbus, Ohio: Center for

Vocational and Technical Education. (ERIC Document Reproduction Services No. ED 011565)

Employer Sponsored Training

Wenig, R. E. & Wolansky, W. D. (1983). *Employer-sponsored skill training*. Columbus, Ohio: National Center for Research in Vocational Education. (ERIC Document Reproduction Services No. ED 232010)

Evaluation

Franchak, S. J. et al. (1980). *Specifications for longitudinal studies*. Columbus, Ohio: National Center for Research in Vocational Education. (ERIC Document Reproduction Services No. ED 187931)

McKinney, F. (1977). *Program evaluation in vocational education: A review*. Columbus, Ohio: National Center for Research in Vocational Education. (ERIC Document Reproduction Services No. ED 149186)

Mertens, D. M. et al. (1980). *The effects of participating in vocational education: Summary of studies reported since 1968*. Columbus, Ohio: National Center for Research in Vocational Education. (ERIC Document Reproduction Services No. ED 199435)

New Educational Directions, Inc. (1975). *Evaluation of vocational technical education. Phase I. A review of the literature*. Crawfordsville, Indiana: New Educational Directions, Inc. (ERIC Document Reproduction Services No. ED 131333)

Pucel, D. J. (1979). *Longitudinal methods as tools for evaluating vocational education*. Columbus, Ohio: National Center for Research in Vocational Education. (ERIC Document Reproduction Services No. ED 173545)

Pucel, D. J. (1980). *Review and synthesis of criteria useful for the selection and admission of vocational students*. Columbus, Ohio: National Center for Research in Vocational Education. (ERIC Document Reproduction Services No. ED 193532)

Spirer, J. E. (Ed.) (1980). *Performance testing: Issues facing vocational education*. Columbus, Ohio: National Center for Research in Vocational Education. (ERIC Document Reproduction Services No. ED 187930)

Stufflebeam, D. L. & Welch, W. L. (1986). Program evaluation—the agony and ecstacy: Review and synthesis of research in program evaluation. *Educational Administration Quarterly, 22* (3), 150-170.

Taylor, C. M. et al. (1979). *Vocational education outcomes; Annotated bibliography of related literature.* Columbus, Ohio: National Center for Research in Vocational Education. (ERIC Document Reproduction Services No. ED 177322)

Ward, C. F. (1970). *The state of accreditation and evaluation of post secondary occupational education in the United States.* Raleigh, N. C.: North Carolina State University. (ERIC Document Reproduction Services No. ED 052364)

Werts, C. E. & Linn, R. L. (1972). *Review and synthesis of educational measurement procedures for studying growth (academic) with the purpose of specifying the appropriate applications for these procedures. Final report.* Princeton, N. J.: Educational Testing Service. (ERIC Document Reproduction Services No. ED 070777)

Forecasting

Bain, T. (1975). *Labor market analysis: A review and analysis of manpower research and development.* New York, N. Y.: Center for Policy Research. (ERIC Document Reproduction Services No. ED 121500)

Kidder, D. (1972). *Review and synthesis of research on manpower forecasting for vocational and technical education.* Columbus, Ohio: National Center for Research in Vocational Education. (ERIC Document Reproduction Services No. ED 060183)

Lewis, M. V. (1980). *An r & d agenda to respond to future needs in vocational education.* Columbus, Ohio: National Center for Research in Vocational Education. (ERIC Document Reproduction Services No. ED 198261)

Futures

Goff, W. H. (1986). *Perspectives on the education and training of the future.* Columbus, Ohio: National Center for Research in Vocational Education. (ERIC Document Reproduction Services No.

ED 272222)
Kadamus, J. A. & Dagget, W. R. (1986). *New directions for vocational education at the secondary level.* Columbus, Ohio: National Center for Research in Vocational Education. (ERIC Document Reproduction Services No. ED 272771)
Kolde, R. (1986). *Secondary vocational education.* Columbus, Ohio: National Center for Research in Vocational Education. (ERIC Document Reproduction Services No. ED 273821)
Rosenthal, N. H. & Pilot, M. (1983). *National occupational projections for vocational education planning.* Columbus, Ohio: National Center for Research in Vocational Education. (ERIC Document Reproduction Services No. ED 229577)

Guidance and Counseling

Clyde, J. S. (1979). *Computerized career information and guidance systems.* Columbus, Ohio: National Center for Research in Vocational Education. (ERIC Document Reproduction Services No. ED 179764)
Herr, E. L. (1977). *Guidance and counseling, vocational education, research and development.* Columbus, Ohio: National Center for Research in Vocational Education. (ERIC Document Reproduction Services No. ED 130161)

Health Occupations

Gillespie, W. & Redford, J. (1980). *Health occupations education: A review of the literature.* Columbus, Ohio: National Center for Research in Vocational Education. (ERIC Document Reproduction Services No. ED 193536)
Holloway, L. D. & Kerr, E. E. (1969). *Review and synthesis of research in health occupations education.* Columbus, Ohio: National Center for Research in Vocational Education. (ERIC Document Reproduction Services No. ED 029982)

Home Economics

Bailey, L. C. (1971). *Review and synthesis of research on consumer and homemaking education.* Columbus, Ohio: Center for

Vocational and Technical Education. (ERIC Document Reproduction Services No. ED 048482)

Chadderdon, J. & Fanslow, A. M. (1966). *Review and synthesis of research in home economics education.* Columbus, Ohio: National Center for Research in Vocational Education. (ERIC Document Reproduction Services No. ED 011563)

Griggs, M. B. & McFadden, J. R. (1980). *The effectiveness of consumer and homemaking education: A review and synthesis of extant data.* Washington, D. C.: Nellum and Associates. (ERIC Document Reproduction Services No. ED 211721)

Nelson, H. Y. (1979). *Home economics education: A review and synthesis of the research.* Columbus, Ohio: National Center for Research in Vocational Education. (ERIC Document Reproduction Services No. ED 179768)

Nelson, H. Y. (1970). *Review and synthesis on home economics education.* Columbus, Ohio: National Center for Research in Vocational Education. (ERIC Document Reproduction Services No. ED 038519)

The Ohio State University Faculty of the Department of Home Economics (1986). *Home economics education: A review and synthesis of research.* Columbus, Ohio: National Center for Research in Vocational Education. (ERIC Document Reproduction Services No. ED 272773)

Individualizing Instruction

Hansen, D. N. (1973). *The analysis and development of an adaptive instructional model(s) for individualized technical training. Phase I.* Lowry Air Force Base, Colorado: Technical Training Division. (ERIC Document Reproduction Services No. ED 092174)

Impellitteri, J. T. & Finch, C. R. (1971). *Review and synthesis of research on individualizing instruction in vocational and technical education.* Columbus, Ohio: Center for Vocational and Technical Education. (ERIC Document Reproduction Services No. ED 058389)

Knaak, W. C. (1983). *Learning styles: Applications in vocational education.* Columbus, Ohio: National Center for Research in Vocational Education. (ERIC Document Reproduction Services No. ED 229573)

Industrial Technology (Formerly Arts/Education)

Buffer, J. J., Jr. (1973). *Review and synthesis of research on industrial arts for students with special needs.* Columbus, Ohio: Center for Vocational and Technical Education. (ERIC Document Reproduction Services No. ED 090394)

Dyrenfurth, M. J. & Householder, D. L. (1979). *Industrial arts education: A review and synthesis of research, 1968-1979.* Columbus, Ohio: National Center for Research in Vocational Education. (ERIC Document Reproduction Services No. ED 185239)

Householder, D. L. (1972). *Review and evaluation of curriculum development in industrial arts education.* Columbus, Ohio: Center for Vocational and Technical Education. (ERIC Document Reproduction Services No. ED 060175)

Householder, D. L. & Suess, A. R. (1969). *Review and synthesis of research in industrial arts education.* Columbus, Ohio: National Center for Research in Vocational Education. (ERIC Document Reproduction Services No. ED 034898)

McCrory, D. L. (1987). *Technology education: Industrial arts in transition: A review and synthesis of research* (4th ed.). Columbus, Ohio: National Center for Research in Vocational Education. (ERIC Document Reproduction Services No. ED 290935)

Placement

Barrow, C. M. (1982). *Job placement programs for the future.* Columbus, Ohio: National Center for Research in Vocational Education. (ERIC Document Reproduction Services No. ED 219504)

Boss, R. D., et al. (1975). *Review and synthesis of job placement literature; Volume I of a research project to develop a coordinated comprehensive placement system.* Madison, Wisconsin: Center for Studies in Vocational and Technical Education. (ERIC Document Reproduction Services No. ED 109428)

Dawis, R. V. & Lofquist, L. H. (1981). *Job satisfaction and work adjustment: Implications for vocational education.* Columbus, Ohio: National Center for Research in Vocational Education. (ERIC Document Reproduction Services No. ED 199441)

Little, J. K. (1970). *Review and synthesis of research on the placement and follow-up of vocational education students.* Columbus, Ohio: National Center for Research in Vocational Education. (ERIC Document Reproduction Services No. ED 037543)

Loudermilk, K. M. & DiMinico, G. (1969). *Instruments for vocational guidance, selection, and placement: A review and synthesis of research in Idaho.* Moscow, Idaho: Idaho Occupational Research Coordinating Unit. (ERIC Document Reproduction Services No. ED 039321)

Strong, M. E. (1975). *Review and synthesis of job placement literature.* Madison, Wisconsin: Center for Studies in Vocational and Technical Education. (ERIC Document Reproduction Services No. ED 109428)

Selected Reviews/Topics

Clary, J. R. (1970). *Review and synthesis of research and development activities concerning state advisory councils on vocational education.* Columbus, Ohio: National Center for Research in Vocational Education. (ERIC Document Reproduction Services No. ED 043744)

Cooper, H. M. (1985). *A taxonomy of literature reviews.* Washington, D. C.: U. S. Department of Education. (ERIC Document Reproduction Services No. ED 254541)

Dessart, K. J. (1983). *A review and synthesis of twelve years of research related to secondary instruction in algebra.* Presentation to Americn Educational Research Association. (ERIC Document Reproduction Services No. ED 228035)

Gideonse, H. D. (1978). *A model for educational research and development: 1985.* Columbus, Ohio: National Center for Research in Vocational Education. (ERIC Document Reproduction Services No. ED 181328)

Greissman, B. E. & Densley, K. G. (1981). *Review and synthesis of research on vocational education in rural areas.* Las Cruces, N. M.: Rural Education and Small Schools. (ERIC Document Reproduction Services No. ED 034632)

Guba, E. G. (1981). *The paradigm revolution in inquiry: Implications for vocational research and development.* Columbus, Ohio:

National Center for Research in Vocational Education. (ERIC Document Reproduction Services No. ED 212829)

Kazanas, H. C. (1978). *Affective work competencies for vocational education.* Columbus, Ohio: National Center for Research in Vocational Education. (ERIC Document Reproduction Services No. ED 166420)

Kazanas, H. C. et al. (1973). *The meaning and value of work.* Columbus, Ohio: National Center for Research in Vocational Education. (ERIC Document Reproduction Services No. ED 091504)

Larson, M. E. (1969). *Review and synthesis of research: Analysis for curriculum development in vocational education.* Columbus, Ohio: National Center for Research in Vocational Education. (ERIC Document Reproduction Services No. ED 035746)

Lewis, M. V. (1969). *Research and development needs of vocational education.* Columbus, Ohio: National Center for Research in Vocational Education. (ERIC Document Reproduction Services No. ED 182493)

Lloyd, R. R. & Rehg, V. E. (1983). *Quality circles: Applications in vocational education.* Columbus, Ohio: National Center for Research in Vocational Education. (ERIC Document Reproduction Services No. ED 229607)

Miller, M. D. (1972). *Review and synthesis of research on preparation of leadership personnel for vocational and technical education.* Columbus, Ohio: National Center for Research in Vocational Education. (ERIC Document Reproduction Services No. ED 064471)

Research visibility, 1967-68, reports on selected research studies in vocational, technical, and practical arts education. Washington, D.C.: American Vocational Association. (ERIC Document Reproduction Services No. ED 20302)

Ross, N. & Kurth, P. (1986). *Model entrepreneurship programs.* Columbus, Ohio: National Center for Research in Vocational Education. (ERIC Document Reproduction Services No. ED 271583)

Solomone, J. J. & Gould, B. A. (1974). *Review and synthesis of research on occupational mobility.* Columbus, Ohio: National Center for Research in Vocational Education. (ERIC Document Reproduction Services No. ED 089097)

Sork, T. J. (Ed.) (1979). *Research in adult education: 1976-1978.*

Columbus, Ohio: National Center for Research in Vocational Education. (ERIC Document Reproduction Services No. ED 179761)

Vetter, L. et al. (1979). *Factors influencing nontraditional vocational education enrollments: A literature review.* Columbus, Ohio: National Center for Research in Vocational Education. (ERIC Document Reproduction Services No. ED 181326)

Warmbrod, C. P. (1970). *Review and synthesis of research on residential schools in vocational and technical education.* Columbus, Ohio: National Center for Research in Vocational Education. (ERIC Document Reproduction Services No. ED 045821)

Wenrich, R. C. (1970). *Review and synthesis of research on the administration of vocational and technical education.* Columbus, Ohio: National Center for Research in Vocational Education. (ERIC Document Reproduction Services No. ED 037542)

Wentling, T. L. (1980). *ARRIVE. Annual review of research in vocational education. Volume one.* Urbana, Illinois: University of Illinois. (ERIC Document Reproduction Services No. ED 221682)

Special Needs/Handicapped/Disadvantaged

Clark, D. M. (1983). *Displaced workers: A challenge for vocational education.* Columbus, Ohio: National Center for Research in Vocational Education. (ERIC Document Reproduction Services No. ED 229579)

Denniston, D. (1983). *Older workers: What vocational education can do.* Columbus, Ohio: National Center for Research in Vocational Education. (ERIC Document Reproduction Services No. ED 229580)

Hamilton, J. B. & Harrington, L. C. (1979). *Review and synthesis of teacher competencies to serve special needs students.* Columbus, Ohio: National Center for Research in Vocational Education. (ERIC Document Reproduction Services No. ED 179738)

Hull, M. E. (1977). *Vocational education for the handicapped: A review.* Columbus, Ohio: ERIC Clearinghouse on Career Education. (ERIC Document Reproduction Services No. ED 149188)

Lockette, R. E. & Davenport, L. F. (1971). *Review and synthesis of research on vocational education for the urban disadvantaged.* Columbus, Ohio: National Center for Research in Vocational

Education. (ERIC Document Reproduction Services No. ED 058390)

Melia, R. (1986). *Vocational rehabilitation: Its relationship to vocational education.* Columbus, Ohio: National Center for Research in Vocational Education. (ERIC Document Reproduction Services No. ED 273822)

Oaklief, C. (1971). *Review and synthesis of research on vocational education for the rural disadvantaged.* Columbus, Ohio: National Center for Research in Vocational Education. (ERIC Document Reproduction Services No. ED 058390)

Reubens, P. (1983). *Vocational education for immigrant and minority youth.* Columbus, Ohio: National Center for Research in Vocational Education. (ERIC Document Reproduction Services No. ED 229581)

Sitlington, P. L. (1986). *Transition, special needs and vocational education.* Columbus, Ohio: National Center for Research in Vocational Education. (ERIC Document Reproduction Services No. ED 272769)

Teacher Education

Adamsky, R. A. & Cotrell, C. J. (1979). *Vocational teacher education: A review of the research.* Columbus, Ohio: National Center for Research in Vocational Education. (ERIC Document Reproduction Services No. ED 179769)

Persell, C. H. (1976). *Testing, tracking and teachers' expectations: Their implications for education and inequality. A literature review and synthesis.* New York, N.Y.: Institute on Pluralism and Group Identity. (ERIC Document Reproduction Services No. ED 126150)

Peterson, R. L. (1973). *Review and synthesis of research in vocational teacher education.* Columbus, Ohio: National Center for Research in Vocational Education. (ERIC Document Reproduction Services No. ED 087898)

Ramp, W. S. & Reeder, R. C. (1970). *An analysis and synthesis of state certification requirements for teachers of secondary trades and industries and postsecondary trade and technical programs.* Carbondale, Illinois: Southern Illinois University. (ERIC Document Reproduction Services No. ED 078142)

Technical Education

Adams, D. A. (1972). *Review and synthesis of research concerning adult vocational and technical education.* Columbus, Ohio: National Center for Research in Vocational Education. (ERIC Document Reproduction Services No. ED 064469)

Anderson, D. A. (1970). *A review and synthesis of technical education research in Oklahoma.* Stillwater, Oklahoma: Oklahoma Vocational Research Coordinating Unit. (ERIC Document Reproduction Services No. ED 039328)

Doty, C. R. et al. (1980). *Review and synthesis of research and development in technical education.* Columbus, Ohio: National Center for Research in Vocational Education. (ERIC Document Reproduction Services No. ED 193526)

Doty, C. R. (1982). *Review and synthesis of research and development in technical education in community colleges, 1978-1981.* New Brunswick, N. J.: Rutgers-The State University of New Jersey. (ERIC Document Reproduction Services No. ED 214568)

Fibel, L. R. (1972). *Review and synthesis of literature on occupational preparation in the community college.* Columbus, Ohio: National Center for Research in Vocational Education. (ERIC Document Reproduction Services No. ED 061416)

Larson, W. E. (1966). *Review and synthesis of research in technical education.* Columbus, Ohio: National Center for Research in Vocational Education. (ERIC Document Reproduction Services No. ED 011559)

Miller, G. G. (1974). *Some considerations in the design and utilization of simulators for technical training.* Brooks Air Force Base, Texas: Air Force Human Resources Laboratory. (ERIC Document Reproduction Services No. ED 097919)

Pemberton, S. M. (1980). *A brief historical review of research on higher education.* Washington, D. C.: Department of Education, Bureau of School Improvement. (ERIC Document Reproduction Services No. ED 205057)

Phillips, D. S. & Briggs, L. D. (1969). *Review and synthesis of research in technical education* (2nd ed.). Columbus, Ohio: National Center for Research in Vocational Education. (ERIC Document Reproduction Services No. ED 036639)

Trade Education

Evans, K. & Brown, A. (1983). *Trade 1. An evaluation of trades education schemes. Synthesis report*. London, England: Surrey University. (ERIC Document Reproduction Services No. ED 228448)

Finch, C. R. (1983). *Review and synthesis of research in trade and industrial education* (3rd ed.). Columbus, Ohio: National Center for Research in Vocational Education. (ERIC Document Reproduction Services No. ED 232062)

Pautler, A. J. & Schaefer, C. J. (1969). *Review and synthesis of research in trade and industrial education*. (2nd ed.). Columbus, Ohio: National Center for Research in Vocational Education. (ERIC Document Reproduction Services No. ED 036638)

Tuckman, R. W. & Schaefer, C. J. (1966). *Review and synthesis of research in trade and industrial education*. Columbus, Ohio: National Center for Research in Vocational Education. (ERIC Document Reproduction Services No. ED 011560)

Transferability

Altman, J. W. (1976). *Transferability of vocational skills: Review of literature and research*. Columbus, Ohio: National Center for Research in Vocational Education. (ERIC Document Reproduction Services No. ED 138834)

Haverland, E. M. (1974). *Transfer and use of training technology: A model for matching training approaches with training settings*. Alexandria, Virginia: Human Resources Research Organization. (ERIC Document Reproduction Services No. ED 109489)

Kirby, P. (1979). *Cognitive style, learning style, and transfer skill acquisition*. Columbus, Ohio: National Center for Research in Vocational Education. (ERIC Document Reproduction Services No. ED 186685, also see ED 174655)

McKinley, B. (1976). *Characteristics of jobs that are considered common: Review of literature and research*. Columbus, Ohio: National Center for Research in Vocational Education. (ERIC Document Reproduction Services No. ED 141638)

Sjogren, D. D. (1977). *Occupationally transferable skills and characteristics: Review of literature and research*. Columbus, Ohio:

National Center for Research in Vocational Education. (ERIC Document Reproduction Services No. ED 146420)

Women

Bowers, E. & Hummel, J. (1979). *Factors related to the under representation of women in vocational education administration: A literature review.* Columbus, Ohio: National Center for Research in Vocational Education. (ERIC Document Reproduction Services No. ED 182462)

Dunne, F. (1985). *Places in the system: New Directions for vocational education of rural women.* Columbus, Ohio: National Center for Research in Vocational Education. (ERIC Document Reproduction Services No. ED 262244)

Kane, R. D. (1978). *Preparing women to teach nontraditional vocational education.* Columbus, Ohio: National Center for Research in Vocational Education. (ERIC Document Reproduction Services No. ED 164978, also see ED 143878)

Kievit, M. B. (1972). *Review and synthesis of research on women in the world of work.* Columbus, Ohio: National Center for Research in Vocational Education. (ERIC Document Reproduction Services No. ED 066553)

The Authors

MELVIN L. BARLOW is professor emeritus with the Graduate School of Education at the University of California at Los Angeles, and director emeritus of the Division of Vocational Education at that university, where he served on the faculty for 37 years. He is also historian emeritus of the American Vocational Association. He served as a member of the research staff for the Panel of Consultants on Vocational Education in 1961 and 1962, leading to preparation of the Vocational Education Act of 1963, and he was the administrative staff director of the Advisory Council on Vocational Education from 1966 to 1968 which drafted the Vocational Education Amendments of 1968.

GERALD D. CHEEK is professor and head of the Department of Technological and Adult Education, College of Education, The University of Tennessee, Knoxville. His teaching experience spans 28 years, including secondary education, technical education, teacher education, and industrial training. He has extensive experience with both developing countries and the private sector in establishing training programs for economic development. He currently is interested in finding more effective ways to form linkages between vocational-technical education and the private sector.

CHARLES R. DOTY is advisor in technical education with the Vocational and Technical Program, Graduate School of Education, Rutgers-The State University of New Jersey. Contributions which he has made to postsecondary vocational and technical education include *Developing Occupational Programs* (1986), *Preparing for Higher Technology: Model Programs in the USA* (1985), *Handbook of Teaching Skills for Industrial Trainers and Occupational Instructors* (1984), *Review and Synthesis of Research and Development in Technical Education: 1968-1978* (1980), and *Postsecondary Staff Development National Conference* (1976). He is presently on the editorial board of the *Journal of Vocational and Technical Education* and the Omicron Tau Theta Research Award Committee.

CURTIS R. FINCH is a professor of Vocational and Technical Education at Virginia Polytechnic Institute and State University. He served previously on the faculties of Ohio State University and Pennsylvania State University and received his doctorate from Penn State. His work experience includes employment as an automotive technician, technical instructor, technical training supervisor, research and development manager, and vocational teacher educator. He has been a Senior Fulbright Scholar in Cyprus (1980) and more recently was a visiting scholar for the University Council for Vocational Education. He has served as editor of the *Journal of Vocational Education Research* and president of the National Association of Industrial and Technical Teacher Educators. His 120 publications have focused on research interests in curriculum, instruction, and personnel development.

ANGELO C. GILLI, SR., is vice-president of IDEAS, INC. His most recent experiences include consultant services for the Center for Productivity and Quality of Working and the College of Education at the University of Maryland. He is the author of textbooks, monographs, and papers in electronics and education. Among his latest writing is *Public Education in Queen Anne's County, Maryland: 1723-1980* and book reviews for several publications. He is retired from the Pennsylvania State University and the Maryland State

Department of Education.

LYNNE GILLI received her bachelor's and master's degrees in Vocational-Technical Education from the State University of New York College of Technology at Utica/Rome. In 1983 she received a doctor of education degree from the State University of New York at Buffalo. Since December of 1982 she has been employed by the Maryland State Department of Education Division of Vocational-Technical Education. She currently serves as a specialist in monitor, review, and descriptive reporting, where she is responsible for the statewide promotion of vocational education and the administration of the Office for Civil Rights Guidelines as they apply to vocational-technical education.

JOHN W. GLENN, JR., is director of the Department of Vocational Technical Education, State University of New York College at Oswego. He is responsible for the administration of a comprehensive vocational teacher education program serving 64 counties in New York state. He is currently a member of the American Vocational Association's Board of Directors and Vice President of the Technical Education Division, and is also a past president of the New York State Occupational Education Association and the National Council for Occupational Education.

JAMES P. GREENAN is associate professor and chair, Vocational Education Section, Department of Education, School of Humanities, Social Science, and Education, at Purdue University. His research focus includes gneralizable skills and special needs, and his instructional focus includes research methods and program evaluation. He has authored numerous journal articles, technical reports, chapters, and other publications related to vocational and technical education. He has also held several leadership positions in the field at the local, state, regional, and national levels. In addition, he has delivered papers and has made several presentations at professional meetings and conferences, and has received national recognition and awards for his research and publications in the field of vocational and technical education.

JOHN H. HILLISON is an associate professor of Vocational and

Technical Education at Virginia Polytechnic Institute and State University. He previously served on the faculty at Western Kentucky University and received his doctorate from Ohio State University. His work experience includes employment as an agricultural education teacher and teacher educator. He has served as editor of *The Journal of the American Association of Teacher Educators in Agriculture* and as president of the American Vocational Education Research Association. His publications have focused on teaching methodology and history of vocational education.

MELVIN D. MILLER is director of the School of Occupational and Adult Education in the College of Education at Oklahoma State University. He is well known for his writings and interest in the area of philosophy and is author of *Principles and a Philosophy for Vocational Education*. He has served in professional positions at Oregon State University and The University of Tennessee, Knoxville. Additionally, he has held various leadership roles related to vocational education, including state president of the Oregon Vocational Association, president of the American Vocational Personnel Education Development Association, and president of the University Council for Vocational Education.

ALBERT J. PAUTLER, JR., is professor in the Department of Educational Organization, Administration, and Policy at the State University of New York at Buffalo. He teaches courses in administration, policy, and instructional systems design for educational leaders. His two most recent books are *Teaching Technical Subjects in Education and Industry* and *Designing Vocational Instruction*. He has consulted with federal agencies, private and public schools, and business. He is the author of over fifty published articles in major educational journals.

DAVID J. PUCEL is a professor of Vocational and Technical Education and head of Industrial Education at the University of Minnesota. He has written two books and a computerized tutorial related to designing curriculum for vocational education and industrial training around the theme of performance-based instruction. He has also conducted numerous research studies and published journal articles and monographs about curriculum practices in vocational education. As a student of the historical development of vocational and practical arts education, he has focused on the evolution of curriculum practices as a reflection of changing societal needs.

JANE RUFF is currently a graduate student at the State University of New York at Buffalo. She received both her bachelor's and master's degrees in vocational education at the same institution. She has been an occupational teacher for twelve years, and is serving her internship in Educational Organization, Administration and Policy as the director of the Erie 1 Teacher Center, under the umbrella of the Erie 1 Board of Cooperative Educational Services. She has served as the teachers' association president for the past several years and as such has become actively involved in all facets of occupational and special education across the state as a member of the New York State United Teachers.

MICHELLE D. SARKEES is an associate professor in the Department of Occupational and Vocational Education at the University of North Texas in Denton. She has served as the past president of the National Association for Vocational Special Needs Personnel, an affiliate organization of the Special Needs Division of the American Vocational Association. She has been involved in vocational teacher education for the past twelve years.

MERLE E. STRONG is professor, Department of Educational Administration and the Department of Continuing and Vocational Education, University of Wisconsin-Madison since 1968. He has also been director of the Vocational Studies Center since 1972, with emphasis on research, development, and leadership in vocational and technical education. His prior experience includes serving in the U.S. Office of Education from 1958 to 1968, as director of the Trade and Industrial Education Curriculum Laboratory, The Ohio State University, from 1955 to 1958, director of vocational and adult education in Sandusky, Ohio, 1951-1955, and teaching in industrial arts and vocational education starting in 1946 following military service in Europe. In addition, he has had international experience in vocational and manpower training in Pakistan, Iran, Sierra Leone, Germany, Peru, Saudi Arabia, and Jamaica.

RICHARD A. WALTER is coordinator of occupational competency assessment and student teaching in the Department of Vocational-Technical Education at the State University of New York College at Oswego. He currently serves as chair of the Trade and Industrial Education Research Committee of the American Vocational Association. His experience in vocational education also includes teaching carpentry and cooperative education at the secondary level, as well teacher education courses at the undergraduate and graduate levels.

LYNDA L. WEST is an associate professor in the College of Education at the University of Missouri-Columbia. She is the director of Missouri LINC, a statewide resource center for educators. She holds a joint appointment in the Department of Practical Arts Vocational-Technical Education and the Department of Special Education. She is a teacher educator, author, national consultant, and public speaker in the field of vocational special needs. She is a former teacher of handicapped and disadvantaged students in an urban school district.